WW2 CODEBREAKING
PEOPLE AND PLACES

This book is dedicated to Eileen Lawrence (Née Hughes), who worked on codebreaking Bombe machines at both Outstation Stanmore and Outstation Eastcote during the last war, and is listed on the Bletchley Park Roll of Honour for her services.

WW2 CODEBREAKING
PEOPLE AND PLACES
A Wartime Glossary

RONALD KOORM

Pen & Sword
MILITARY
AN IMPRINT OF PEN & SWORD BOOKS LTD.
YORKSHIRE · PHILADELPHIA

First published in Great Britain in 2024 by
PEN AND SWORD MILITARY
An imprint of
Pen & Sword Books Limited
Yorkshire – Philadelphia

Copyright © Ronald Koorm, 2024

ISBN 978 1 39905 349 5

The right of Ronald Koorm to be identified as Author of this work has been asserted by him in accordance with the Copyright, Designs and Patents Act 1988.

A CIP catalogue record for this book is available from the British Library.

All rights reserved. No part of this book may be reproduced or transmitted in any form or by any means, electronic or mechanical including photocopying, recording or by any information storage and retrieval system, without permission from the Publisher in writing.

Typeset in Times New Roman 10/12 by
SJmagic DESIGN SERVICES, India.
Printed and bound in the UK by CPI Group (UK) Ltd.

Pen & Sword Books Limited incorporates the imprints of Atlas, Archaeology, Aviation, Discovery, Family History, Fiction, History, Maritime, Military, Military Classics, Politics, Select, Transport, True Crime, Air World, Frontline Publishing, Leo Cooper, Remember When, Seaforth Publishing, The Praetorian Press, Wharncliffe Local History, Wharncliffe Transport, Wharncliffe True Crime and White Owl.

For a complete list of Pen & Sword titles please contact
PEN & SWORD BOOKS LIMITED
George House, Units 12 & 13, Beevor Street, Off Pontefract Road,
Barnsley, South Yorkshire, S71 1HN, England
E-mail: enquiries@pen-and-sword.co.uk
Website: www.pen-and-sword.co.uk

or

PEN AND SWORD BOOKS
1950 Lawrence Rd, Havertown, PA 19083, USA
E-mail: uspen-and-sword@casematepublishers.com
Website: www.penandswordbooks.com

Contents

Foreword vi
Introduction vii

GLOSSARY
People 2
Commentary on People 66
Places 80
Commentary on Places 170

APPENDICES
Abbreviations 186
British Y-Station Listing 188
Overseas Listening Stations (examples) 190
Terms and Names 191
Author's Note 196
Points of Interest on Intelligence and Codebreaking 197
Experiences of a Codebreaking Wren During Wartime 200
Selected Papers of Alan Turing 202

Sources 204
Bibliography 205
Other Acknowledgements 211
Museums of Interest in England 212

Endnotes 213
Index 221

Foreword

Never has the need for gathering and processing intelligence been so important in the twenty-first century. This glossary reflects back in history, mainly to a period when Britain and its allies were with their backs against the wall, the Second World War. The horrific events during that time and the aftermath of it showed that lessons needed to be learned; that it would be futile to go to war again, at least on that scale. But world wars arise from relatively local acts of arrogance, occupation of nations, confiscation of land, and oppression.

As I was writing the draft for this volume of the glossary, Ukraine was still at war with Russia. War in post-Second World War Europe would have been unthinkable only a year or two back, and yet here we are again. Intelligence remains crucially important for both sides of that conflict. Also, for the other world states and countries who are looking on, to see whether there is a threat to themselves. Those responsible for gathering and processing intelligence have been working overtime. There will be so much data to collect. The key problem will be filtering it and ensuring that nothing important is missed. The methods used since the Second World War might have changed somewhat. The equipment now is more modern, and we rely much more on the digital age, the internet, social media, satellites, drones, and many other modern technological achievements. Some of that technology owes its development to the many brilliant minds of people who worked on systems during the last war, and the post-war period. GCHQ, the British cornerstone of protection and interception of threats to our nation, has a great deal of work to do in these uncertain times, and with few people being aware of its important history and development that has seen it become the complex organisation of the present day.

History is so important and relevant to today. It is why I could see a need for a glossary on intelligence and codebreaking, to pull together many different aspects of the subject and to attempt to achieve something that is reasonably balanced in content, readable, and informative. I do hope you find something of interest within it. Consider comparing the situation all those years ago to today's world and challenges. There will be many analogies relevant to today from the historic past.

It was in 2019 that HRH Queen Elizabeth II unveiled the plaque on Watergate House, London, to commemorate the beginning of GCHQ a hundred years earlier. I believe that GCHQ, or its equivalent, will stay in existence for as long as the United Kingdom remains as there is a continued need to protect the state in these challenging times.

Introduction

While there are countless articles and books available about the Second World War and intelligence, a select number of them tend to be quite specialist in content. This series of books forms a concise glossary of codebreaking, and associated subjects, including intelligence gathering, deception, some wartime luck, and considerable technical brilliance by a few. The first book, *People and Places*, looks at those individuals who contributed to the development of codebreaking activities, those who may have been in a support role, creators and modifiers of encoding and decoding machines. You will discover a combination of both military and civilian personnel, including inventors, engineers, politicians, generals, and admirals. Some of them will be well-known, others less so. A proportion will be on the side of the enemy during the Second World War, aiming to rely on secret messages and intelligence in order to defeat Britain and its allies. There will be people in a few 'neutral' countries during wartime, and we may establish that neutrality can change over time. Even neutral countries are targeted for intelligence by adjacent states. Some individuals will appear to have minor, or even trivial roles compared to people like Alan Turing, mathematician and codebreaker at Bletchley Park, but they all have one thing in common in that they made a difference to the outcome of the war. Remarkably, many of these individuals had little or no idea how significant their contribution to the war effort would be in the bigger picture of things. The fear is that many might become obscure and forgotten over time. This book goes some way in recording the names and identities of some who would otherwise probably be forgotten about. The reader will find among the 'people chapter', a range of individuals, including engineers, mathematicians, accountants, data processors, prime ministers, managers, inventors, spies, trainers, telephone engineers, amateur radio 'Ham' listeners, and many others. Not all of those will be British, and we do have to recognise the contribution to encoding and intelligence of those who fought against us during the war. The Poles were particularly active in assisting the British to attack the German Enigma encoding machines. Across the pond, in the USA, progress was also made by several individuals, and by organisations that helped the war effort in analysing enemy intelligence. This glossary is part of their deserved recognition for their efforts and their perseverance. While the timescale for the glossary is the Second World War period, I have also included people and places that precede the war, as well as several, selected post-war entries. Deception, and the art of deception, also features.

Within the 'Places' element of this book, the author has tried to achieve a balance of both the well-known, together with some less well-known places and locations both in Europe and elsewhere that were pertinent and relevant to codebreaking and intelligence. Most have heard of Bletchley Park, but several locations are much more obscure. A sizeable support network, established over the period of the war and beyond, assisted Bletchley Park to gather and process intelligence from Europe and elsewhere. The biggest challenge for the author has been to avoid the omission of relevant locations and people, at the same time having to draw a line to avoid requiring many hundreds, if not thousands, of pages. The purpose of this glossary is to give the reader key information about a person or place relevant to codebreaking and intelligence, and where relevant, deception of the enemy. It does not venture into extreme detail, which may be available in other books by a variety of established authors. This glossary becomes a reference book, identifying links between people and places, a clarification of who did what, where and when. Where opinion is given by the author, it should be readily apparent that it is purely opinion. Some of the entries in this glossary will be much longer than others, perhaps recognising the significance or contribution of that person or location with more detail and background.

Some of the entries include individuals such as WRNS personnel, or Wrens, and many of those may be on the Bletchley Park Roll of Honour, which can be viewed online. The roll is for those people who contributed to wartime codebreaking and intelligence work, and also includes people who designed, built and modified codebreaking equipment like those at Dollis Hill working for the Post Office Research Engineering Station. It must also be appreciated that not everyone who was involved has come forward or is on the Roll of Honour. Not all Wrens became members of the Association of Wrens,[1] and therefore some may have dropped through the net. As time passes, fewer of those who were active during the war on this area of specialist work survive. Eventually, we will all have to rely on visiting museums such as at Bletchley Park and TNMOC.[2] Listening to a real person who was there, during the war, is the preferred way of understanding the challenges they faced in a time of great uncertainty. Bletchley Park periodically holds veteran days with talks and lunches for those on the Roll of Honour, and this is an excellent way of telling people that they have not been forgotten about. That their contribution was and still is valued for their service all those years ago. I am honoured to have spoken and communicated with a few of them.

Events in Europe and elsewhere in the world at the time of writing have confirmed that nothing is certain between nations, that stability in Europe can change in a moment, and there becomes a greater need to understand your enemies, collecting and gathering intelligence and processing it to be one step ahead. The modern age of digital processes and computers has accelerated the development of systems and machines, but historically, a great deal of concepts and ideas were formed prior to, and during, the Second World War, in the sphere of intelligence. This was further developed post-war with organisations such as GCHQ and the NSA.[3] During the later war much of the focus was around the approach and build-up to D-Day, and the deception tactics applied by the Allies to improve the odds of success. The Germans, our principal enemy at the time, were expert engineers and developers of equipment and systems, but did not anticipate how well organised Britain was in terms of

INTRODUCTION

collecting and processing intelligence. Nor did they anticipate the brilliant minds here who would analyse and penetrate the encoding systems the Nazis had developed. Luck played a part too, but overall, it was a concerted and combined team effort.

When we choose to, the UK and our allies can become a formidable opponent to threats from abroad in wartime, and even in peacetime, although how one defines 'peacetime' is debatable in the twenty-first century. Of course, codebreaking and intelligence gathering did not stop at the end of the Second World War. The development of modern technology and computers, the threats of 'hacking' software and teams of spies who plan covert operations makes it as valid a concern today as it was back then. At the time of writing there have many alleged 'hacking' attempts and cybercrime against Ukraine by a foreign power.

The entries in this volume of the glossary are, where possible, in alphabetical order, surnames first. The description is a summary of that person or place/location, relevant to intelligence and codebreaking. Most of these are centred around the Second World War, but several are pre-war and others post-war, into the 1950s, with one or two beyond that period. Dates for people are provided where possible. Some of the people mentioned are still currently with us at the time of writing. At the end of the entry there may be a mention of another person, persons, place or places, as a cross-reference that could provide further relevant information for the reader. As Bletchley Park was such a focal point for intelligence processing and codebreaking, I have limited the number of references at the end of entries with 'See *Bletchley Park*', to avoid multiple repetition. Following each main chapter, a commentary is also included, to further enhance the information.

The numbers of people associated with Bletchley Park alone run into the thousands, and we therefore can only provide a small sample of names and individuals here from that site during wartime to demonstrate the wide range of special skills that several of the workers applied in their jobs. The reader is referred to the Bletchley 'Roll of Honour' for a listing, but even then, not everyone who worked there on codebreaking or support services may be listed. The nature of this glossary is that there will be a degree of overlap and links to other entries, and indeed other future glossary volumes in the series. For example, if there is a location or place that was the basis of an organisation with relevance to the Second World War and codebreaking or intelligence, that organisation may well appear as a separate entry in another volume. This enables the reader to read as much or as little as they require, finding out more detail and obtaining a better understanding of that topic or subject. To take another example, Alan Turing, probably the best well-known individual in terms of Second World War codebreaking, will have entries under his name as an individual but also in 'Place' under Bletchley Park, and under organisations such as GC&CS. He, of course, interacted with several others during wartime and may also be referenced in those separate entries, too.

Some of the entries here are focussed on gathering intelligence, deception, and deception techniques. This is relevant due to the feedback and intelligence that was intercepted during the war as to whether the enemy had fallen for a particular and specific trap created by the Allies, or vice versa. It is one thing providing a deception technique and putting it into operation, but not always easy to establish if it achieved its objective. Did it really fool the enemy, or was it a complete waste of time and resources? That intelligence would be gleaned from a combination of sources: troop radio communications; open enemy broadcasts to the public; locating marked-up enemy maps, reports, and documents; intercepting Enigma-encoded or Lorenz-encoded Morse, and non-Morse[4] transmissions via listening Y-stations, and then sent on to Bletchley Park and its outstations. It is included here in this glossary as being part of the overall picture on intelligence and how it was acted on effectively. One or two 'Places' have been taken from organisations such as BTM, which was a factory and successful company before the war. It would flourish while supporting Bletchley Park in its manufacturing of codebreaking machines and accessories but was situated within the city of Letchworth. Strictly speaking, BTM was not a geographical 'Place' like Letchworth, but a series of buildings within that town. However, I have taken the view it almost became such a place, so significant was the factory, and its achievements.

The sources of information for this glossary are broad and wide-reaching sources. Books, articles, lectures, the National Archives, discussions with some who worked in this specialist field during the war or later years, museums, records, associations such as the Association of Wrens, and many others. While there is detail in the text against many entries, I have tried to balance the glossary so that it does not become overwhelming. Readers will use the glossary in different ways to benefit them and their search for knowledge. Having had a book previously published in 2020 on codebreaking outstations,[5] I continued writing down more notes after reading a further range of books and articles and having several in-depth conversations with others. What surprised me was that I was uncovering lots of different bits of additional information over time, and then piecing them together. That changed the balance, and my understanding of the subject, and put a different angle on the various topics. Situations can change extremely quickly in wartime, and that was certainly true of the considerable challenges to the codebreakers and cipher specialists on both sides. The pressure on many of them was considerable. Politicians and military commanders were anxious for more intelligence and in a timely fashion. That was not always possible, and there would have been some dark days in the huts at Bletchley and elsewhere when things would not go our way.

The contribution made to the Allied success during the last war by numerous nations and countries has not always been properly recognised in the past. Britain and the United States had a particularly close bond and there were ample opportunities to share intelligence, including exchange of personnel, such as the 6812th and 6813th US Signals detachments, some who went to Bletchley Park, and others who went to operate Bombe machines at codebreaking outstations such as Eastcote. There would be close connections between Bletchley and Washington, as well as many of the developing factories and organisations, in the race to produce better codebreaking and intelligence solutions during the war. Although there is much mention of the WRNS personnel, or 'Wrens', in this glossary, there were also invaluable contributions via the WAAF and ATS. RAF, GPO and Foreign Office personnel also contributed enormously.

INTRODUCTION

Dedication

This book is dedicated to Eileen Lawrence (née Hughes), one of the many Wrens who worked on several codebreaking outstations during the last war. She, like most others of her generation, is extremely modest about her achievements and those of her colleagues. They just saw it as doing their job. But the incredible team effort that occurred made a huge difference to the outcome of the war. Her daughter and grandchildren must be very proud of her. In years to come, they may probably better appreciate how important her role was in the bigger picture of things during the war. Eileen now has the commemorative medal issued by GCHQ for her wartime services, and a certificate from Bletchley Park. Bletchley holds a veterans' day from time to time, to bring together the people who were involved during the last war. Eileen attended one such event in September 2022. At that event, there were a total of nineteen veterans who had some involvement in codebreaking or in a support role.[6] Not everyone who contributed in wartime codebreaking or support is on the Bletchley Role of Honour, but many are.

I am fortunate that Eileen has also shared some of her wartime personal experiences with me, and within an appendix to this glossary on People and Places she has provided some information on something of her life as a Wren. This brings home the fact that people listed in this book are, or were, individuals who helped to change the world, sometimes in a small way, but mostly for the better.

If this glossary helps you, the reader, to understand certain aspects of what happened during the Second World War in the fascinating world of intelligence and codebreaking in bite-sized chunks and inspires you to investigate more then it has been worthwhile for me, the author, spending countless hours to research, and write it. Most importantly, convey your new knowledge and enthusiasm to your children and grandchildren, so that they too may one day learn about those special, skilled, talented men and women who made a significant difference to working in the last war, and helped to maintain our freedom all those years ago.

GLOSSARY

People

Aitken James M. (1908–1983). Scottish cryptographer at Bletchley Park who worked in Hut 6 on decoding the Enigma machines. He studied classics at Edinburgh University. Aitken was an accomplished chess player and Scottish chess champion over several years. Part of a Bletchley Park chess team against Oxford University, Bletchley won comfortably. He became a PhD, a graduate of both Oxford and Edinburgh. Post-war he worked for the Foreign Office in Cheltenham. As a point of interest, Aitken's namesake A.C. Aitken, from New Zealand (and no relation assumed), had a photographic memory, and would be able to recall mathematical Pi to 1,000 decimal places, a most unusual and incredible feat. For a brief time, he also worked at Bletchley Park, so it was a coincidence that two brilliant men with the same surname worked there. It is not known if they met each other at Bletchley, but it is possible.

Alexander Hugh (1909–1974). Codebreaker and cryptographer at Bletchley Park, arriving there in 1940. He worked in Hut 6 with many other famous codebreakers. It was in 1941 that he transferred over to Hut 8 and worked under Alan Turing on Enigma Naval intelligence decoding. He became deputy director of Hut 8. His cryptographic colleagues would include Gordon Welchman, and Milner-Barry. He would work later on attacking and decoding Japanese codes. After the war transferred to GCHQ at Eastcote, Middlesex, a base that had previously existed as the largest codebreaking outstation supporting Bletchley Park during the war.[1] He received promotion to Head of Section 'H' (Cryptanalysis section) at GCHQ in 1949. In the early to mid-1950s, GCHQ would relocate to Cheltenham.

Batey Mavis (Nee Lever) (1921–2013). See **Lever**, Mavis.

Baudot Emile (1845–1903). Inventor of the Baudot code system in 1870 and patented in 1874. This was later to form the basis of non-Morse messages during the war as used by the Nazis for transmitting German high command secret messages using advanced encoding teleprinter machines. It was a binary code using dots and crosses. This was considered to be the first form of digital communication. The Baudot code was based on a much earlier code developed by Carl Friedrich Gauss and Wilhelm Weber in 1834. The Baudot code was not designed for a teleprinter but used a special manual keyboard that was quite complex to design and use. It was the Germans who adapted it for teleprinter use for wartime military use. The Baudot code adapted for wartime use was more efficient than traditional Morse

PEOPLE

code and used a combination of some thirty-two permutations for letters and several punctuation symbols. A revised version was devised in 1901 by a fellow called Murray, and hence the later Baudot–Murray code.

Blagrove Edith Gordon (Née Lowe) (1895–1979). Superintendent and Head of the WRNS (Wrens), during wartime, and in charge of HMS *Pembroke V*, secret base at Bletchley Park and codebreaking outstations with WRNS personnel. Married to Admiral Henry Evelyn Charles Blagrove, later married to Patrick Eric James Brind (1892–1963). Became Lady Brind. Commencing in 1940 and 1941 based at HMS Cochrane II, which was supply and accounting base for tenders at Rosyth, Scotland. From July 1941 to 1943 became chief officer of WRNS based in West of Scotland HMS St Andrew. October 1943 in Charge of WRNS based at HMS Beaver, a Royal Naval Base in Hull. From May 1944 in charge of HMS *Pembroke V*, secret base at Bletchley Park and outstations. From October 1945 in charge of WRNS based at HMS Drake, a Royal Naval Base in Devonport.[2] See *Greenwich*.

Blake George (1922–2020). A spy who worked for security agencies in Britain and was working for the Russians after the Second World War. He was born in the Netherlands. Blake worked for the Secret Intelligence Service, MI6, in 1944, after serving in the Royal Navy. He would interrogate U-boat captains when in northern Germany, before studying languages at Cambridge, including Russian. He was tasked with collecting intelligence from North Korea, China and Communist Russia. Taken prisoner in Korea, he gradually became a communist from his experiences there, and he offered his services to the Russian secret service as a spy. His excuse was that he watched the horrific bombing of people in Korea, and this changed his mind about the West and their intentions. From that point on he had sympathies with Russia and with Eastern communist states. He had spent three years in captivity in Korea but was released and came back to Britain a hero. Blake was based in Berlin for some time after the war ended. He passed over numerous British and Allied documents to the East Germans and Russians. He later betrayed the American and British underground tunnel and phone tapping in Berlin in 1956, known as CIA *Project PBJOINTLY*, to the East Germans and Russians,. Blake had given the Russians the identities of many British agents, some of whom were executed. Eventually, Blake was caught, arrested and sent to Wormwood Scrubs prison in London.[3] He was sentenced in 1961 to forty-two years' imprisonment, but only spent five years behind bars. He escaped one night to return to Russia and was never recaptured. The night he escaped from Wormwood Scrubs, 22 October 1966, Blake and his accomplice in the getaway car crashed into the rear of an Austin A35 van around the corner from the prison on the main road. In that van sitting in the back was the author of this glossary, and his much older brother who was driving. I saw Blake and his accomplice clearly from the rear window of the van, through the windscreen of the car, but he was not recognised, and as he had only just escaped from prison within minutes of the incident, there was no alarm out for his capture. The van hit by Blake's car pulled over to the side of the road to exchange insurance details. Unsurprisingly, the getaway car with Blake inside accelerated at high speed down the main road to escape the situation. That evening, the BBC television news broadcast that a famous Russian spy, George Blake, had escaped from Wormwood Scrubs prison. The Prime Minister was informed of the incident, and a national manhunt for him started, but was unsuccessful. The getaway car impacted with an Austin A35 green van with seats in the back.[4] It was many years ago, but that impact of seeing Blake staring out from his getaway car is still vivid in my memory. He was smuggled out of the country in a camper van. The men who planned Blake's escape, at one time being inmates of Wormwood Scrubs prison, were cleared at the Old Bailey by the jury, after writing a book on how they assisted Blake to spring him from the Scrubs' jail. This was a strange verdict where the perpetrators had not denied their involvement, and had written an account of it publicly, for all to read.

Blake died in 2020 at the age of 98 and was buried in Moscow as a national hero. President Putin of Russia stated that: 'Colonel Blake was an outstanding professional of special courage. He made a truly invaluable contribution to ensuring the strategic parity and preservation of peace on the planet.' The West had a different view and would take decades to address and correct the damage caused by Blake in his role of a spy. His espionage for the Russians was carried out while in a position of trust. Blake never acknowledged formally that he had betrayed Britain as a spy as he stated he had never truly belonged to Britain. The security services in Britain and the West had been complacent, and Blake would not be alone in taking advantage of such complacency. See *Burgess*. See *Cairncross*. See *Blunt*.

Blunt Anthony (1907–1983). A Russian spy and soviet agent employed in Britain during the war. One of the 'Cambridge Five' who compromised Britain's national security. Blunt was an art historian. He was recruited to MI5 during the war, and fed Enigma-decoded Ultra secrets to the Russians.

Bourne Ruth (née Henry) (b. 1926). A Wren (WRNS) Bombe operator under *Pembroke V*, Special Duties X, engaged at Bletchley Park and specifically at Outstation Eastcote, designated HMS *Pembroke V*, on codebreaking Bombe machines. Bourne also assisted in decrypting Enigma messages at Bletchley. At the age of 18 in 1944 she commenced her codebreaking career, signing the Official Secrets Act. At the end of the war, in 1945, she was also used to de-solder the wiring on Bombe machines, appointed to be 'wire destroyer', with other Wrens, based on instructions from Winston Churchill to destroy the machines. Bourne was awarded the Legion d'honneur by France for her contribution to codebreaking during the war. She is on the Bletchley Park Roll of Honour, along with other Wrens and people who provided support in codebreaking during wartime.

Burgess Guy (1911–1963). A famous spy who worked for the Russians in the 1950s and '60s in Britain. After being recruited by a Russian agent at Cambridge, he agreed to work for the Russians and obtain Government documents and information that would benefit the Soviets. He penetrated Foreign Office departments and shared secrets from Section D of MI6 with the Russians, a propaganda division, compromising Britain's security. After working a stint for the BBC, he joined MI6.

PEOPLE

Burgess was later known as one of the 'Cambridge Five', a group of recruited spies for the Russians, who penetrated British intelligence and individually exposed Britain's security to varying degrees. He defected to Russia in 1951 together with another spy, Donald Maclean. See *Cairncross*. See *Blake*.

Cairncross John (1913–1995). A civil servant and spy who worked for the Russians in the 1950s and '60s in Britain. He worked within Bletchley Park and managed to pass secret material and data across to the Russians. This included the decoded German intelligence on the plan for the battle of Kursk. He would be one of the 'Cambridge Five' individuals who were spies based in Britain. Although he gave a limited confession about his activities after the war, he was given immunity from prosecution. Cairncross would eventually escape back to the East, and Russia. Some reports have indicated that his espionage activities at Bletchley Park during wartime years were known about and monitored.

Canaris Wilhelm (1887–1945). Appointed head of the *Abwehr* (German Secret Service) in 1935, Canaris had a key position in intelligence gathering and communication across Germany and the occupied nations during the Second World War. In the First World War he was a naval officer. Prior to the war, he supported General Franco in the Spanish Civil War. This was a training ground for the Nazis to perfect their techniques in overrunning Poland and other countries. In 1944 he was transferred, and he apparently shielded conspirators against Adolf Hitler. Eventually he was tried by the SS and executed for his involvement in the failed attempt on Hitler's life. See *Germany*.

Caughey Catherine. WRNS. A Wren on Special Duties X at Bletchley Park. She joined the Newmanry section and worked as one of the Colossus machine operators from early 1944.[5] She took charge of the teleprinter room in the Park's Newmanry, where advanced non-Morse messages would be intercepted at Knockholt in Kent. These would be the Tunny messages, and only relatively few intercept stations would be able to record them and convert them into punched tape for further processing. See *Knockholt*.

Churchill Winston (1874–1965). Prime Minister of England and UK during the Second World War. When he married his wife, Clementine, in 1908 he stayed at Highgrove House[6] in Eastcote, Middlesex, for his honeymoon, or at least part of it. A stone's throw from Highgrove was a site with several open grazing fields and no buildings. If Churchill would have ventured over the old public footpath from Highgrove, he would have come across a five-bar gate overlooking the fields. Churchill would have been surprised that in thirty-five years' time from then,[7] the largest codebreaking outstation supporting Bletchley Park would stand on that site, with over a hundred codebreaking machines, the brainchild of Alan Turing and Gordon Welchman, jointly. Churchill was aware, during the war, of the need to be one step ahead of the enemy and find out what they were planning, by intercepting enemy intelligence. He visited Bletchley Park to find out how things were going and was surprised to later receive a letter from four mathematicians from Bletchley, without their boss's knowledge, asking for more resources, in order to keep up with the volume of enemy messages that had to be decoded. Churchill responded by agreeing to their request without question. He famously wrote on the request for his staff 'ACTION THIS DAY'. Not all leaders would have taken the request seriously, and many would have only responded to requests for resources through official management channels.

Churchill understood the relevance of decoding enemy intelligence, whether it be from the Nazis, the Italians, or the Japanese. He asked for all decoded messages to be provided to him each day at Downing Street, but that was impractical due to the volume. Many of the messages were minor trivia, and the management needed to sort them into those that were significant, filtering out the low-level messages. As a compromise, a summary was provided for Churchill in a buff folder each day. With a military background in the First World War, Churchill had a reasonable understanding of the priorities in wartime: to ensure that the resources were there for the population in terms of food, fuel, medicines, supplies and materials; that armaments, vehicles, fuel, and food had to be brought in from the USA by convoy, and negotiate the U-boat threat, which was Churchill's worry; to ensure that Bletchley Park and its supporting infrastructure worked as intended, and were able to intercept, with some degree of consistency, the Nazi Enigma messages. He would meet in the underground Cabinet rooms in Whitehall to discuss military strategy, immediate threats to the population, and progress.[8] As an alternative, he had Cabinet rooms in Dollis Hill, north London, known as the Paddock, but did not use them frequently, as they were damp, cold and uncomfortable. Churchill had to fight against other politicians who wanted appeasement with Hitler, but he would have none of it. He built up a friendly relationship with the King, and confided in him regarding his decisions being considered. Churchill worked with the War Cabinet, supported by Committees of Chiefs of Staff. This would bridge across the Admiralty, War Office and the Air Ministry. Parliament would be consulted on certain matters but as surprise was essential against the enemy, statements in Parliament had to be carefully scrutinised beforehand.

Over the wartime years, Churchill acted as a true leader for Britain and the free part of Europe, wrote and gave memorable speeches to the nation, raising morale in the darkest of times, during the Blitz and U-boat attacks. Churchill realised that, until America's intervention after Pearl Harbor, Britain was on its own against Hitler. Stalin became an ally of Britain and the West when Hitler invaded Russia under Operation Barbarossa. Churchill almost rejoiced when America was attacked by Japan at Pearl Harbor, bringing it into the war, as he knew it would be a close ally and support Britain. The gathering, decoding and analysis of military intelligence was essential to the success of defeating Hitler and the Axis powers, also later Japan. Churchill would try brief military incursions in France to see how the troops might fare, but with disaster ensuing, and a bloody nose. D-Day was some way off, and by then advanced Nazi machines had to be dealt with by Bletchley, with the help of several supporting organisations, including the engineering arm of the Post Office.[9] Churchill agreed to spread the risk at Bletchley using satellite outstations to process enemy messages, to avoid the calamity of a possible Luftwaffe attack at Bletchley potentially wiping out Britain's intelligence and cryptographic capability.[10] He could not afford that risk. He would need to be kept informed if any of those outstations were put out of action for any length of time. Secrecy was paramount. Leaks to enemy agents could not be allowed. How much Churchill knew about the detail of the 'Robinson' and 'Colossus' decoding machines, is not known but he would have been told about the threat of advanced machines and the approach to tackle the intelligence arising through them. He did not need the detail, only the results and progress. There were others to worry about the detail of the design and build of those machines. Leaders cannot get involved in fine detail.

Churchill did not trust Stalin, but at the time it was convenient for Russia to be an ally of Britain rather than an enemy. There is some hypocrisy here, as Russia invaded Poland two weeks after the Nazis, yet Britain did not declare war on the Russians. Probably a wise move at the time. Churchill met at Tehran with Roosevelt and Stalin to discuss strategy against the Nazis. Stalin wanted a second front, but that was not ready yet. Churchill instructed others to set up a transmitter, 'Aspidistra', which transmitted programmes in 1942 to try to convince the Nazis that the war was not going their way and they would be suffering heavy losses in future. It would be somewhat the equivalent of the propaganda transmissions from Lord Haw-Haw in Germany transmitting to the Allies. However, it did not make much difference, and other more practical methods were needed to stop Hitler. There would be several deception operations that Churchill was keen on implementing, such as *Operation Mincemeat*,[11] which did have some degree of success in the Mediterranean, fooling the Germans at a crucial time and potentially saving many Allied lives.

Churchill would have secret conversations from the Cabinet War Rooms across the Atlantic to President Roosevelt, on a semi-regular basis. Churchill preferred to use the Red scrambler phone but was told not to use it as it was insecure. The Americans designed and built a relatively secure voice-communication system and installed one unit in the basement of a famous London department store. It was enormous, used many kilowatts of electrical power and needed air-conditioning to cool it. Apparently, from records, Churchill didn't care much for the system known as SIGSALY,[12] but it worked, and was highly complex, run by an American team of signals engineers and officers. There were also links back to the American Embassy and 10 Downing Street, but the bulk of conversations using this highly complex Vocoder system would have been via the Cabinet War Rooms in Whitehall.[13] Churchill continued to use this system for transatlantic phone calls when Roosevelt died, and President Harry Truman took over the reins. In April 1945, Churchill would speak to President Truman over the SIGSALY link, and spoke for two hours, the longest call ever made over the system. This would be top-secret equipment, systems and technology for a further thirty years, under the Official Secrets Act.

Churchill was instrumental in supporting Bletchley Park and the codebreaking infrastructure in Britain, taking an interest and enabling resources to make it happen.[14] He had visited Bletchley Park and Dollis Hill during wartime, but there is no record of him visiting the codebreaking outstations, even though he was aware of their existence. He received regular reports on progress on codebreaking. Churchill will be remembered for his famous speeches and oratory, to the nation and to the House of Commons. He died in the 1960s when Britain and England in particular, was rebuilding and restructuring after the war years, and was given a state funeral in London.[15] Churchill made a significant contribution to the defeat of Hitler during the last war, under extremely challenging circumstances. He was aware of the need for the processing of intelligence against the enemy by whatever means necessary: covert operations, decoding machines, Y-stations, using spies, obtaining financial and material support from your allies, such as under Lend-Lease opportunities, and many others too. Arguably, one of the greatest leaders that Britain ever had. See *Roosevelt*. See *Truman*.

Clarke Joan (1917–1996). English cryptanalyst and numismatist who was a codebreaker at Bletchley Park during the Second World War. Clarke had obtained a double first degree in Maths at Cambridge. She was recruited into GC&CS by Gordon Welchman, at Bletchley on 17 June 1940. She quickly obtained promotion as a linguist and worked on Naval Enigma codes cracking many of the settings for the Enigma cipher in Hut 8 at Bletchley. She was proficient in using the Alan Turing 'Banburismus' system in her codebreaking work. Receiving further promotion at Bletchley in 1944, and now head of Hut 8, Clarke became friendly with Turing, and they became engaged. However, Turing broke off the engagement as he confessed he was a homosexual. They remained good friends afterwards. Due to the efforts of Clarke and her team, they reduced the shipping convoy losses in the Atlantic to around one-fifth of what they had been previously. Clarke spent a time at GCHQ Eastcote after the war. She married a retired army officer in 1952, spent some time living in Scotland and went back to GCHQ in 1962, which had then relocated to Cheltenham. Clarke is well-known in codebreaking circles for her connection with Alan Turing, and her competence in codebreaking at Bletchley Park in what was, at the time, a male-dominated circle of mathematicians and specialists. See *Turing*. See *Bletchley Park*.

Cooper Joshua Edward Synge [Josh] (1901–1981). Cryptographer at Bletchley Park, joining as an assistant in 1925. 'Josh' Cooper was qualified in advanced Russian language skills, and this was used to the Allies' advantage, working on Russian diplomatic ciphers and naval codes. He worked as the head of the air section from 1936, interested in Luftwaffe operations and intelligence. He was made a CB and CMG for his wartime services.

Cumming Mansfield (1859–1923). Sometimes referred to as 'the Father of SIS', the British Secret Intelligence Service. His involvement at SIS was between 1909 and 1923. It is apparent that SIS started to be used as a term in or around 1920. Cumming made SIS an international service covering the world. Originally, he was a Naval officer, working his way up in early developing organisations between Foreign Office and Military intelligence. His reports on intelligence at SIS were termed CX reports. As Chief of the SIS he was known as 'C'. The term MI6 was used during the Second World War but is now disused, and SIS is the most relevant intelligence service to reflect it.

PEOPLE

De Grey Nigel (1886–1951). A codebreaker fluent in French and German, who worked at Bletchley Park during the last war. De Grey studied at Eton, then Roehampton in the early part of the twentieth century. He saw action in the First World War in Belgium, trained in the Royal Naval Reserve and was transferred to Naval Intelligence at Room 40 in Whitehall, which would eventually develop into GC&CS at Bletchley. James Alfred Ewing would recruit codebreakers to build up the intelligence and signals expertise and selected De Grey as one of the team. A new section termed the Intelligence Exchange would have De Grey as its head. It was a form of coordinating and project management role to bring together the daily cryptographic output from Bletchley Park. This would encompass naval, military, air, commercial, Russian, French naval, and other sections.

Prior to this, it was De Grey and two other codebreakers including Dilwyn Knox,[16] that managed to decipher a message from the German Ambassador to the German embassy in Mexico, which would become famous as the Zimmerman telegram. The contents of this telegram would soon bring America into the First World War, and the handling of the intelligence was extremely sensitive to avoid Britain being implicated over how the information was accessed. The Germans were encouraging Mexico to wage war on the United States. The date was 16 January 1916. The decryption of the telegram was the most significant piece of codebreaking of all the German messages in the impact it would eventually have on one of Britain's major allies. On 23 February, a few weeks after the telegram was decrypted, De Grey had to demonstrate the decoding of a fresh copy of the telegram for the Americans, to prove it was genuine and that the threat from Germany and Mexico was real. By April that year, the United States was at war with Germany alongside Britain, France, and others. Mexico did not attack the US, however, which would have been a mistake. De Grey was later made an OBE and received other formal awards for his cryptographic services during the war. He worked on Russian intercepts as the Cold War developed and became Deputy Director at Bletchley Park. For all his achievements, he will always be remembered for his part in decrypting the Zimmerman telegram in 1916, and showing the highly sensitive content to his boss, which helped to change world history. See *Dilwyn Knox*.

Denniston Alastair (1881–1961). The Head of Bletchley Park from 1939 to 1942, being the headquarters of cryptographic and intelligence work known as GC&CS, the Government Code and Cipher School. Technically, he was head of GC&CS from 1919. Bletchley Park was established as a top-secret base in the Buckinghamshire countryside, away from prying eyes, and filled with specialist mathematicians and cryptographic analysts, and support personnel, trying to break into enemy encoded messages such as those based on the Nazi 'Enigma' machine developed by Arthur Scherbius. Denniston was a Scot, well educated in both Germany and in Paris. He cut his codebreaking teeth in Room 40 in the Admiralty, some years before taking up his role at Bletchley. Even after the First World War ended, the Government required Room 40 to continue its work in codebreaking, and it was merged with Ml 1b from the army and became GC&CS in 1920.

Denniston was keen on relocating to Bletchley Park in 1939 due to its relatively close links to Oxford, Cambridge and London, and contacted the top universities to seek out the core of his codebreaking team. These included mathematicians such as Alan Turing, Gordon Welchman and Dilwyn Knox. Denniston had been involved in important meetings with the Poles and the French in Warsaw at a codebreaking conference, to discuss methods and systems in codebreaking activities. In 1941, Denniston was unimpressed when he found out that four members of his team had bypassed his management and had privately written to Winston Churchill, requesting more resources at Bletchley Park as a matter of great urgency. However, Churchill responded positively and made those additional resources available. This change would move Bletchley Park forward much faster than otherwise would have been the case, and Denniston eventually saw the benefit this would bring his organisation and personnel. Denniston had serious doubts in the early years as to whether the complex German naval codes could be broken. However, due to the perseverance of his team of mathematicians, significant progress was made.

When Denniston was director, four US officers visited to discuss cryptographic matters and share some information. They would bring with them an analogue 'Purple' Japanese encoding machine. This greatly excited the people at Bletchley. At the time, in February 1941, America was still not at war, unlike the British. Those at Bletchley and senior politicians in the know, i.e. Churchill, were somewhat reluctant to allow these overseas visitors to see the Turing/Welchman Bombe machine, as it was top secret. Not even Churchill had been to Bletchley at that time. However, it was decided to share the secret with the two army and two naval officers. Considerable time was spent showing them the Bombe at work, processing a message, with many questions asked and answered. The fear for the British was that if such information got back to the Nazis then they would have changed their encoding machines and systems almost immediately. It was a risk, but a risk worth taking. As it turned out the Americans would later, with help from J. Desch and the National Cash Register Company, produce their own version of the British codebreaking Bombe, a more efficient machine by all accounts, and which could tackle four-rotor Enigma machines.

By February 1942 Denniston had been replaced by Commander E. Travis. Travis modernised Bletchley Park and expanded the personnel to include large quantities of men and women, with varying roles. It became a mix of military personnel and civilians, unusual for wartime, as an operational base. See *Y-stations* and *Worldwide Y-stations*. See *Desch. See Travis.*

Desch Joseph (1907–1987). Electrical engineer and an inventor of a range of various electronic equipment from 1939 to 1953. He was of German heritage and his parents worked on blacksmith-type equipment and trades. His key role during the Second World War was as the Research Director for the NCML in Dayton, Ohio, USA, and the development of the American Naval Bombe codebreaking machines to complement the British Bombes at Bletchley Park and the five outstations. Defence contracts were issued in 1940 via the National Defense Research Committee. These would be four-rotor codebreaking machines for the US Navy, principally to counter the U-boat threat affecting shipping in the Atlantic. The improved Bombe machines were designed and built at the National Cash Register factory in Dayton. Some American naval officers had basic drawings of the British Bombe to work from, but they would be heavily modified. The codebreaking machines would be supplied to OP-20-G, and the laboratory would be in Building 26 at NCR, which would have armed guards on the perimeter. His laboratory would become the United States Naval Computing Machine Laboratory. Although it appears that Desch had been promised a prototype to study for the design, he never received this, so had to use intuition and research to design in modifications and build the machine, using whatever blueprints he could lay his hands on.

Joseph Wenger, a rear admiral in the US Navy, would also drive forward the production and need for this modified codebreaking Bombe machine, convincing the authorities to find the $2 million for the project. Desch was unconvinced of using valve tubes for the switching of the new machine, and advised the Navy against this, due to the vast numbers of valves that would be required. The final design would be a combination of mechanical and electronic items. Desch was interested in new ideas and technology, and studied with some interest British physicist Charles Wynn-Williams' research and papers on thyratron gas-filled tubes for counting. He would develop his own versions in the USA, and some were used for counting purposes in the Chicago Manhattan Project.

Over the years, Desch would take out many different patents for inventions of electrical and electronic equipment, from calculating machines to measuring instruments and impulse transmitters. Back at NCR, he would oversee the stage from design and building the first Naval Bombe machines to a production run of some 121 American four-rotor Bombes. They would be built by a large group of women, some six hundred WAVES, or Women Accepted for Volunteer Emergency Service. There would also be 100 Navy officers and enlisted men, plus civilians. The units would be tested and transported to Washington for operation. Alan Turing would visit NCR in Dayton in December 1942. Two experimental Bombes were ready in operation by May 1943. Designs for full production would be completed by April 1943, operation of US Naval Bombe machines starting by early June. Each Bombe would be 7ft high by 2ft deep by 10ft long and weigh 5,000lb. Building 26 would be used between 1942 and 1946. By all accounts there would be thirty-two rotors on the front and the same on the back of the machine, and rotor speed on the fastest rotor could reach some 1,725 revolutions per minute, reducing the processing time of message settings. Although built to target naval Enigma machine keys, some reports indicated a further additional fifty Bombes would later be built to interrogate army and air force keys.

The NCR Desch-led laboratory at Dayton grew significantly in numbers of staff personnel, from around twenty staff to over one thousand by 1944. Desch was formally recognised for his inventions and services by several organisations. President Harry Truman would award Desch the Medal of Merit in 1947, but he would not be allowed to discuss the detail as to what it was for due to security issues and restrictions imposed by the Government at the time. Few NCR engineers and naval officers had complete knowledge of the project that Desch had worked on, to produce the US Naval Bombes and the purpose of them. One of the US Naval Bombes is in the National Cryptologic Museum in Maryland.

Post-war, Desch would patent an electronic calculator in 1946 and with his colleague Mumma they applied for the patent of what might be considered as the first modern digital computer. However, Tommy Flowers in England could not talk about his Colossus machine, which was working in 1944 at Bletchley Park, and was top secret, using thousands of valves as switches. After the war had ended, Desch would help to develop the NCR 304, the first completely solid-state, (i.e., non-valve) transistor-based computer. He would be recognised formally by the NSA/CSS Hall of Honor for his services. From a career that started off testing radios for General Motors, and then moved into work with teleprinters and communications, he had learned and developed his skills and knowledge to such a degree that he became a key player in American wartime codebreaking, although he himself had no real experience in that field. His real expertise was in applied electrical and electronics, to solve problems using new materials and technology, borrowing ideas from others and developing them further to form a practical use. From remote controls to electronic calculators, to sophisticated electronic counting machines, Desch was a specialist and innovator who made a difference to the war effort. His use of Wynn-Williams' research demonstrated his flexibility of approach and his acceptance to learn from others. See *Dayton, Ohio*. See *Charles Wynn-Williams*.

Dönitz Karl (Admiral) (1881–1980). Commander of the *Kriegsmarine* or German Navy, Dönitz oversaw the Nazi U-boat threat in the Atlantic and elsewhere from bases in France and Germany. U-boats attacked Allied convoys and shipping in order to cut off valuable supplies and resources for America, Britain and Canada, as well as being active in the Mediterranean. Dönitz would supersede Admiral Raeder in early 1943, becoming Grand Admiral of all German naval forces. A master stroke by Dönitz was to require an upgraded version of the Enigma encoding machine for his U-boats to add a fourth wheel rotor, to increase the number of permutations of the settings of the machine.[17] This additional new rotor, however, would not be interchangeable with the original three. This caused Bletchley Park's cryptographic team major headaches and stopped them breaking into naval Enigma encoded messages for several months, until some code books were captured by the British in October 1942. Dönitz was Supreme Commander of the Nazis and would succeed Hitler in 1945 for a short period before his capture and the German surrender.

Reports indicate that when Dönitz was a British prisoner of war during the First World War he came up with the idea of wolfpacks of submarines, as he had been active in submarine warfare. He would later refine and develop those techniques to perfection, crippling the Allies in the Atlantic and Mediterranean and destroying millions of tons of shipping. Communication would be via Enigma encoding machines used for brief periods, to limit the possibility of Allied interception of radio encoded messages. U-boats would communicate via radio nets, which were

PEOPLE

termed 'Diana' and 'Hubertus', with six radio transmission frequencies to choose from. Ironically, 'Hubertus' was the patron saint of hunters, and appropriate for the task of torpedoing Allied shipping en masse. The positioning of U-boat pens on the French Atlantic coast made it easier for them to reach the enemy convoys. Due to air superiority, centimetric radar technology and a lack of German resources, the U-boats would lose their effectiveness. The breaking of the Enigma codes by Bletchley Park would make a difference but would not be as significant as perhaps other advances made by the Allies. It would be in May 1945 that Dönitz instructed Jodl of the OKW to sign the formal German surrender in Reims, France, at the end of the war, resulting shortly afterwards in Victory in Europe Day, or VE day.[18] See *Germany*. See *Hitler*. See *North Atlantic*.

Du Boisson, Dorothy. WRNS. A Wren from 1943 and sent to Bletchley Park. Engaged in the Newmanry during the pre-Colossus period, she operated the 'Robinson' or Heath Robinson earlier machine attacking the settings of Lorenz Nazi teleprinter encoding machines. Eventually she would move across to operating the Colossus Mark 1 and later the Mk 2. Dorothy became a registrar in the Newmanry's Operations Room and would help to distribute tapes that contained the encrypted coded messages. See *Flowers*.

Eisenhower Dwight D (1890–1969). Supreme Allied Commander for European Forces who took back Europe from the Nazis, along with help from the Russians. Later to become President Eisenhower, better known as 'Ike'. Eisenhower had to discuss strategy with Churchill, Montgomery, and others to ensure the best chance of success at D-Day in June 1944. This would depend on intelligence received from a large number of sources, including the French Resistance, double agents and from Bletchley Park intercepts and decoded messages. The codebreaking Bombes, Robinson, Colossus Mark 1 and the Mark 2 advanced codebreaking machines would play an important role in the build-up to D-Day, the latter Colossus machine arriving only days before the major assault on Normandy. Eisenhower approved the final D-Day Plan in May 1944 at a boys' school in Hammersmith, London, which had been requisitioned for the use of the military. At that meeting were Churchill and King George VI. The school has since been demolished. A commemorative plaque exists on the boundary wall of the site, recording this key event in the war. It was Eisenhower that approved the message to be sent to the Nazis on the early morning of D-Day by double agent 'Garbo' advising of the mass movement of ships across the English Channel towards France. This was a huge risk for the Allies, but part of a well-conceived plan to tie large Nazi Panzer divisions down in Northern France, awaiting an assault across the Pas-de-Calais that would never materialise. See *'Garbo'*. See *USA*. See *Churchill*.

Ellis James (1924–1997). Cryptographer, engineer and developer of a public key cryptographic cipher system in the 1970s. This system was inspired by reading a paper issued by Bell Laboratories, which had worked on the voice encoding/decoding SIGSALY system, whereby noise was added and then subtracted to conceal a voice message. Ellis worked for GCHQ in the 1970s and developed his ideas to achieve practical objectives, many being secret and classified. Clifford Cocks and Malcolm Williamson were two mathematicians that became involved in Ellis's ideas. The NSA became aware of Ellis's work and generated much interest in his papers and the team that worked on solving cryptographic problems with cipher keys. It wasn't until the end of the twentieth century that acknowledgement of their significant contribution to GCHQ in the development of ground-breaking cryptographic secret systems could be mentioned publicly.

Ewing, James, Alfred (1855–1935). Working with British Admiralty and within Room 40 on intelligence operations, he helped to establish the Y-stations, or listening stations, around Britain, and later elsewhere abroad. These were to listen to friend and foe, in order to obtain advance warning of military operations against the British Empire, and to intercept encoded messages. Ewing was a well-educated engineer who graduated from Edinburgh University. He rose rapidly within the Admiralty and had various teaching positions abroad before the start of the war. In 1902, he was the Director of Naval Education. His background included study of magnetic properties of metals, as a physicist. Ewing had various nicknames while at Room 40, including 'Eavesdropper Ewing', 'The Cipher King', and 'The U-Boat Trapper'.[19]

Fairbanks Jnr, Douglas. (1909–2000). Famous as an American actor, but also as a highly decorated soldier and officer. He was appointed by the President to be an envoy to South America and also commanded various warships in naval battles. However, his main contribution was in helping to develop the area of technical deception during the war, and utilising collected intelligence in the deception operations. Fairbanks, who was initially in the US Navy Reserve, was asked in 1941 by British naval officer Lord Louis Mountbatten to establish a deception programme for the British. Mountbatten was already aware of the use of sonic deception techniques for commando raids, to draw enemy fire away from attacking soldiers. Fairbanks's popularity as an actor meant that he had to do most of his innovation and planning work back in America with US troops. Some tests were carried out and training took place on the west coast of Scotland. Fairbanks was instrumental in helping to evolve various deception techniques using a variety of methods. Detailed tests with troops on a beach were carried out near New Jersey, and in one test scenario, at Sandy Hook island in 1942, American soldiers were visibly confused as to which direction an attack was coming from due to the various sounds and noises transmitted. Observers included both Fairbanks Jr and various military senior officers. It was recorded as a success.

The division that was eventually formed comprised carpenters, actors, sound technicians, painters, camouflage artists and others. A 'Ghost' army, 23rd Headquarters Special Troops, was formed to support those in the battlefield and take away fire from approaching forces using complex deception techniques. Fairbanks Jr had the advantage of having worked in the film industry and was aware of special effects. He had the vision that this could work in wartime if enough detail was incorporated to make the deception realistic. Fairbanks Jr was also well-connected with senior politicians and senior officers due to his acting fame. In 1943, the top brass instructed a unit to be formed specifically to deceive the enemy in beach landing operations, comprising a unit of almost five hundred men, both officers and enlisted men. These would be termed 'Beach Jumpers'. The impact of such activities in battle would be closely monitored as to their success or failure and communicated back to HQ command. This intelligence would be invaluable for the Allies with regard to the enemy positions and movements affected by the deception strategy. These specialists would train at Camp Bradford in Virginia. Fairbanks used his skills and experience to give guidance on technical detail during deception operations and training. Dummy soldiers were also developed to be dropped by parachute, to confuse the Nazis defending positions. Referred to as *gummipuppen* or dolls, the American versions, known as 'Oscars', would be technically different to those used by the British 'Ruperts'[20] when landing around Caen in France in the period just prior to the D-Day landings. Exploding and firing from a distance, they could appear convincing to an enemy in darkness or poor light, creating the illusion of being under attack.

Deception techniques were used on a small, medium and large scale during the war, and Sicily was one location where this aided Allied forces landing on the beaches. July 1943 saw the deception team attack with a combination of air-sea rescue boats and MTBs with audio sonic broadcasts from high-powered horn speakers and smoke launchers. Interception of German broadcasts and intelligence indicated they had fallen for the trap and had 'repelled' an invasion of forces at the location where the 'Beach Jumpers' approached. Action was also seen in southern France in August 1944. These combined deception techniques, some developed to an incredible technical and scientific level, saved Allied soldiers' lives, caused chaos and confusion to the enemy, and took enemy resources away from key battle positions giving the attacking forces time and space to reach their objectives. It is an example of how specialist and highly skilled peacetime trades and professions can convert successfully to wartime action.[21] The 23rd HQ Special Troops organisation was top secret, and only declassified in 1996. See *USA*. See *Normandy*.

Fenson, Harry. Engineer at the Post Office Research Establishment at Dollis Hill, north-west London. He joined the inner circle of engineers with Tommy Flowers in 1942. He became involved in the Heath Robinson decoding machine, and later the Mk 1 and 2 Colossus computer. He was responsible for the machines at Bletchley Park, and also later post-war had a part in assisting Flowers design the Premium Bonds National Savings computer ERNIE. This machine was truly random in terms of output and checked periodically by an independent actuary. See *Flowers*.

Fletcher Harold. A codebreaker who worked in Hut 6 at Bletchley Park. He had been a Cambridge mathematician recruited from the University, like so many others.

Flicke Wilhelm (1882–1946). A German cryptographer during the Second World War. He worked in Lauf, analysing signals and intelligence from the Russians, Poles and the Western Allies. Papers seen from Flicke written in 1945 indicate he and some others suspected that either agents had betrayed the Germans at Crete, in the

Mediterranean, or alternatively that the Enigma cipher had been compromised and broken. A report and translation of a paper by Wilhelm Flicke by Anglo-American TICOM in 1948, outlined his operating procedure at an intercept station in some considerable detail. Flicke had been a member of the LAUF intercept station of the Signal intelligence agency of Supreme Command German Armed Forces. Flicke would write substantial accounts after the war of the processes, methods and progress made when he was in post. 'War Secrets in the Ether – Part III' dated 1953, translated from a previously restricted and classified document, is available online via the NSA. It was only declassified by the NSA in July 2014. In that account, Flicke gives his opinion as to how well organised were the German intelligence services, and it is apparent that Hitler had imposed certain protocols and directions that made the organisation far less efficient than it could have been. Reports of intelligence intercepts were only authorised to be read by certain chief officers but the volume collected meant this was impossible. Items would be then stored in safes, away from prying eyes, and periodically a purge of intelligence papers would be organised, with the destruction of huge amounts of intercept data that may well have been useful if matched with other relevant intercepts. By comparison, Bletchley Park considered it essential to introduce the creation of an intelligence database, using Hollerith tabulating machines initially at Bletchley, and later at Drayton Parslow off site.[22] The resources to run and manage that database was, however, considerable in terms of storage space, equipment and vast numbers of personnel. Only in this way could there be connections made between different intelligence intercepts collected the and building up of a picture for commanders to progress their strategic aims against the Nazis. Flicke did not agree that the German intelligence services were poorly organised, but maintained that the restrictions imposed by Hitler did not help or assist those officers with the expertise to collect, decode and analyse enemy intercepts.

Flowers, Thomas (1905–1998). A Post Office engineer who studied at night school in Woolwich, and who made equipment for Bletchley Park and other units. Flowers was born in East Ham, London. He studied at Woolwich Polytechnic, enrolling in 1922, and passed his intermediate examination in engineering in 1926, then joining the telephone branch of the Post Office. In 1930 he joined Dollis Hill in research and explored and experimented with the use of valves in the making and breaking of telephone connections. In 1934 Flowers had used 3,000–4,000 tube valves to control one thousand telephone lines, an advanced piece of technology for the time. Each line would have three or four valves. His background in the late 1930s on experimental digital data storage for telephone exchanges would prove to be extremely useful in his later work for the Post Office, and of enormous assistance to Bletchley Park. Flowers would first meet Alan Turing in 1939, the year Turing joined Bletchley Park. Turing wanted Flowers to build a relay-based machine that would have some connection to the new Turing Bombe codebreaking invention. But Flowers' machine attachment was not used at Bletchley Park. His most important role during the war was in designing and building (with some considerable Post Office engineering assistance) the Colossus advanced codebreaking machine to tackle the Nazi Lorenz teleprinter encoders.

PEOPLE

The development began when Turing introduced Flowers to his colleague, Max Newman, who managed a section at Bletchley Park named the Newmanry. That department concentrated on using machines where possible to tackle the new advanced Nazi encoding machines. Following use of a less sophisticated and unreliable machine, the Robinson, for which Flowers had built certain parts and components, Newman approached Flowers and asked if he could assist in building something better, and one that was much more reliable. That initial meeting culminated into a long-term project, with Flowers designing and building the enormous and complex Colossus. It was built at the Post Office Engineering Research Station unit in Dollis Hill, not far from Willesden, in north-west London. In effect, Newman had the mathematical and cryptographical knowledge as to what needed to be achieved to break the advanced Nazi encoding machines, and Flowers had the technical knowledge as to how to achieve this in practice using many valves as switches. Flowers would fall out with Gordon Welchman from Bletchley Park, and there would be significant differences of opinion on approaching and solving technical problems. However, the Colossus machines were very successful and when reassembled at Bletchley Park were tested a considerable number of times and worked well.

Flowers had designed and built the world's first semi-programmable digital computer at a time when computers did not exist. Flowers had to assemble a team of support engineers from the Post Office Engineering Research Station, abbreviated as PORES. Also, some of his engineers from the Midlands were brought in and he had the full support of his boss, Radley. However, all was not perfect, as there were mutterings from Bletchley Park management as to the reliability of the new machine as it was based on valves. Flowers had studied the use of tube valves as switches, effectively digital switches, in a world and a time whereby valves were only used commonly as amplifiers. The vast number of valves needed to make Colossus work was considerable, expensive and could potentially fail in operation. Flowers was fortunate to have management support in terms of time, manpower and resources to design and build this innovative codebreaking machine, but he ended up forking out £1,000 of his own money to purchase key components to finish the project. The Mk 2 Colossus took around nine months to design and build, a timescale that was compressed after criticism as to the length of the project within Bletchley Park. It was delivered from Dollis Hill a few days prior to D-Day, a critical time for gathering enemy intelligence.

After the war, Flowers was not given the opportunity to work on computers at PORES, and went back to making systems and equipment for telephone communications. He became head of the Switching Division. From 1950 to 1964 he was Staff engineer, and often would deputise for the Controller of Research. He left PORES in 1964 and retired in 1970.

In 1993 Flowers went on a short course on digital personal computers and information processing, run by Hendon College. He passed the course and received a certificate to state that he was competent in the use of basic personal computers. It is not known if others on the course were aware of his achievements for the Post Office and Bletchley Park, as he probably had to sign the Official Secrets Act when working on codebreaking equipment and it would have been considered a breach of that Act and a criminal offence if he had told others of his involvement, even if it was some years after the war had ended.[23] The course would have been based on personal computers using modern solid-state transistors, and not valves. If the attendees of that course had known that Flowers had worked on valves as digital switches, and not transistors, it is likely they would have been astonished that a computer could work reliably with valve technology to produce many operations at great speed.

After the war ended Flowers received a £1,000 prize for his involvement in the invention of the technology, an amount that effectively reimbursed him for the money he had used to finish completing Colossus Mark 2. He would not have been impressed, especially as he would not have been allowed to tell others exactly what that prize was for. In 1950, Flowers worked on electronic telephone exchanges, and the first of these was Highgate Wood. In the 1960s Flowers worked on and designed the Premium Bonds computer ERNIE. This was designed to create random numbers in a sequence and had to be sufficiently robust such that no one could establish a pattern to win the jackpot with some form of cheating system. ERNIE stands for Electronic Random Number Indicator Equipment. It is based on thermal noise of transistors with both voltage and heat fluctuations, with independent monthly testing to ensure it is truly random. That definition is *statistically* random.

Flowers tried to obtain funding to build another version of Colossus and develop it, but failed in this venture, partly as he was still under the Official Secrets Act and could not talk about Colossus with anyone, and partly because his bank didn't believe such a machine was possible. We can therefore state that in his post-war years, although employed at the Post Office Engineering Establishment on converting telephone exchanges, he was probably frustrated, and not able to utilise his depth of knowledge and skills to the full.

Flowers is remembered via some street names, including one at Dollis Hill, Flowers Close. Another, Flowers Avenue, is at the site of the previous Outstation Eastcote and GCHQ. He was made an MBE for his work. In 1975 his invention of Colossus, the world's first semi-programmable computer based on valve switching technology, was formally recognised when the British Government declassified it. He developed and pioneered the first electronic telephone exchange for the Post Office, which was also a significant achievement, and brought about a change in British telecommunications, moving it into the digital age. Americans have claimed in certain books and publications that they were the first to build and operate an electronic computer, but Flowers and his team constructed the world's first semi-programmable computer, Colossus, during wartime using valve tubes as switches.

BT unveiled a bronze bust of Flowers at its research site at Martlesham Heath on the seventieth anniversary of the engineering division of the Post Office (the predecessor of British Telecom), recognising his contribution to technology, computing and innovation. See *PORES*. See *Bletchley Park*. See *Newman*.

Foss, Hugh (1902–1971). A British cryptanalyst at Bletchley Park during the last war. He was one of the first to propose a way of cracking the Enigma machine. Foss applied Turing's technique to establish the wheel orders on Enigma, known as 'Banburismus'. He went on to crack Japanese codes very successfully. The date 8 May was celebrated at Bletchley as Foss Day, the date when he intercepted a complex encoded message, working on it until November of that year and eventually succeeding. He led the Japanese cryptographic section on naval intelligence and built up a large team at Bletchley. Foss was sent to America in 1943 to assist with cracking Japanese naval codes and managed to crack the naval attaché code system, Coral. After the war, Foss worked for GCHQ, retiring in 1953. See *Turing*.

Freeborn V. Frederick (1897–1977). A civilian manager who worked at BTM in Letchworth, Hertfordshire, but was later asked to head up a new section running Hollerith punched card machines. Freeborn was Head of the Hollerith Section and Chief of Bletchley Research Department with the British Tabulating Machine Company (BTM). The Hollerith Machine Tabulating Section (punched card section) was originally in one of the huts at Bletchley, Hut 7, from around 1940, then moved to Block C from November 1942. Freeborn was tasked to manage this section, building up a large number of skilled personnel, mainly women. He would list the equipment inventory he required to do the job required of him.[24]

However, the volume of cards collected was enormous, increasing daily, and Bletchley needed the space. In 1942 it was decided to relocate the Hollerith section to the village of Drayton Parslow, around 4 miles from Bletchley Park. BTM occupied a large house in the village and huts were erected nearby for workers, who were Hollerith operators. Freeborn had close relatives who were section heads in the Hollerith department. BTM had sold Hollerith machines under licence from International Business Machines (IBM) in the USA around the world to the British Empire.

The department employed a process of filing punched cards, taking them and processing them through large Hollerith machines, collating them, and using them to collect and distribute a great deal of intelligence.[25] It was an early search engine, pre-dating Google and other search engines by many decades, although it was not computer-based. This intelligence assembly and processing often listed what appeared to be trivial information by itself, but when put together with others could identify new information useful to the Allies. There would be cryptographic and statistical data, together with a considerable amount of personal data of German officers, possibly identifying links between units. It was, in essence, a large card-based database, capable of being searched and filtered down. Bletchley needed to send information to Drayton Parslow, and to additionally receive back requested data for searched information. Freeborn identified several female staff with a special aptitude for the work, and promoted them, although at hardly any pay increase for the added responsibility. Bletchley Park wanted to dictate how the section was run, how information should be processed, and when information came back to Bletchley. Freeborn resisted this level of interference from codebreaking HQ and did his own thing, managing his busy team under pressure, troubleshooting problems that arose daily, and running an extremely efficient set-up.[26] Later, John Tiltman at Bletchley would act to prioritise messages to be Hollerith-processed and reduce the conflicts that had arisen. Tiltman was the Chief Cryptanalyst at Bletchley Park. The work was done on shifts and would be continuous day and night. This was due to the vast number of messages received via Enigma intercepted by listening stations. There was even little respite on Christmas Day, when work largely went on until late afternoon. The Hollerith section had engineers for any repairs needed to the noisy machines. The staff were a mix of ATS women, Wrens and some civilians, too. The section expanded to over five hundred staff by the end of the war. Punched cards were later used in early computers after the war, followed by punched tape on spools and reels. The tabulating section team would be known as the Freebornery.

Prior to his involvement at BTM Freeborn had been engaged in the East Surrey Regiment of the British Army in the First World War. Freeborn had an aptitude for understanding the use and operation of Hollerith machines, how to apply them to a problem, and organising staff efficiently. He appears in the Bletchley Park Roll of Honour for his unique services supporting codebreaking during wartime. A detailed description of how they were used is available.[27] See *BTM*. See *Letchworth*. See *Drayton Parslow*. See *Bletchley Park*.

Fricke Walter Ernest (1915–1988). A mathematician, astronomer and cryptanalyst who worked for the Wehrmacht during the war. He would study cipher systems in some detail. The German Army cipher office was OKH-Chi, and he worked there developing new ciphers for use by the military. Fricke would also study and adapt ciphers developed by British codebreaker John Tiltman, who was based at Bletchley Park. See *John Tiltman*.

Friedman Elizebeth (1892–1980).[28] American female cryptographer who worked on a variety of intelligence and exposed a number of spies working in America. In the early years of her career she would assist the authorities to clamp down on liquor manufacturing and sales during prohibition. Both she and her husband, William, would become early pioneers of cryptography and intelligence analysis during the First World War, when few would be giving it priority. They took charge of the US Department of Ciphers at Riverbank Laboratories, and it was here they supported the US government and trained staff. The couple would move to Washington in 1921 for the War department.

By the time of the approaching Second World War they were supporting the US Coastguard looking for spies in South America who would be a threat to the United States. Jointly they decrypted German Enigma transmissions, and also shared solutions, processes and ideas with those at Bletchley Park. The section they would work from was termed Unit 387, being the Coastguard Cryptanalytic Unit. In the 1940s Elizebeth led a team to identify German spies reporting on shipping movements of Allied vessels in South America. The Coastguard was able to use this information and pass it on to government agencies for action and monitoring. In 1942, J. Edgar Hoover, responsible for the FBI, compromised security by inadvertently tipping off Nazi spies during an announcement. Transmissions stopped and the Friedmans had to pick up the pieces afterwards and start making new progress. However, by the end of 1942 Elizebeth had been able to decipher and crack three separate Enigma machine codes, which was a major achievement at the time and astonished her colleagues.

PEOPLE

Elizebeth Friedman acted as expert witness in a large number of cryptographic and espionage cases, and became somewhat of a minor celebrity, mainly because it was rare for women to hold such esteem and positions in such a specialist field that was dominated by men. While her husband gained much of the acclaim for his involvement and achievements, Elizebeth would contribute greatly to the decoding of ciphers and intelligence. The volume of encrypted messages decoded by the pair would be in the thousands. She managed to track down an important SS agent who had eluded the official agencies acting for the government such as the FBI and law enforcement teams. Friedman would also expose a spy known as the 'Doll Woman' who had been sending information to Japan. This was a female agent with a cover of trading in antique dolls who had been sending Japan status reports of ships at Pearl Harbor for some time before the attack. The agent, Velvalee Dickinson, would be arrested and charged based on the evidence that Elizebeth had collected against her. Elizebeth would work for the International Monetary Fund (IMF) after the war, and set up security systems for the organisation. Her husband became very ill in 1941 and never fully recovered from a cognitive mental condition. She would spend time caring for him, during and after the war.

Her Christian name, Elizebeth, was spelt differently to the traditional spelling of Elizabeth, and was decided by her mother for personal reasons. J. Edgar Hoover did give the Friedmans sufficient credit for their work in locating villains and spies, and pretended that the FBI had achieved more than it had as regards penetrating the spy networks, when the Friedman pair had actually done a lot of that work themselves. This was more about politics at the time.

Elizebeth's initial interest in cryptography and the cracking of ciphers had been nurtured in the early years of her life by a librarian who had discussed with her an eccentric millionaire, George Fabyan, who was looking into a Shakespearean code-cracking project. Fabyan offered her a job and she moved to the Riverbank Laboratory in Geneva, Switzerland, where she met her husband. It was only when the First World War started that Fabyan offered the services of some of his researchers to the US Government.

Elizebeth, a scholar of literature, poetry and Shakespeare, could never have predicted that her love of the classics would bring her into the area of cryptography, and assist the war effort across two world wars. Her skills included an uncanny ability to recognise patterns, and she could predict solutions based on her intuition, which was often accurate. From exposing drug smugglers, to identifying spies, to acting as an expert witness in the US law courts, and supporting government agencies such as the FBI, she will go down in history as an extraordinary woman who made a significant impact in the world of cryptography and intelligence. See *USA*. See *Japan*.

Gano Stanislaw (Colonel). Chief of Second Department of Supreme Commander's Staff in London in 1941. A Pole, he was instrumental in establishing a wide intelligence network across occupied Europe, also North and South America and North Africa. Some of his methods were so successful as to be used and adapted by intelligence organisations today. Gano instigated the destruction of secret papers and documents at a secret location, St Paul's Boys School in Hammersmith, London, by his Polish intelligence staff when the war ended. See *St Paul's School*.

Garbo (1912–1988). A code name for a Catalan/Spanish double agent for the Allies during the Second World War, who was actually named Juan Pujol Garcia. He became known for his deception of the Nazis when he pretended to be working as an agent for them, passing secrets and intelligence. Garbo was the British name allocated to him by the authorities, but the Germans called him Arabel. The high point of his career was when he contacted the enemy on the early morning of D-Day to tell them that ships were leaving harbour in England en masse, but to be aware there was a large army remaining in the south-east, possibly awaiting the main assault across the Pas-de-Calais. This message was received eventually by Hitler and his key generals, also Field Marshal von Rundstedt based in France. Garbo extracted large sums of money from the Nazis for 'expenses', which was siphoned back into the Allied war effort against the Nazis. He established a large number of fictitious agents supporting him across Britain and convinced the enemy that they were supplying him with accurate intelligence.[29] Garbo made a few errors in communication with his Nazi controller, messaging them one day that up in Glasgow 'the men would do anything for a litre of wine'. Of course, Glaswegians were more likely to drink beer, and they would not be finding wine in litres in Scotland. However, fortunately such errors were overlooked by his handler. Garbo would pretend that some of his agents working under him in Britain would fall sick or even be captured and find replacements for his spy network. All this was pure fiction, but the Nazis had no idea of his deception.

Garbo had a British controller monitoring his messages and checking to verify he had not changed his allegiance to Nazi Germany. He would use secret ink in letters sent to Portugal or Madrid, and then intercepted by the Nazis, with reports communicated to Berlin. He wrote 315 letters to his German handler, and averaged 2,000 words each letter. It is somewhat surprising he was not given an Enigma encoding machine by the Nazis. It was the case that when intercepted in Spain, his messages would often be encoded via Enigma by others and transmitted to Berlin for studying by the German high command. This, then was a potential weakness in the security of his messages. Garbo had obtained the confidence of his German handler and he was sent substantial funds he had requested 'for expenses'. Garbo was awarded an Iron Cross by Hitler for his services, and later an MBE by the British; the only person ever to be awarded medals for services by both Britain and the enemy.

He left to travel to South America as the war developed after the D-Day assault.[30] He was then fearful for his life, in case the Nazis ever located him and realised he was a double agent. His efforts, managed by a MI5 handler in the UK, made a significant difference in the days building up to D-Day and for some weeks afterwards, when key Panzer divisions were held back by the Germans awaiting an assault from the Allies across the Channel that never materialised. It bought the Allies invading Normandy precious time. This was the culmination of the Operation Bodyguard deception, and supported via Fortitude South, which helped to deceive the enemy at a crucial time in 1944. Garbo (or Pujol) did come back to England to receive his MBE, but was always looking over his shoulder and was never really very comfortable in public after his exploits in wartime with the British, following his clever deception tactics with the enemy. There could always be Nazi sympathisers hiding who would see him as a traitor to the Führer and wish to dispose of him, so he had to be careful for his personal safety. See *Garcia*. See *Von Rundstedt*. See *Pas-de-Calais*.

Garcia Pujol Juan (1912–1988). A Catalan and double agent for the British and Allies during the Second World War, who was instrumental in deceiving the Nazis on D-Day as to the location of the main armed forces. His code name allocated was Agent 'Garbo'. See *Garbo*.

Golombeck Harry (1911–1995). A codebreaker at Bletchley Park working in Hut 8, and a high-level master chess player, which was to influence his career and win him awards for his participation in the game at world-class competitive status. He was awarded an OBE in 1966 for his contribution to chess, having been British chess champion three times, narrowly missing a fourth title in 1948. Working on naval Enigma challenges initially at Bletchley, he would additionally work in other sections as the war progressed. See *Hut 8, Bletchley Park*.

Good Irving John (Jack) (1916–2009). Good's original name was Gudak, having been born of Jewish–Polish parents. He worked at Bletchley Park as a mathematician codebreaker along with Michie, Turing, Newman and others. He had been to Cambridge and was an expert in specialist areas such as Fourier analysis in mathematics. It took time for him to settle in Hut 8 at Bletchley Park as part of the codebreaking team. He was a proficient chess player and used the game to help cement friendships with other players in the codebreaking huts. He had some success with statistics and application to the naval Enigma intelligence, sharing ideas with Turing and others. Good was later to work on German High Command enemy intelligence, known as 'Fish', under Max Newman at the Newmanry. This was assessing how best to use the machines for the first part of the codebreaking of non-Morse enemy messages. As Good was heavily involved in statistical analysis, and had considerable expertise in this area, he proposed changes to the Colossus codebreaking advanced machine, which made it even more efficient and reduced calculation time. Good became principal statistician at Bletchley and used his exceptional skills to advance codebreaking techniques and develop new systems to eliminate the millions of permutations of settings of Enigma and other encoding machines.

Post-war, Newman recruited Good to work on the new computer being designed and built at Manchester University. He went on to work at GCHQ from 1948 to 1959, but became frustrated and wrote numerous publications on many different subjects. He became a consultant for IBM and also did some work at Princeton. His interest in artificial intelligence had been growing over time, following discussions with Turing, Newman, and others. Indeed, in 1965 he wrote and published a significant academic paper about the possibility of a machine becoming far more intelligent than man; the concept of machine learning on an exponential scale. A worrying thought. He became a Doctor of Science at Cambridge and then at Oxford, then moved to the USA in 1967 to work on research projects. He would become a research professor in statistics at the Virginia Polytechnic Institute and State University.

Good was appointed as a technical adviser on AI on the Stanley Kubrick film *2001: A Space Odyssey* from the original book by Arthur C. Clarke. He advised Kubrick on the HAL 9000 computer in the film, which had a large red 'seeing eye'. The film showed the computer becoming a significant threat to mankind. This was to result in him achieving a major membership award in the film industry (the Academy of Motion Picture Arts and Sciences), and was most unusual for a mathematician, statistician and a highly competent codebreaker. He selected a car number plate in the USA that not only incorporated his initials but was prefixed 007.

Grabeel Gene (1920–2015). American mathematician and a cryptographic expert who initiated the Venona project in 1943. This was an intense detailed study that lasted until around 1980, analysing messages and intercepts to try to identify spies and agents acting against states in the West. This became even more expanded post-war during the Cold War period. Breakthroughs in various foreign embassies identified infiltration of the political and security services of Western powers, and one such suspect activity was identified in Canberra, Australia. Worldwide investigation arose from a few initial suspicious messages intercepted, and then resulted in exposure of numerous enemy spies acting for foreign powers. Outstation Eastcote, in Middlesex, England, which had been a codebreaking outstation during the latter part of the Second World War, and then became GCHQ, became involved in the investigation of thousands of messages, some using machines and cryptographic equipment. This was top secret at the time and involved liaison with not just the British Government security services but also the NSA and equivalent security services in various parts of the world. Funding was made available in later years for GCHQ Eastcote to carry out investigations and probe into historic messages that had been filed. Eastcote was but one single location around the world working on the Venona project with fairly limited numbers of staff for several years.

The original orders to Gene Grabeel had come from a colonel in the Military Intelligence Service in the US in February 1943. As a result of the project developing and exposing more individuals, the Western powers were shocked and disturbed as to the extent of infiltration by foreign agents into their organisations, buildings and sites, many having access to highly sensitive documents. Encrypted messages going back decades would be analysed by cryptanalysts for suspicious wording or phrases, and linking them to other incriminating text. Much of the evidence was of Russian espionage activity. British, US and many other states had been targeted by Russian espionage since around 1942. Many spies were identified, but not all were exposed for various political and other reasons. Some working within the British intelligence services escaped back to Soviet territory.

PEOPLE

Grazier Colin (1920–42). Famous for his brave action to capture enemy Enigma material from a sinking German U-boat, *U-559*, and who sadly drowned. The information was passed to a young Tommy Brown, only sixteen years old, who salvaged the enemy prize, and later would assist Bletchley Park with code books. Grazier lost his life alongside Lieutenant Antony Fasson from HMS *Petard*, in October 1942, and they were posthumously awarded the George Cross medal for their unselfish act of extreme bravery. The submarine was off the coast of Egypt when HMS *Petard* managed to intercept it. The prize of the German Short Weather cipher code book and the Short Signal code book were recovered from the disabled U-boat, although it was too late to recover Nazi equipment from the sinking submarine and the two men perished in the action. The swim across to the submarine was at night in pitch darkness and would have been terrifying. The added relevance of this event was that the Nazis had a fourth-rotor version of the Enigma machine, which Bletchley Park had no success in analysing and decrypting. Capturing those Nazi Enigma code books made all the difference to the cryptographers and mathematicians at Bletchley Park, who were then able to use them to assist them in cracking the four-rotor messages.[31] It would be only a few weeks before Bletchley Park had those captured code books in their possession. The young Tommy Brown, the sailor who managed to get the code books back to HMS *Petard*, was later awarded the George Medal.

Hall William (Captain) (1842–1895). Led the cryptographic team that cracked the Zimmerman telegram code that led to the US entry into the First World War. He was based in Room 40 O.B. in London, working for GC&CS. The telegram was copied to the Americans, who saw the potential threat to them from Mexico and Germany. The British had to be careful not to divulge the source of the telegram.

Harris Lionel Brigadier (Sir) (1897–1971). Head of Signals Unit for GCHQ in 1941, and later appointed Chief Telecoms Engineer to General Eisenhower of SHAEF. Engineer in Chief of the GPO between 1954 and 1960. He was an expert in relays in automatic switchboards, telex and converting telegraph systems into teleprinters. Post-war became Controller of research at Dollis Hill. Knighted in 1957. See *PORES*.

Harris William (Colonel) (1918–1950). General Jake Devers, Commander of the US Army at HQ, would bring in Colonel 'Bill' Harris to advise on the technical deception trickery that might be needed for the D-Day invasion. That is, the deception part of Operation Overlord. There would be fake radio transmissions and use of small dummies that appeared to be soldiers. Dummies had apparently been used by the Nazis in Holland previously for deception, and from a distance would appear to be quite realistic, particularly at night or in poor-visibility conditions. Dummy soldiers would be used by both the Americans and the British but using very different designs. Arguably, the British versions had more detail. General Omar Bradley would have coordination meetings and challenge the effectiveness of using dummies. On his orders, more realistic versions would be constructed, and then approved for use. Bradley and Devers gave the approval for creating a 'Ghost' army, comprising one armoured division and two infantry divisions. Tennessee was chosen for the camp to establish this group of men and arrange the training. The unit mobilised in January 1944. It would have a variety of tasks to help deceive the enemy, divert fire away from more valuable troops and divisions, and create much noise, military sounds and activity to create panic among the Nazi divisions and soldiers. They would inflate and position dummy tanks, armoured cars, lorries, and vehicles, and make grinding metal against metal noises to simulate the erection of Bailey bridges to cross rivers. The inflatable vehicles would sometimes be established as a type of diorama, or scene, which could be observed from a distance by German officers or Luftwaffe spotter aircraft to report back to HQ as to the Allied positions. The plan was to encourage the Germans to incorrectly move Panzer divisions, tanks and men, and take military resources away from valuable targets. It was still a risky process and had to be carried out to the rule book to be fully effective. It was a form of 'fake news' for the enemy, which could crop up at any time and anywhere. Some decoy equipment had explosives incorporated, so that they would destroy the evidence before the enemy could find out what was going on if they overran Allied positions. The division created was listed as the 23rd Headquarters Special Troops. It would incorporate signals personnel, camouflage experts and combat teams. Many tradespeople were used including carpenters, electricians, sound engineers, artists, painters. There was even a cardboard air force.

Radio intelligence would be essential in the field of battle to listen in to the enemy and establish if they were 'taking the bait'. German-speaking radio listeners were essential. Some transmissions of the enemy would be via Enigma, and these were much more challenging for the Allies. Breaking enemy codes and ciphers in the middle of a field, with Nazi '88 shells passing over, was highly impractical. The 244th Signal Company (Special) would be the 23rd Signals radio wireless communication link. There would also be some training and administration in Warwickshire. They would have SCR radio equipment with ranges up to 100 miles. There would be short-range receivers, too. Combined with American audio deception using high-powered horn loudspeakers with substantial range, the enemy would be confused as to the direction of the Allies approaching in France, Belgium and Germany on several occasions, and the deception was deemed to be a success. The overall picture would be monitored by Allied listening stations, deciphered where encoded by Enigma transmissions, and reported back to the commanders in charge.

Hayes Richard (1902–1976). Irish cryptographer and state librarian during the last war, who cracked important Nazi ciphers and codes, including the Görtz code, following the capture of a major Nazi spy. See *Ireland.* (*Places*)

Hayward Gill (1917–2011). Electronics engineer who joined Tommy Flower's engineering research Post Office group in 1944. Joining the Post Office engineering department as an apprentice, he would help to develop the speaking clock.[32] Hayward would be given special responsibility for the British Tunny machines.

He worked on developing secret bugging devices in Egypt before working on codebreaking machines at Dollis Hill. Post-war he would work on top-secret voice-encoding systems at the research branch. Hayward used his extensive knowledge and expertise to assist the volunteers and enthusiasts at the National Museum of Computing to reconstruct various codebreaking machines, and would also meet with Tony Sale, who went on to build the Colossus computer replica. The designer of the electronic security seal in the 1980s, Hayward proved he had a wealth of experience, including in speech-encoding cipher systems, which was to be invaluable in the development of advanced electronic systems and equipment.

Hebern Edward H. (1869–1952). An American inventor who, arguably, invented the first rotary-based encoding machine in 1917, and started construction of it in 1918. He was rather late in applying for patents compared to others, only applying for a US one on his machine in 1921. He apparently received the patent in 1924, several years after others had had patents granted for rotary-based encoding machines. His name is not widely known and, like many inventors, he was overlooked due to some poor decisions on applying for the appropriate paperwork, and inadvertently passing the baton of innovation to others.

Hitler Adolf (1889–1945). Austrian-born and German politician. The leader of the Nazi Party, Reich Chancellor for Germany, and the leader of the German armed forces during the Second World War. Hitler was keen on keeping messages confidential between the armed forces and the Enigma encoding machine was an important tool, but information was still only passed across divisions on a need-to-know basis. Hitler wanted a more secure system than even Enigma for transmitting and receiving messages across the German High Command, and that is how Lorenz and the advanced encoding machines were brought into use. These would give Hitler and his generals added comfort that the information in messages could never be decoded by the enemy or 'cracked'. How wrong he was. These messages were only for the High Command, including Hitler himself, and only generals, field marshals and similar high-end military officers were permitted to send and receive messages using these complex advanced machines. The British called the Nazi transmission links Tunny, and gave them fishy names such as Sturgeon, Jellyfish, Bream, Gurnard and others. These high-level secure messages would have key strategic information that only Hitler and his commanders knew, and this might include the order of battle, fuel depot resources, panzer division allocation information, dates and times for attacks, and counterattacks against the enemy. This information was like gold dust for the Allies if intercepted correctly. Hitler and his generals had no clue that the Allies were reading their messages, mainly sent by high-speed radio transmission using Vernon–Baudot code, via advanced encoding teleprinter machines. Hitler had the opportunity during the war to fund early computer/machine technology of a type, using valves, proposed to the Luftwaffe by certain academics such as Konrad Zuse, but the Nazis ignored those requests. Hitler was far more interested in funding and advancing the technology of the V1 and V2 rockets to bring Britain to its knees.

At first Hitler's ace card was the U-boat attacks in the Atlantic. That worked for a period with great success, sinking enormous quantities of Allied shipping, both merchant and military. Bletchley Park had limited success with decoding the Enigma messages to and from U-boats, but eventually a range of factors upset the U-boat strategy, including various radar developments by the Allies.

The problem with technological development and advanced scientific techniques is that it is hard for a non-mathematician or layperson to appreciate what they might be used for in a world war situation, and they would be seen perhaps to use up valuable resources and be given low priority. By comparison, Churchill was not a mathematician or a cryptographer, but understood the importance of being one step ahead of the enemy with technology as a tool. The infrastructure in Britain with Bletchley Park as HQ overseeing the analysis of enemy messages and 'cracking' the latest Nazi advanced encoding machines would have surprised and shocked Hitler. He never knew what we were up to, and relied on a false sense of security, together with complacency, along with his senior staff. At one stage in the war, Bletchley Park cryptographers were reading Hitler's personal messages and instructions to his high command generals and staff. Hitler and his commanders were fooled by communications from British double agents as D-Day approached.

Hitler will probably go down in history as the single individual who was the cause of more death and destruction than any other. Studying Second World War statistics provides a shocking reality to the losses across many different countries. In terms of losses, Russia suffered most, but that is no consolation to others or the Jewish or Roma people who lost their lives after being pursued by the Nazi war machine. Hitler was stopped by the combined Allied armed services of the British, Canadians, Commonwealth countries, Poles, French, Americans, Russians, and many others, working together, aided by the interception and analysis of military intelligence to provide a clear, military advantage . See appendices for tables of wartime losses by each nation.

Hollerith, Herman (1860–1929). Inventor of the American Hollerith punched-card pin-box tabulator, which was used for large-scale census processing, and later on for collating and storing intelligence information at Bletchley Park and at Drayton Parslow nearby. The Hollerith Section was managed by a BTM senior manager, Frederick Freeborn. BTM in Letchworth had the licensing rights for the US-designed Hollerith machines. This was to be of great assistance to GC&CS at Bletchley Park in processing and managing large amounts of collected data, which could then be connected to, or paired with other data. Some of this information was trivial and minor, but when connected with other relevant data may have given clues to the Allies as to German people in the armed services, politicians, locations, buildings, resource planning, troop movements, or other useful information.

Hollerith was the son of a German immigrant, a statistician and inventor in the United States, who saw the need for a relatively fast data-processing machine that was electro-mechanical in operation. As a young man he taught mechanical engineering at MIT and experimented with punched-card technology. His machine was highly successful and sold around the world as well as being available on a rental basis. BTM would later contract licensing rights to market the machines across the British Empire. In 1924 Hollerith's established company was renamed International Business Machines, or IBM, and that organisation then largely dominated the modern computer sector after the war, using punched cards for data entry and later magnetic tape. Hollerith saw the need for data processing on a large scale and was probably ahead of his time. He would invent the first automatic card-feeding system, and one that was both robust, and reasonably reliable. The Hollerith machine he developed was based on binary mathematics, helping to enable the digital age of technology in the early twentieth century. His machines were used on a large scale in England and played their part in helping the Allies to neutralise Nazi Germany during the war over time. See *BTM,* See *Freeborn.*

Hollingberry Betty Morrison (b. 1923). A Wren who worked on codebreaking Bombe machines at Outstation Eastcote, Middlesex, in 1943–45. At the time of writing in 2023, Betty was approaching her hundredth birthday, and has seventeen grandchildren. After the war, she lived in Eastcote and Pinner, west London. She appears on the Bletchley Park Roll of Honour. Betty is also recognised by the Royal British Legion for her war service.

Hooper Leonard (1914–1994). Later Sir Leonard James Hooper, knighted. From 1965 to 1973 he was director of GCHQ, Britain's signals intelligence agency, based in Cheltenham, Gloucestershire. He worked at Bletchley Park during the war as a codebreaker within GC&CS, the forerunner of GCHQ. Prior to becoming director, he was deputy director at GCHQ. In the 1970s he worked in the Cabinet Office on UK intelligence coordination.

Hughes Eileen [WRNS] (1926–2023). A Wren who worked on Bombe machines at two codebreaking outstations, being Outstation Eastcote and Outstation Stanmore. Later, she relocated to Scotland to a WRNS base. Like several Wren codebreakers, Eileen is on the Bletchley Park Roll of Honour for her wartime codebreaking services and has received her commemorative medal from GCHQ. She was but one of the 1,676 Wrens on codebreaking 'Special X' duties, and signed the Official Secrets Act at the time. Her bases would be identified as HMS *Pembroke V,* as codebreaking outstations, specific to the naval administration for the WRNS. They were all shore-based operational bases. During the latter part of the war, she was transferred to RNAS Donibristle, a Fleet Air Arm station near Fife in Scotland. After the war, Eileen worked for MI5, and had to sign the Official Secrets Act for a second time. Eileen agreed to give a brief summary of her experiences during the war as a Wren and this is contained within the appendices of this glossary. See *Appendices.* See *Outstation Eastcote.*

Ireland Eleanor (WRNS). Joined the Wrens in 1944. She was posted to Bletchley Park, and worked with others in the Newmanry, and operated the large Colossus computer machine until the war ended. She helped break up the machine on instruction by Churchill when war ended. This would have been a frustrating instruction to follow through given the amount of time spent in training on and operating the machine.

Irvin, Leroy Leslie (1895–1966). An American ex-stunt pilot who set up a factory making parachutes during the war, in Letchworth, Hertfordshire. This was known as Irvin Airchutes. Irvin liaised with the Spirella factory down the road to subcontract parachutes there, prior to Spirella being largely taken over by BTM for making components for the Bombe decoding machines. Irvin formed the Caterpillar Club, whereby if you bailed out of your aircraft and survived using one of its parachutes you were entitled to be listed as a member of the club and probably given a free drink too. In excess of 20,000 people were allegedly saved by an Irvin parachute. See *Spirella*. See *Letchworth*.

Jeffreys John R. (1916–1944). Mathematician and codebreaker. Developed a system at Bletchley Park, GC&CS, using stacks of perforated paper to help analyse ciphers and code settings to crack the German Enigma machine. Settings were the first stage in setting up the Enigma encoding machine, and the equivalent of the combination to the safe, to enable the messages to be read. These perforated sheets, or Jeffrey's sheets, were different from the Polish *Zygalski* sheets, developed by them when they were working on the Polish-designed and built Bomba machine earlier. Jeffrey's sheets helped to eliminate various permutations and combinations of Enigma rotors and a reflector component. Jeffreys was eventually based in Hut 6 at Bletchley, in charge of the development and processing of the sheets, and worked alongside Gordon Welchman. Polish cryptographers applied and used his perforated paper system in 1940 to help crack Enigma messages in France. Jeffreys became seriously ill with both tuberculosis and diabetes as the war progressed and died in hospital in 1944.

Jenkins Roy (1920–2003). Joined Bletchley Park in 1942 as a codebreaker and was tutored by Donald Michie among others. He worked on deciphering Tunny intercepts until the fall of Berlin. Post-war he had a successful career as a senior politician and minister in Government. He became a Labour MP, and then changed parties and joined the SDP, and then the Liberal Democrats. Jenkins was Chancellor of the Exchequer from 1967 to 1970 and later Home Secretary in the Labour Government. He became the President of the European Commission in the late 1970s. During wartime he was billeted in Bedford, and there is a blue commemorative plaque on the house where he lodged, which recognises his codebreaking at Bletchley.

Jones Elwyn (Sergeant). Responsible for maintaining Bombe codebreaking machines, and overseeing RAF mechanics, at Bletchley Park, he was probably the most experienced in this specialist field. He would also visit outstations and be responsible for RAF mechanics there. It would be likely he would pass on his technical knowledge in this area to RAF and other engineers as well as informing the Wrens working on the Bombes at both Bletchley and the outstations how to carefully align the fine wire contacts that were incorporated within each rotor wheel. He is mentioned in Gordon Welchman's book *The Hut Six Story*, which indicated there were some 15 million wire brushes that had to make electrical contact as the drums rotated on the codebreaking Bombe machines. Jones wrote to outstation personnel at the end of the war, such as at Outstation Stanmore, thanking them for their contribution to the war effort. There is information to indicate Sergeant Jones operated the very first codebreaking Bombe when it was operational.

Jones Reginald Victor (Dr) (1911–1997). A physicist and scientist, studying at Oxford and obtaining an honours degree and later a Doctorate in Philosophy. Initially working for the Air Ministry at RAF Farnborough and as a scientific officer, he later became Assistant Head of the Scientific section and department of SIS from 1941 to 1946, and technical advisor to Churchill. Briefly, he was based at Bletchley Park in 1939 in Hut 3, for a short period before moving on. He was sometimes referred to as the father of electronic warfare, applying different technological methods to problem-solving during wartime. He would evaluate and report on enemy equipment and systems, finding weaknesses to explore. Countermeasures were designed, tested and applied in practice to defeat the enemy technology. These included attacking the transmitted *Knickebein* radio navigation beam used by the Nazis to assist the Luftwaffe. This involved him detecting and finding the transmission frequencies, then bending and neutralising it with a technical solution using equipment carried in Allied aircraft. He also worked on 'window' or 'chaff', metal foil strips of a specific length to interfere with enemy radar, together with fellow scientist Joan Curran. Post-war he became a professor of Natural Philosophy at the University of Aberdeen. Jones was made a CBE and a Fellow of the Royal Society for his achievements. He wrote an autobiography, *Most Secret War – British Scientific Intelligence 1939–1945*, which was well received and the basis of post-war lectures and TV documentaries.

Keen Harold H. (Doc) (1894–1973). Senior, and later Chief Engineer at BTM British Tabulating Machine Company during the war, based in Letchworth, Hertfordshire. He designed the codebreaking Bombe from an engineering viewpoint, directed the assembly of Bombe machines and modified versions of the Bombe codebreaking machines at the factory. He was promoted to be head of the Experimental Section at BTM before the war and worked on punched-card technology, which was probably the main expertise and business of the factory, selling systems around the world and helping to manage the collection of census data for various countries. This was all about 'number crunching', so Keen took on the challenge of designing and building the Bombe machine to Turing and Welchman's requirements enthusiastically. One must appreciate there were no handbooks or blueprints for such experimental new machines, so Keen had a great deal of personal responsibility for the success of the project. The factory was spread over several buildings, although there was a large main building in Icknield Way, Letchworth, where all the modules and components came together for assembly.

Keen was nicknamed 'Doc', as he carried a bag around with him, appearing to look like a doctor on call.

During the First World War, Keen had taken on a non-flying role as an engineer supporting bombers in the Royal Flying Corps. He had joined BTM in 1912 after studying electrical engineering in London. Keen had a skilled team of engineers under him and had the task of meeting tight time and quality targets to construct and build the Turing/Welchman Bombe machines. These would then be sent to Bletchley Park initially, and later to the five codebreaking outstations, including three country house bases, plus Stanmore and Eastcote. The first completed Bombe, named 'Victory', was sent to Bletchley in March 1940. It was the first of over 200 Bombe machines to be sent around England to codebreaking sites. The majority went to the outstations and not to Bletchley Park, which concentrated on the mathematics, looking for 'cribs', or clues in the enemy messages, and processing the data from the outstations. Keen had to implement modifications to the Bombe, either those suggested by Turing or Welchman, or in some cases, his own suggestions. One specially modified Bombe was 'Giant', a combination of four individual Bombe machines on a frame, which was too unwieldly to move and eventually became split into four individual machines. 'Giant' was an attempt to make a 'super-Bombe', faster and achieving a higher rate of data processing to eliminate permutations of the Enigma settings. It was not a success.

BTM Letchworth was visited from time to time by Turing and Welchman from Bletchley to discuss progress of manufacture of Bombes with Keen. In the official Bombe registers held at the National Archives, several of the entries have 'HSK' against many of the named and numbered Bombes. This stands for 'High Speed Keen' machine. H.J. Morton was Keen's principal assistant at BTM, where the Bombe manufacturing project was known as Project 'Cantab'. A dinner was held after the war by management to thank BTM staff, and a letter of thanks sent to staff by Chairman Raleigh Philpotts. He issued key staff with certificates and diplomas for their services, at a time when the Bombe and the background to it was still officially under the Official Secrets Act. After the war, Keen was awarded an OBE for his services. Various photographs of the factory at BTM at various times pre-war and post-war can be seen at the Garden City Heritage Collection and Museum at Letchworth (or their website archive online). These photos give an idea of the arrangement of the factory, personnel and conditions. However, no photographs are available at the museum of Bombes being manufactured or assembled due to the secret nature of the work during the war. *See BTM.*

Kesselring Field Marshal (1885–1960). A senior Nazi officer during the war, he is of interest because a convoy of six German signals communications trucks with SZ42 Tunny machines was captured in Germany along with the operating crew. Previously, it was thought that the advanced encoding teleprinter attachments would be in fixed locations in buildings due to their physical size, weight and complexity. It was a surprise for the Allies to therefore find and capture a unit with Tunny machines on the battlefields of Europe. Each truck contained radio transmitters, aerial antennae, radio receivers and encryption machines. There would be two bunk beds in each vehicle. The driver of the vehicle and an operator would have to set up the equipment. Although a highly complex encoding/decoding system and much more advanced than Enigma, it could be operated more efficiently than the latter and the errors made were far fewer. The entire group of six communication caravans left Augsburg on 16 May 1945, complete with twelve prisoners, and went overland and across the Channel to Bletchley Park. It transpires that this unit was the field communication circuit between Berlin and OB West for the German High Command. This was a great coup for the Allies and of great interest to the experts at Bletchley Park.

Knox Dilwyn (Dilly) (1884–1943). Chief cryptographer, codebreaker and a senior manager at Bletchley Park, Knox established a special team, including several enthusiastic female codebreakers, teaching them the basics and supporting them to develop their skills further. His protégés would include Mavis Lever among others, who had great success in breaking many enemy codes. He had assembled the people who cracked Italian naval Enigma codes. Lever and Keith Batey would work together and come up trumps, impacting at the Battle of Matapan in Britain's favour. Prior to this in 1941 he had broken the German Abwehr Enigma.

Instead of being a mathematician like so many others at Bletchley, Knox had a background of Classics at Cambridge, and unusually was an expert papyrologist. In his early years he would work at Room 40 on intelligence, before Bletchley Park was established, and assisted with the cracking of the famous Zimmerman telegram, which influenced the USA becoming involved in the First World War. Knox would spend hours in the bath in Room 53, evaluating codes and ciphers using the steam and humidity to focus his thoughts on Enigma problems.[33]

In his early time at Bletchley, before the outbreak of war, he played a role in attending meetings between the French, Poles and British, which eventually led to the analysis of the Enigma encoding machines at Bletchley. This was only possible due to the work the Poles had done earlier, and with a stroke of luck when the French obtained some code books and information that was passed to the Poles for investigation. Knox would work out the wirings of the Enigma K Italian naval machine as far back as in 1937. Knox developed a technique called 'rodding' using algebraic methods to break part of Enigma after reading technical reports by colleague Hugh Foss.

Knox developed a special section at Bletchley termed 'Intelligence Services Knox', or ISX. It would specialise in decoding and establishing wiring circuit connections on a number of Enigma machines that generated messages, including *Abwehr* Enigmas. The first decrypted message in this respect would occur on Christmas Day, 1941. The output from his section was considerable and many messages were cracked by the team. There would be in excess of 140,000 decryptions of Abwehr-based messages at Bletchley Park by the end of the war. Knox would ensure the Poles had the appropriate perforated sheets to assist decoding of Enigma even if it meant disagreements with Denniston at the top of Bletchley's management tree. Knox would establish a special and newly devised method, using the perforated sheets. This method involved looking for clues termed 'cillies', aiding the process of breaking Enigma codes.

By all accounts Knox was rather absent-minded, occasionally overlooking and forgetting his family commitments, concentrating on his work at Bletchley.

His contribution to development of teams at Bletchley Park to analyse enemy encoded messages and to develop and manage cryptographic systems was considerable. Additionally, he gave several women a unique opportunity to demonstrate their ability, competence, enthusiasm and drive when trusted with challenging cryptographic tasks in Hut 8 under his direction.

He will go down in history not only for his success as a cryptographer and codebreaker, but also for his empowerment and trust given to his female staff, at a time when this was most unusual and the more important jobs were usually given to men. Some of his staff were new to the job and needed mentoring but learned quickly under Knox's direction and encouragement. He allowed his staff to ask questions, making some mistakes, but to learn from them quickly.

Knox apparently damaged his eyesight years earlier when he researched fine papyrus texts in museums and libraries. He became seriously ill during his time at Bletchley, and while he did try to maintain an involvement with his team, working from home, he eventually died, and was a huge loss to his staff and the Bletchley Park organisation.

Mavis Batey, nee Lever, being a star pupil of Knox, wrote a particularly interesting biography on him after the war. *See Lever.*

Koch Hugo (1870–1928). A Dutch inventor who applied for patents on a rotary-based encoding machine in 1919. While there has been some controversy about who was first to make such a machine, the detail indicates that Arthur Scherbius, the Enigma inventor, was awarded patents in 1918, a year earlier than Koch. This has been confirmed in an article 'An error in the history of rotor transcription devices' (Source: Springer link) and the application date of 23 February 1918, when soon afterwards he approached the German Navy on the subject of rotary encoding machines and his patent. Many of Koch's patents on rotary machines would later be acquired by Scherbius just prior to the latter's premature death.

Kroger Bruno. A cryptologist who wrote reports on the Enigma machine, including, allegedly, for the Swiss authorities. However, he was an intelligence officer for the Third Reich. His name appears in TICOM reports regarding Nazi research and security. He had identified the weaknesses of the Enigma K model (similar to the discoveries made at Bletchley Park, of which he had no knowledge). After capture in Germany he was transferred to the USA due to his importance and knowledge of cryptographic techniques and became the chief cryptologist on German for the Americans. In TICOM reports Kroger is referred to as a specialist in the team of cryptanalyst Erich Huttenhain.

Laughton Matthews Vera (1888–1959). Director of the WRNS from 1939, awarded an MBE and made a Dame after the war. She retired in late 1946. Born in Streatham, London, as a young woman she attended King's College. When she initially applied to the Admiralty to join the Navy as a female member, she was refused and told that women were not allowed. Compare that today, when women not only can join the Navy, but carry out the same tasks and hold the same positions as men. In 1917, when the WRNS was established, she volunteered for service, and was put in charge of a training establishment at Crystal Palace, London. She rose through the ranks, being promoted to lieutenant commander and responsible for some 250 Wrens. It was Laughton Mathews who persuaded the Admiralty that the Superintendent Wrens should wear four blue stripes. She would eventually wear the equivalent stripes of a rear admiral. This was her way of demonstrating to the Royal Navy that men should not have it all their own way, and her staff were worthy of recognition and promotion for ability and effort. Laughton Mathews was instrumental in creating a new uniform for the Wrens complete with a tricorn hat. In 1939, the HQ for the Wrens was a building in part of Trafalgar Square. Interviews and assessments would take place there and elsewhere.

While the WRNS were disbanded in 1993 under MoD restructuring, there is currently an Association of Wrens, with many active retired members, and a journal, *The Wren*. Many ex Wrens have been incorporated on to the Bletchley Park Roll of Honour for codebreaking or support activities during the Second World War.

Lever L. Mavis (1921–2013). Lever, who later married a British codebreaker, Keith Batey, and became Mavis Batey, was a successful codebreaker during the Second World War. In 1940 after joining Bletchley Park, she assisted Dilwyn Knox, better known as 'Dilly'. He recognised talent and particularly female aptitude in looking for patterns in messages and 'cribs' or clues. He had a number of codebreaking protégés, one of whom was Mavis. He was always able to support his team players, and encouraged them to try various approaches to break the message codes. One of her key moments was in cracking Italian messages relevant to the Battle of Matapan in 1941, giving key strategic information to the British fleet in the Mediterranean about a forthcoming surprise attack against a Royal Navy convoy with key supplies that was approaching Greece. Her astute approach to codebreaking and recognition of Italian phrases along with her codebreaking logic helped the fleet avoid a disaster, and turned the tables on the Italian Navy with substantial losses when they were surprised by the British. The admiral was so pleased he went to Bletchley Park to shake hands with Dilly Knox and with Mavis. She had a little assistance from her future husband Keith Batey, also working at Bletchley and together they made a formidable team. Her knowledge of German was extremely useful, having studied the language in London before the war commenced. When the war ended, she spent time in Eastcote when it was becoming GCHQ, previously the site being a supporting codebreaking outstation. This may have been at a time when she had transferred into the diplomatic service. Later, she became a gardens historian, and was awarded an MBE in 1987 for her work on the preservation and conservation of gardens.

Lovell Alfred Charles Bernard (Sir) (1913–2012). Physicist, research electronics engineer and later, an astronomer, with significant involvement working on radar research at TRE in Malvern during the war. Lovell worked on the advanced H2S radar system for aircraft and had to access a crashed Hudson aircraft in 1942 to recover top-secret experimental equipment. He was to go on after the war to design and build the largest steerable radio telescope in Britain. While Lovell was not a codebreaker, his research work made considerable progress for radar research in wartime. Lovell was heading a team of specialists at TRE to identify surfacing enemy U-boat submarines at night. He worked on a system termed ASV, Air to Surface Vessel Radar, and this had a significant impact on reducing convoy losses through the detection of enemy submarines. This system avoided detection by the enemy METOX equipment and U-boats had little or no warning when Allied aircraft approached and attacked. This was possible through the applied use of centimetric frequency radar. This innovation, arguably, had a proportionately greater impact on locating enemy U-boats than the codebreaking of Bletchley Park at the time. The combined effort of his TRE team on radar together with Bletchley Park's work made a huge difference to turning the tide of the war in the Allies' favour.

Lovell was also extremely valuable to the British Government post-war due to his specialist expertise in radio communications and radar systems. The Jodrell Bank radio telescope that he established was also used during the Cold War period for part of the British early-warning system to detect a nuclear attack from Russia. Lovell claimed to be a target for assassination by the Russians, for his knowledge and expertise, and claimed that he narrowly escaped an attack on his life while abroad on business. He was given an OBE in 1946 for work on the H2S radar and received numerous scientific awards throughout his post-war career. He was knighted in 1961. TRE was an important secret research and test organisation in the English countryside, which incorporated several physicists, including *Charles Wynn-Williams*, and assisted Bletchley Park in modifications to the codebreaking Bombes, and later, more advanced machines.

Lywood Oswyn George William G. (Air Vice Marshal) (1895–1957). Developer and inventor of the Typex machine for the RAF that was initially used in 1939 to decode Enigma messages. It was an improved version of the Enigma encoding machine and would be further developed during the war. Machines would be sent across the world, including to New Zealand, where two machines were purchased initially and supplied to Wellington and Auckland. Lywood became Chief Signals Officer for HQ Coastal Command in May 1936, and Chairman of the W/T Board in 1937. He would later become Principal Deputy Director of Signals in 1940. Known initially as RAF Enigma with Typex attachments, the device would be developed further and would be impenetrable to German attack to decipher the system or understand exactly how it worked due to the modifications made. Commencing with around thirty units initially, it would be made in the thousands and improved over time. Bletchley Park would have teams of women operating the Typex machines to decipher Nazi and Italian enemy messages after the message settings were established, usually by the codebreaking machine outstations or by a cryptographer by hand using clues or 'cribs' at Bletchley. An advanced cipher machine was later produced to ensure that it could be used more easily between the British and Americans, exchanging cryptic messages, and this was termed the Combined Cipher Machine, or CCM. The type 23 Typex was modified for use with the Combined Cipher Machine.

Maclean Donald. A spy who worked for the Russians after the Second World War while based in Britain. One of the 'Cambridge Five'.

Masterman John Cecil (1891–1977). Chairman of the 'XX', Double Cross, or Twenty Committee in London during wartime. This was established from (MI5) British Security Services, using experts from the Admiralty, RAF, Army and civilians, and arranged operations in counter-espionage and deception. It was situated in St James' Street in central London, and in a former MGM building. The committee was featured in the 2022 feature film *Operation Mincemeat*, regarding the deception plan against the Nazis in 1943 regarding the attack on Sicily. Enemy agents were frequently identified and then 'turned' or blackmailed to become double agents working for Britain and handled by trusted individuals to monitor the activities when sending or receiving messages, often using secret invisible ink. Bletchley Park intercepts of enemy intelligence would prove to be invaluable to the Twenty Committee. Activities in Washington, USA, on Enigma decrypts also assisted the Allies. Ironically, British technical experts would sometimes upgrade, improve or replace German double agents' radio transmitters, to be sure the transmissions reached Germany. Masterman was made an OBE in June 1944. He would write and have published a book in 1972 on *The Double-Cross System in the War of 1939–1945*. This book had to have certain pages of the draft removed for state security reasons. In 1974, the lid would be lifted on Bletchley Park's activities and the public would learn what was achieved during the war, previously under the Official Secrets Act.

Menzies Stuart (Sir) (1890–1968). Later, Major General. Head of MI6 from 1939 to 1952, the Secret Intelligence Service. He would provide Prime Minister Winston Churchill with daily summary transcripts of enemy intelligence collected and deciphered via Bletchley Park and other sources. He would help coordinate the Ultra intelligence for distribution to the appropriate commanders and chiefs of staff. It would be Menzies who helped modernise the organisation of Bletchley Park and build up resources to meet the constant challenge of collecting, processing and distribution of enemy intelligence in the war years.

Michie, Donald (1923–2007). Later Professor Donald Michie, he was an important and talented mathematician, engaged at Bletchley Park on codebreaking together with Alan Turing and others. Michie was born in Burma and studied at Rugby School, later going to Oxford University. After his initial education in 1943 he trained in cryptography. He modified the Mk 2 Colossus advanced codebreaking machine just prior to D-Day to make some improvements. This had been delivered to Bletchley Park just days prior to the invasion. Michie knew Turing well and regularly played chess with him. They would discuss ideas on codebreaking and mathematics together. They were both intrigued by the concept of machines working for mankind, machine learning, and with artificial intelligence. In many ways, they both were ahead of their time intellectually. Michie also worked closely with Jack Good and Max Newman at Bletchley. Part of his time at Bletchley was spent working in the Testery, a specialist section that challenged the Nazi advanced teleprinter machines and helped to break their codes to establish the settings. Additionally, he had carefully nurtured new codebreaker, Roy Jenkins, later to become a famous politician after the war. Developing a machine system known as Menace, which automatically played noughts and crosses, the author was surprised when a BBC programme demonstrating it at a lecture failed to credit Michie for it.

Michie went on after the war to study anatomy and worked with his wife on the subject of genetics, which was about as far removed from codebreaking as was possible. Together with his wife, Anne McLaren, he established the modern basis for invitro-fertilisation, using intensive studies on mouse genetics. This development impacted on many couples who had difficulty conceiving, and improved success rates in conception significantly. However, the subject of artificial intelligence was never far from Michie's mind.

Michie became the director of the University of Edinburgh's Department of Machine Learning and Intelligence, and that was linked to the computer unit of the university. After Turing's death and even before, he led teams and commissions on Artificial Intelligence or AI on a worldwide scale. He was head of numerous organisations but did not always agree with how others saw AI developing, such as the Japanese. Michie worked with several external companies and organisations writing and developing papers, systems, and furthering the road to medical science and AI. He worked with GEC in the 1970s and the author's schoolfriend briefly met him in Scotland on a project. (GEC were involved in developing advanced medical and scientific equipment among others). According to the schoolfriend, Michie was a pleasant, easy going and unassuming man. Never once did he appear to patronise others who were less well-informed than him in his specialist fields of science, machine learning and mathematics. Sadly, Michie and his wife died together tragically in a car accident in 2007 in England. He was a great loss to the UK but left a legacy of the need to pursue AI to help society achieve greater things. A remarkable individual with skills and knowledge across a wide range of topics. If Turing is 'the father of computing', then Michie is 'the father of Artificial Intelligence' in the author's opinion.

Milner-Barry Stuart (1906–1995). Recruited at Bletchley Park by Gordon Welchman in 1940. Milner-Barry was one of four at Bletchley who signed a letter to Churchill explaining how fragile the system was for codebreaking at Bletchley, and that more resources were needed immediately to make a difference. His other colleagues included Alan Turing, Gordon Welchman and Hugh Alexander. Churchill acquiesced immediately to their request. Like most of his colleagues, Milner-Barry was a formidable chess player, a champion at school and at Cambridge, and used that skill to discuss concepts and ideas with others, such as Hugh Alexander and

Turing. In late 1941 he was made deputy head of Hut 6 by Gordon Welchman, a co-developer of the codebreaking Bombe machine. Milner-Barry would take charge of Hut 6 in autumn 1943. There, he would work with his colleagues and attack the German Army Enigma and the Luftwaffe ciphers, leaving others to deal with the German Navy in Hut 8. Exceptionally good at chess, puzzles and similar, he developed techniques to expose cribs or clues in the messages that eventually led to their analysis and decoding. Over time, the Enigma machine had been further developed with a higher level of security and many more permutations of the settings. Milner-Barry tackled these challenges together with his expert team, and achieved a considerable amount, taking on a high level of responsibility. Milner-Barry took charge of computer policy for the Treasury in the mid-1950s and had a good understanding of data processing post-war. He was awarded an OBE in 1946 for his wartime service at Bletchley Park and other awards in 1962 and 1965.

Morell Head of the telegraph and teleprinter unit at Post Office Research Establishment, at Dollis Hill, north-west London. Approached by Max Newman, he worked on a substantial part of the design of the 'Robinson' machine, as an engineer. They commenced work in January 1943 and operated from June that year in the Newmanry at Bletchley Park. Another part of the machine had been designed by Charles Wynn-Williams, who was based at TRE in Malvern. Tommy Flowers, the later designer of the Colossus machine, was not particularly impressed by the Robinson, but did contribute to it.

Morgan 'Jerry'. Bletchley Park's expert on the Hagelin cryptographic machine. The Italian Navy used a model C38 Hagelin machine for encoding messages.

Morse Samuel (1791–1872). Inventor of the Morse code communication system using dots and dashes and inventor of the telegraph. The Morse code system was widely adopted across the world using transmission of dots and dashes in a specific sequence to create letters using brief dots and longer dashes. It would be used as the basis for military intelligence transmissions during the Second World War, some plain and many later encoded via a specific cipher for secrecy. Listening stations, or Y-stations, would intercept radio waves with Morse code, and write the letters and words down to be passed on to other agencies. The weakness of an enemy transmitting in Morse code was that a country many hundreds or even thousands of miles away would be able to listen in to the transmitting radio frequency and take down the message. This is why encoding with ciphers became necessary and the sophistication of these increased rapidly over time, such as with the German Enigma machines.

The original telegraph was used to assist transport systems such as the railways, shipping, etc., and provide messages over very long distances in a robust way. It was around 1844 that Morse first used his telegraph with a version of Morse code. International Morse code was adopted in 1865, for worldwide uniformity. Samuel Morse could never have seen the vast use of his Morse code system in wartime, the ciphers adopted, and the machines designed and built such as the

British 'Bombe', to decode enemy ciphers and codes. Morse code transmissions are vulnerable to deterioration in certain adverse atmospheric conditions. Skilled Morse code operators can achieve a rate of around forty words per minute. Modern communication techniques are superseding Morse code as a way of international communication for maritime and associated sectors.

Mussolini Benito (1883–1945). Italian leader, known as Il Duce, during the war. Italy declared war on the Allies 10 June 1940. The fascist dictator became an ally of Adolf Hitler and the Nazis but made a considerable number of errors that came to fruition when attacking with substandard armed forces. His actions in British Somalia (East Africa), Egypt, Greece and Albania destabilised Germany's hold on the Mediterranean area, necessitating substantial reinforcements of Nazi troops in central Italy to hold back the Americans and British. Mussolini was a frustration for Hitler. His strategic ambitions included Corsica, Tunisia, the Balkans, and Egypt but Mussolini's forces were heavily compromised. A large proportion of his merchant fleet had been seized when the war commenced. His army was well below standard, and the level of training relatively poor compared to the Germans. Equipment was inadequate for the battles and coordination of his armed forces inadequate. His navy was severely reduced at the Battle of Matapan, when intelligence on decoded Italian messages decrypted at Bletchley Park identified a surprise attack against the British was about to occur. This was used to Allied advantage and the tables were turned against the Italian navy.[34]

Wherever Mussolini's armies attacked, whichever region or country, they were pushed back with heavy losses and many soldiers becoming prisoners of war. Almost a quarter of million Italian soldiers would be captured between 1940 and 1941 across Libya and East Africa. By July 1942 Mussolini had been considered sufficiently incompetent to have a motion of no confidence passed against him by his people. Sicilians probably started the lack of enthusiasm for him, as their area was relatively quickly occupied by the Allies. He was deposed and put in custody but rescued by the Nazis in September 1943. Mussolini was eventually executed by Italian partisans by firing squad in 1945. An Italian Enigma machine once owned by Mussolini is in the Bletchley Park Museum. It is marked A1214 and was made in 1932. It appears to be a four-rotor Enigma machine from photographs. See *Mavis Lever*.

Myers Kenneth. Engineer at the Post Office Engineering Establishment in Dollis Hill, north-west London, working under the direction of Tommy Flowers on Colossus Mk 1. He joined the team in 1943. At the beginning of 1944 he transferred to Bletchley Park, where he was tasked with installing, testing and maintaining the codebreaking machinery. Post-war, he worked on the coordination and sequencing of London's traffic lights.

Newman Max (1897–1984). Senior codebreaker and mathematician, who worked at Bletchley Park and managed the Newmanry, a specialist section using codebreaking machines with a team of men and women to analyse enemy messages. He arrived at Bletchley Park in the autumn of 1942 to help the war effort, having been a lecturer previously. He was initially reluctant to accept the appointment, and planned to leave earlier than most, although circumstances changed in his favour. The key machines that were used for attacking the advanced machines included the Robinson, and later the Colossus semi-programmable electronic computer using thousands of valves as digital switches. Turing would introduce Newman to Tommy Flowers, a talented Post Office Research Station engineer, to discuss the possibility of designing and building a new and specialist machine to improve the Robinson. Essentially, they were testing to eliminate the enormous number of permutations for the start position of the teleprinter to arrive at the correct one. That was the key to the success of Colossus, the new machine. This was built over several months at Dollis Hill and enabled Bletchley Park to challenge the advanced German teleprinter encoding machines such as Lorenz and others. It would contain 1,500 valves in the first version and many more in the later version. This design was only made possible by the initial analysis work carried out by Bill Tutte, who had analysed the non-Morse messages by hand, using different processes, and worked out the configuration of the rotors and wiring of Lorenz. This was done even though he had never seen the Lorenz machine before. The Newmanry was the initial stage, using advanced British-built and designed machines to attack the settings of the encoded messages, and then to pass the partly deciphered settings over to another specialist section, the Testery, managed by Ralph Tester. The combined efforts of both of these sections would reveal the deciphered messages sent from the German high command. Newman had studied maths at Cambridge University before the war, and his father was a German emigree.

Newman would become Alan Turing's tutor and lecturer at Cambridge. He served in the First World War as a Paymaster. Newman was a competent chess player and played with those at Bletchley Park during the war, including with his ex-pupil Turing. He later worked at the University of Manchester on computer development and established the Royal Society Computing Machine Laboratory. In 1948 the 'Baby' was produced, a new computer, and incorporated stored programme technology. Newman was a serious pianist and musician, and he achieved a high standard in all his work. The course of the war may have been rather different had he not met up with Tommy Flowers of the Post Office Research Station and suggested a decoding machine should be built to tackle the advanced enemy systems, based on the logic of Bill Tutte's analysis of Lorenz. Newman was offered an OBE for his services during the war.

Neumann John Von (1903–1957). Mathematician, and a consultant to the US Army on aerodynamics and ballistics research. He came to Britain in 1943 and considered large calculation methods, looking for solutions to his mathematical challenges on projects during wartime. He was arguably one of the first mathematicians to have programmed large mathematical calculations. He would liaise with American Engineer G. Stibitz of Bell Laboratories about electrical relays and the use of them for calculation machines. Neumann worked on the US atomic bomb project and had negotiated to use an IBM machine in 1944 for calculation purposes. It wasn't the mathematics that eluded him but the need for calculations of vast amounts of mathematics and at speed that became the critical objective. Neumann would become involved and attend various meetings related to the ENIAC machine, the Electronic Numerical Integrator and Calculator, based at the University of Pennsylvania. However, although it contained an enormous quantity of valves, it was still unfinished at the end of the war. ENIAC was used on calculations for the forthcoming hydrogen bomb and would be compared to Colossus, the British semi-programmable computer. There would be substantial differences between the two, but this was all part of a learning curve for people like Neumann, who may not have even been aware of the existence of Colossus at the time due to the secrecy imposed by the British Government. Neumann would go on to become involved in monitoring and advising on the second electronic machine in the summer of 1945, called EDVAC, or Electronic Discrete Variable Calculator.

Across both sides of the Atlantic, there would be great minds pursuing advanced calculating machines around the same time, but with different approaches, and collaborating with a range of specialist people. While Neumann was originally concerned with mathematical calculations on the trajectories of bullets and missiles for the US Army, his career brought him down a rather different road, where he and others saw the need for some form of programming of machines to solve different problems. Alan Turing had these ideas too, as did others in Britain and Germany. A draft report on the EDVAC by Neumann made comparisons between the machine and the human brain and nervous system. Neumann had read Turing's 'On Computable Numbers' paper, and that had inspired him.

O'Grady, Dorothy (1897–1985). A London-born female Nazi spy who was based in Sandown, on the Isle of Wight. She was a Nazi sympathiser and would walk to the cliffs at Culver Cliff, where there was a command post for anti-aircraft guns. She would then flash a torchlight to transmit signals, possibly via Morse code, out to sea. She was also caught interfering with and cutting cables and wires to telephone equipment on the island. School children would be bribed by her to obtain information on military guarded installations on the island. Maps of military installations were confiscated from her on her arrest. She had a long history of prosecutions for theft, fraud and prostitution. On the mainland, O'Grady was interrogated by MI5, tried and convicted of espionage and treason under the Treachery Act. She was fortunate to escape the hangman's noose or a firing squad, and spent her sentence in Holloway prison in London. She also appeared to be a masochist, and prison officers were alarmed at the lengths she would go to in order to satisfy her personal desires. She died in an assisted care home.[35]

Page, Gwendoline (b. 1925). A 'Special Duties' Wren during the Second World War. She was brought up in Hertfordshire and studied at the Barnet Queen Elizabeth Girl's Grammar school. Working at Bletchley Park during the war in the Naval section, and indexing U-boat signals, she became highly proficient at this task. She was put into a difficult position when her work discovered that her brother's ship was being dive-bombed in the Mediterranean, but could not act on the information due to the need to keep the fact that Enigma had been cracked secret from the enemy. Thankfully, her

PEOPLE

brother survived the ordeal. Page was later transferred to Colombo in Ceylon, now Sri Lanka. That base may have been HMS *Anderson*, on the island. This was helping decode Japanese military intelligence messages sometime after VE day. After the war, she became a housing officer in Vanuatu in the South Pacific. She moved back to Norfolk eventually and was the author and editor of *We Kept the Secret – Enigma Memories*. This book is about the Special Duties X Wrens across different locations and bases. One of the author's contacts, now an ex-Wren, knew Gwendoline during the war.

Patton George S. (General) (1885–1945). United States Army General who commanded the Third Army in France in 1944. When the Second World War commenced he commanded the 2nd Armoured Division and had firm ideas about mechanised armies and support strategy for troops. This was based upon his work in the First World War, when he trained tank commanders and took tanks into battle. At one point he was injured in battle but recovered.

Patton was identified by the Allies via radio transmissions and other means as the general in charge of FUSAG, the First US Army Group based in Southern England. This was false intelligence aimed at the Nazis and maintained that Patton and his army were soon about to come over the Pas-de-Calais, with an amphibious landing in northern France. This was a fictitious army, but a deception plan using Patton's name for the head of FUSAG convinced the Germans that he and his troops would attack the Calais area. The enemy respected the American general, who had a reputation for winning battles and driving his troops forward at some pace. Patton was famous for not only being a ruthless general, but also for once striking some enlisted soldiers who had suffered shellshock in action and were recuperating when he inspected them. He apologised for his action. The FUSAG deception locked-in various German Panzer divisions in northern France in June and July 1944. The intelligence intercepts by the Allies via both Enigma and Lorenz encoding machines became essential feedback as to what the enemy was planning on the approach to D-Day, and the weeks afterwards in July and August 1944. The non-Morse message intercepts at Knockholt of the *Jellyfish* Nazi communication link to Paris from Berlin were of particular interest. These made use of the Colossus Mk 2 codebreaking machine, which had just been delivered to Bletchley Park by the Post Office Engineering Research team, led by Tommy Flowers.

Patton saw action in the Mediterranean area, particularly North Africa, also Sicily, and he led the drive forward to capture Messina. He commanded the US 7th Army in the assault on Sicily. His determination and drive saw Allied forces penetrate deep into Germany after racing through France and creating openings for advancement. For a brief time in 1945 he would command the US 15th Army, but unfortunately died in a car crash in December that year.

Payne Diana. A Wren who worked at Bletchley Park, although she initially started off at Outstation Wavendon on Bombe codebreaking machines. Her comment on Wavendon, which was a country house and grounds, was that there no real security as compared to Bletchley Park. High windows in huts would prevent noise being heard outside of the Bombe machines operating. Payne would phone through readings from the Bombes, following a Bombe-run processing session, to the controller at Bletchley. She was taken to BTM in Letchworth to watch the Bombes being constructed, a most unusual privilege for both a Wren and a woman during wartime, given the intense secrecy on the factory installation. A further transfer to Outstation Stanmore occurred in 1943, where there more than 500 Wrens plus headquarters staffing. A big change from Bletchley Park, where there were a mix of civilians and military personnel, which was quite unusual. Stanmore was run purely as an onshore naval station, managed and staffed by Wrens. Payne was promoted and put in charge of ten Bombe codebreaking machines, with a couple of assistants and an office. She would see special instructions from Bletchley's codebreakers called Menus on a regular basis and give instructions for her staff to set up the cables and connectors at the back of the machine and load the rotor drums onto the Bombes. Quite a responsibility. Wavendon closed in January 1944.

Philpotts Buller Raleigh (Sir) (1871–1950). Chairman of the British Tabulating Machine Company (BTM) in Letchworth during the war. Under his direction was Chief Engineer H. Keen, who designed and built the Bombe codebreaking machines in the Letchworth factory. Philpott provided a name for the project, Cantab, and a special celebratory dinner and function was held at the end of the war as a thank you to his staff, board, and colleagues. He arranged for certificates and diplomas for achievement to be awarded to selected staff. His note to staff referred to the appreciation by the Lords Commissioners of the Admiralty, for the rapid and efficient production of the Cantab equipment, which made such a significant difference in the outcome of the war. Even a Cantab titled menu was produced for the dinner. One wonders if the pudding included a Bombe dessert. Raleigh Philpotts was awarded a knighthood for his services to the country in engineering, and his key engineering staff awarded OBE and MBEs. His chief engineer, Keen, obtained a large number of patents for inventions and designs while working for the company.

Pujol Juan Garcia. See *Garbo*.

Radley W. Gordon (1898–1970). Assistant Staff Engineer of the Research Branch, at PORE or PORES, the Post Office Engineering Research Station at Dollis Hill, north London. Radley was the boss of Tommy Flowers, the engineer who eventually designed and built Colossus. It was Radley that was approached by Flowers when the idea of Colossus was tabled, following a meeting with Max Newman of Bletchley, and resources were needed urgently in order to proceed. Radley had much faith in Flowers and gave him the go-ahead to build Colossus. This was despite some at Bletchley Park having their doubts and concerns that such a machine could ever work or be reliable. Indeed, it was far more reliable than the Robinson codebreaking machine ever was, which Bletchley had relied upon to break the Lorenz machine, and similar advanced encoding machines. Various groups of research existed at the site including telegraph, switching and physics.

PEOPLE

The switching group was led by Tommy Flowers. From 1951 to 1953 Radley would hold the position of Engineer in Chief.[36]

Radley was knighted after the war and was Director General of the Post Office between 1955 and 1960. We are fortunate that he kept detailed personal war diaries, and these can be accessed online (at the time of writing) via a BT website celebrating his achievements. These were marked as top secret even after the war. Radley had the difficult and challenging role of keeping his staff motivated at a time of war and uncertainty, and finding resources to enable the research and development to continue at PORES. The building at Dollis Hill was the first permanent one for the engineering personnel, and they moved into it in 1933. It has now been converted into residential flats. The Post Office Engineering research branch relocated to Suffolk in the 1970s. BT, now a major private company in telecommunications and the internet, is the modern equivalent of the Post Office engineering division. The company acknowledges the contribution made by Post Office engineering staff, including Radley and Flowers, among others. The Post Office Research Station became BT Research Laboratories, and later Adastral Park. In 1942 Radley stated, 'Never has there been a time when so many knew so little about so much,' indicating the enthusiasm and hunger for technological research.[37]

Rejewski Marian A. (1905–1980). A Polish codebreaker and mathematician. As part of a team of Polish cryptographers, he analysed and deduced the wiring for the early Enigma machine, and this information was passed on to other countries, including Britain, who were able to use it to establish systems to decode message settings by hand. In 1938 the team had built a machine to decipher the settings, termed Bomba. Some have said this name was from a certain Polish ice cream. The development of such a machine meant that as Enigma became more secure and sophisticated over time, another decoding machine was designed and built by the British, the Bombe. It is said the Turing/Welchman-designed Bombe worked differently to the Bomba, and the only similarity was in the name, which may have come from the Polish machine. It is essential to recognise the contribution made by Polish mathematicians and others in the fight against Nazi encoding machines such as Enigma. Their work saved the British valuable time.

Rochefort, Joseph, (Captain) (1900–1976). A naval cryptographer who would lead Project 'Station Hypo', a specialist team at Pearl Harbor, Oahu, Hawaii, against the Japanese, and have great success contributing to intelligence relevant to The Battle of Midway in June 1942. He would include within his team, codebreakers Elvin Urquhart, and Thomas H. Dyer. See Midway. See United States of America See Pearl Harbor. See Japan.

Roberts Jerry (Captain). (1920–2014). A military officer, cryptographer and codebreaker who worked at Bletchley Park on advanced codebreaking activities, such as deciphering the Lorenz SZ40 machine. He was a founder member of the Bletchley Park Testery, a specialist section involved with the manual decoding of advanced Nazi encoding machines. These were completely separate from the Enigma suite. Roberts was critical of the machine section that operated prior to handing over data to the Testery, stating that the machines and work in the Newmanry received too much recognition, but the hard work was in his section, and required careful logic, aptitude, pattern recognition, and perseverance, but was somewhat overlooked by the mystique of the new codebreaking machines, such as Robinson and Colossus. This viewpoint is completely understandable, and arguably, correct. It's the equivalent of showing someone the NASA Saturn rocket that took men to the Moon in the 1960s, and then showing them the boffins, scientists and engineers who did the calculations to get the astronauts there. Most people are far more impressed with the rocket, the machine, than with the calculating personnel behind the scenes.

Roberts was multilingual and spoke fluent German, which helped enormously in his work. He produced a book, *Lorenz*, after the war and outlined some of the issues and challenges that Bletchley Park encountered with tackling the complex form of messages received via the Nazi teleprinter attachment. His book was published when the machines had been declassified. Roberts was interviewed by journalists and the BBC about his time at Bletchley breaking codes and his contact with mathematician Bill Tutte, and that originally they thought Tutte, working alone at Bletchley, was just gazing into the air, considering a problem. However, Tutte came up with the eventual solution on how the Lorenz machine worked, a major breakthrough that helped change the war in respect of gathering enemy intelligence from the German High Command. Even messages from Hitler were eventually intercepted, deciphered and read.

Roberts worked with others including Donald Michie and Captain Roy Jenkins, although they were often on different shifts. After the war he participated in the War Crimes Investigation Unit in Europe, seeking out Nazis for trial. Roberts appeared in a documentary on Bletchley Park and was filmed walking through some of the dilapidated huts and rooms, discussing his work during the war. Roberts was not one to join in with the clubs and social events at Bletchley Park, so was a bit of a loner. His work became his main objective, and he achieved great things in the Huts and the Testery.

Roberts was made an MBE after the war for his services in codebreaking. Prime Minister David Cameron wrote to him in November 2012, advising him of his award in the New Year's Honours list and thanking him for his efforts in codebreaking during the war. HM The Queen, when awarding his MBE at Buckingham Palace, apparently commented that she remembered meeting him at Bletchley Park. Jerry Roberts was 92 when he received his MBE. In the same year, 2012, the hundredth birthday anniversary of Alan Turing, Roberts gave a substantial number of talks and lectures at King's College and at Bletchley Park on his work. He died in March 2014.

Roosevelt Franklin D. (1882–1945). American President at the start of the Second World War, and at the trigger event of the Japanese attack of Pearl Harbor that forced the US into the war. The US would become formal allies of Great Britain and its European and Asian allies. Initially, Congress approved war against Japan for their action. Nazi Germany and Italy then declared war on the United States on 11 December, only a few days after the attack on Pearl Harbor. Roosevelt would ensure the Lend-Lease programme option was available to provide financial support for countries including Britain and Russia. Millions of US dollars and armaments would be made available to shore up those fighting against the Axis powers for the duration of the war. Roosevelt would communicate with leaders Winston Churchill and Josef Stalin. Churchill would sometimes speak with Roosevelt on the American-designed and built SIGSALY voice-encoding system. Churchill got on well with the President and trusted him. There was generally a meeting of minds in the way forward, and Roosevelt saw the destruction of Nazi Germany as a priority, even though Japan had attacked the USA. Churchill was delighted that the Americans had been brought into the war, as that gave him confidence in terms of resources, men, funding, armaments, fuel, materials and equipment.

Roosevelt was not a well man, and suffered from polio, so was mobility-impaired and used a wheelchair. He is reported to have stood up at a meeting of politicians and military commanders with great difficulty when the Japanese attacked the country at Hawaii to make a point as regards the resolve of the American people. He won four presidential elections and was President from 1933 until his death in 1945, when Harry Truman took his place. A famous photograph has Roosevelt sitting next to Churchill and Stalin at the Yalta conference. His administration would establish the Pentagon in Washington. The atomic bomb, which would help to end the war in the Pacific, would also be enabled and supported by him, but remain top secret until its detonation at Hiroshima and Nagasaki. Under the President's administration, American-built and designed naval Bombe machines would help to counter the naval Enigma threat, and the U-boat threat in the Atlantic. Not all American generals or commanders saw eye to eye with their British Allied equivalents, but the bond between the two nations was strong and together they rid Europe of Nazi oppression.

Rozycki Jerzy (1909–1942). One of three Polish mathematicians and codebreakers who were successful in penetrating the workings of the Nazi Enigma encoding machine before the war. This work assisted the British at Bletchley Park considerably. He was initially employed in the Poznan Cipher Bureau in Poland, even though he was still studying as a student, and monitored German radio and phone messages. Later he worked alongside Marian Rejewski and Henryk Zygalski, two mathematicians who would eventually design and build a decoding machine, the Bomba. The three would be the first outside Germany to demystify the workings of the Enigma encoding machine. Before the Second World War they would decipher the code used by the German Navy. By 1932 they would be reading the German military Enigma codes and deciphering military messages, on what was supposed to be an unbreakable enciphering machine. Information would be shared later with the British, which gave Bletchley Park an advantage in attacking Enigma. In the summer of 1939 these three Polish mathematicians and cryptographic analysts would meet with the French and British including Dilwyn (Dilly) Knox, a codebreaker who would work at Bletchley Park in England. A few months later, in September 1939, Germany would invade

Poland, and trigger Great Britain, as Poland's ally, to declare war on Germany. The timing of that earlier meeting was critical in gathering important information on the Enigma encoding machine.

At the start of the war, the three remained in Paris and decoded German messages relevant to Norway and France. They shortly after moved to Algiers in North Africa as the Nazis advanced in France. Bletchley Park's Director, Alistair Denniston, requested they come to the site having heard of their achievements, but France was not keen to let them travel and had use for them nearer home. Rozycki died in 1942 after a ship he was travelling on sank in a gale.

In 2000, Rozycki was awarded a Polish honour medal, the Grand Cross of the Order of Polonia Restituta, for his services to Poland as a cryptographer. A memorial was established for him in the crypt of the Pantheon in Warsaw, Poland, as his body was never recovered after the sinking of the ship. In 2007, a monument was unveiled in Poznan castle to the three mathematicians, on the date of the seventy-fifth anniversary of the breaking of the Enigma encoding machine.

Sale Anthony (1931–2011). Famous engineer and codebreaking machine enthusiast behind the reconstruction of the replica Colossus codebreaking machine at Bletchley Park in the late twentieth and early twenty-first century. The reproduction machine is currently within the National Museum of Computing (TNMOC) in Block 'H' at Bletchley Park. The reproduction and rebuild of Colossus was based on a handful of photographs, and possibly the odd faded and torn piece of a blueprint that might have escaped the purge on destroying drawings after the war had ended. Also, the project was made possible with the recollection by key people of how Colossus worked, and how it was fabricated. All this information became an important and essential part of the project. The reconstruction was done on a voluntary basis, with little money, which had to be raised by volunteers. The Bletchley Park Trust was established in 1992. The rebuilding project for Colossus took around thirteen years, and was necessary as all the machines were dismantled and destroyed immediately after the war, with the exception of two units that were transferred to GCHQ Eastcote and then later on to Cheltenham in the early 1950s. These two, termed 'Red' and 'Blue', both Mk 2 machines, were broken up and dismantled in the 1960s.

Volunteers travelled from all over the country for several years to make their contribution to build the machine. It is a working replica, and demonstrations are given by TNMOC from time to time for the public and for members of the organisation. Information suggests that the original Colossus (i.e. non-replica) took between three to eight hours to produce the target data, known as the *de-chi*, and that this was much faster than if the analysis had been performed by codebreakers by hand. Professor Jack Copeland had confirmed that the majority of messages were broken within two to six hours during wartime.

Scherbius, Arthur (1878–1929). A German-born electrical engineer from Frankfurt who designed and built the famous Enigma encoding machine and improved it over time with numerous modifications. With his father a businessman, Scherbius had studied for his education at the Leibniz University in Hannover, and in Munich, and had achieved a doctorate of Engineering (D.Eng.), so was respected for his engineering knowledge. He completed his studies in Hanover by March 1903. A paper on Indirect Water Turbine Governors demonstrated his ability to research and come up with ideas and problem solving. His inventions included bizarre items such as electric pillows, but also useful products and designs such as ceramic heating parts and asynchronous motors. He worked for a number of companies across Germany and Switzerland.

While Scherbius was possibly, and arguably, not the first to invent a rotor-based encoding system (the Dutch were also involved with encoding rotor-based systems), he acquired various patents and issued new ones on the Enigma machine in 1918. His first company had the name *Scherbius and Ritter*. He started building the machines in his factory, in Berlin, initially in small quantities. This was fortunate, as initial interest was lethargic. The Enigma was manufactured by *Chiffriermaschinen Aktiengeselschaft*, which Scherbius had founded. This was effectively 'the Cipher Machine Joint Stock Company'. The design of Enigma, using three rotor wheels, was based on a rotary machine initially invented by Dutchman Hugo Koch.

The initial Enigma machine was extremely bulky and heavy, weighing around 50kg. It was sold for a considerably high amount of between 4,000 and 5,000 Reichsmarks. That was far too expensive for many potential clients and it had to be extensively redesigned and modified to reduce the weight, physical size and cost. Eventually they were modified and used by the German railway network, the Italians, and even the Swiss. The demilitarisation of Germany due to the Treaty of Versailles and the ease of travel between nations made it easier to sell the new, innovative product. Scherbius's idea was to sell the product initially to banks and finance houses, as a means for secure communication between them. However, in many ways, it was possibly too early to introduce a machine such as Enigma, as Germany and other countries had problems with locating sufficient resources to get their economies moving again. The German Foreign Office would decline a meeting with Scherbius, saying it was not interested. They did not have the funds for it. The German military gradually became interested in using its potential for communications in the German Army, later the German Navy, and the Luftwaffe.

The first model of Enigma was called the model 'A'. It was also known as *Die kleine Militärmaschine* (the small military machine). The Enigma was displayed at a major exhibition for postal services in 1923, and the marketing literature stated that the system of encoding and decoding used was so robust as to be completely unbreakable. This was at a time when communication across distances was traditionally by telegrams. The Enigma was, therefore a different, relatively secure approach to sending confidential information over distances. However, the original machines had not sold well, due to their cost, bulkiness and weight.

Scherbius would reorganise his factory, making it much more efficient than previously. The improvements reduced the cost of making the Enigma, and therefore a reduced sales price attracted investors and potential customers. The original machine weight and material content was also reduced, making it much more portable, and practical for using it anywhere, even on a ship. The Enigma model 'A' was produced commercially in 1924. Once the military found a use for it and became interested sales rocketed, and it was a challenge to manufacture enough machines for everyone who required them. (The British evaluated Enigma for military use but thought it 'unworkable in the field'.)

When the German military became seriously interested in his invention, Scherbius was told the commercial sales had to cease, as they would otherwise compromise the security of the armed forces. This inventor had made for the German army, with his modifications, probably the most cryptographically secure encoding/decoding system in the world at the time. Based on a three-wheel-rotor Enigma, and together with other key design features, the machine-encoded settings would amount to permutations of approximately 158.9,000,000,000,000,000,000. This was far more advanced than other available systems and the strong security clearly appealed to the German military, particularly the army.

Scherbius never fully realised how significant his design was, and never became aware of the efforts the Allies made to challenge and to break Enigma as a system, as he died in a horse and carriage accident in 1929 when he was only fifty years old.[38] He had sensibly acquired Koch's patents on rotary encoding machines a couple of years prior to his death. After his death, others took over the running of his company and further developed the Enigma models for the Nazis.

Without Arthur Scherbius, there might have been no need for our codebreaking outstations, or for Alan Turing's 'Bombe' machines, and perhaps, a very different structure to Bletchley Park as the HQ for British codebreaking. Some of Scherbius's papers, inventions, developments and discoveries are still used today for the production and design of asynchronous motors. It should also be stated that in America, Holland and in Sweden, Scherbius had competitors and rivals working on inventions for rotor-based encoding/decoding machines. Scherbius's acquisition of numerous patents from others, particularly the Dutch, put him in a strong position overall. There are some disputes online as to whether he genuinely was the first to design a rotor-based machine. The dates of actual patents around the world in that time period help to clarify some of these arguments. See *Hugo Koch.*

Schmidt Hans T. (1877–1948). A German who worked in the Reichswehr ministry. Schmidt had made contact with the French in 1931, and supplied a range of important intelligence papers, manuals and documents regarding codes and ciphers. These would include information on the Enigma machine and were like gold dust for the French and their allies. Schmidt was short of money and disillusioned with the government and his treatment in the Ministry, and effectively sold the intelligence to the French. Captain Gustave Bertrand of French intelligence accepted Schmidt's offer of information. Although highly suspicious of his motives at first, he was eventually trusted not to be a double agent for the Germans. Schmidt would be nicknamed 'Asche'. Things improved even more for the French when Asche passed over useful Enigma keys for the autumn months in 1932. These would essentially be the settings for the Enigma. Asche's contact was a French agent code-named 'Rex'. The information supplied, however, did not enable the French to break into Enigma, and they needed experienced Polish cryptographic experts for that. They now had the Enigma manual, operating instructions and the key settings. The intelligence from Asche was then passed on to the Poles in 1932, and they made good use of this, checking intercepted radio encoded messages. Information was then analysed to reveal the wiring arrangement of the Enigma rotors, those being selected from a code book and listing relevant dates, giving instructions to the operator on setting up the machine. By 1938 the Poles could read German signals from around 75 per cent of the Enigma intercepts from the Wehrmacht (army), plus other sources, at least for a time. Schmidt was eventually exposed to the Gestapo as a traitor and spy by his 'Rex', arrested and executed. Enigma was made more secure as time progressed but this was an excellent starting point for the Poles and French and ultimately would benefit Britain and Bletchley Park, the latter not yet established. GC&CS was always on the lookout for ways into the new cipher systems and machines. The Poles took Enigma seriously but not everyone else did, at least, not until the approach of the Second World War. See *Poland.*

Schreyer Helmut (1912–1984). A German engineer who built an advanced electronic computer based on a design by Konrad Zuse. He approached the German High Command with his equipment but was turned down. It appears that Hitler was only really interested in weapons of mass destruction such as the V1 and V2 rockets and advanced jet planes. Like many others, Hitler could not appreciate the concept of machines that saved time and resources, as it was not as tangible to him as a rocket engine or a missile that could help destroy the enemy. Schreyer would assist, Zuse, a civil engineer, to help resolve complex calculations of structures using the new technology. It would be in 1936 when Schreyer would consider the use of valve tubes as electronic switches, a very modern concept at the time. This would be very similar to the ideas of Tommy Flowers, when he approached the building of Colossus in England at Dollis Hill in the mid-1940s. One could say that Schreyer was ahead of his time, in the same way that Turing had thought of machine learning, or Flowers with his advanced Colossus design.

At first, Zuse could not comprehend such a concept of using valves as switches. This situation changed over time and he accepted the idea, although it was criticised by others. The problem was that many valves would be needed to build a computer to do anything worthwhile, and 2,000 valves would be required for this machine. Relays were used for some prototypes, but they did not respond fast enough. It was Schreyer who suggested the use of valves as digital switches. The Luftwaffe was approached by Zuse, but he was turned down. The concept and ideas were too difficult for non-electronic engineers to comprehend. If they had accepted the idea and given Zuse and Schreyer a chance of building their computer, the outcome of the Second World War may have been very different. Zuse and Schreyer would have to wait until 1958 before their electronic computer would come to fruition. Schreyer would experiment with film and projectors and use punched film to communicate data, much like punched cards could be used. One machine for mathematical calculations using this method was completed in 1938.[39] See *Zuse.*

Siemens, Carl Friedrich von (1872–1941). Entrepreneur of the Siemens factory and organisation during the last war, which manufactured many components and specialist equipment for the military services. He was the director in charge until his death 1941. Under the company name Siemens and Halske they also manufactured an important encoding machine, the *Geheimschrieber* or T52 machine. The development of the machine was more advanced than the Lorenz and more secure. This model was eventually used by the Kriegsmarine (Navy) and the Luftwaffe for sending secure messages. It was very heavy and not intended to be mobile or transported. However, later on, as the war progressed some machines were installed in vehicles and military wagons. One version, the T52d, was extremely secure, and Bletchley Park had little opportunity to make progress with it, not helped because most of the messages were sent by landline and could not be easily intercepted. Bletchley Park relied principally on its listening stations, such as at Knockholt, intercepting non-Morse messages from Lorenz machines over the radio waves.

Controversially, Siemens used forced labour to expand the organisation during the war, in order to meet the targets imposed upon them for delivery of equipment and supplies. They argued that as much of the normal German workforce had been called up to fight in the armed forces, leaving large gaps in the workforce, there was little choice but to comply. They apologised after the war, made a formal statement of apology in 2017, and paid compensation to surviving persons and the families of those affected. Siemens made reliable relays, among other equipment, and the British studied them in detail, at BTM in Letchworth and probably at the Post Office Engineering base in Dollis Hill, north London. They copied the design, with some modification, and inserted them into the Bombe machines to produce better efficiency and speed of operation. Some of the Bombe registers may indicate modifications to certain Bombe machines in 1943 and beyond. The first Siemens relays were installed at Outstation Eastcote in early 1944. One might even say that German precision engineering via Siemens helped the British win the war.

The Siemens company had been in Britain since 1843 and had a presence in London from 1850. Post-war there were various company mergers, and it became Fujitsu-owned in 2009. It is a substantial international company in the twenty-first century, with engineering expertise and a highly skilled workforce. See *OSE Outstation Eastcote*.

Sinclair Hugh Admiral (Sir) (1873–1939). Established the Secret Intelligence Service and the basis of GC&CS, which was later to develop to become GCHQ in 1946. Sinclair was an intelligence officer and a Director of British Naval Intelligence in the inter-war years. His reports to the British Government on Hitler before the start of the war were probably not taken seriously, but he did foresee him to be ruthless, cunning and potentially unstable in his actions, which was to prove true. He organised GC&CS to relocate to Watergate House in the Strand, twenty years before Bletchley Park would be used as HQ. Sinclair would later acquire Bletchley Park as the basis for GC&CS in 1938 but died of cancer the following

PEOPLE

year. He would not live to see the Bletchley Park establishment develop into a major codebreaking and intelligence HQ during the war years. See *Bletchley Park*.

Slowikowski Mieczyslaw Z. (Major) (1896–1989). Polish intelligence officer nicknamed 'Rygor-Slowikowski'. He would help to make the North African Allied Operation Torch operation in 1942 successful due to his team's interception and gathering of enemy intelligence. Experienced in military action during inter-war Polish–Russian conflicts, he rose in the ranks to become a major, with an interest in finding enemy weaknesses, such as codes and ciphers. This started with collecting Russian intelligence while in Ukraine before the Second World War. He would later establish a section of intelligence experts in Algiers, mainly of Poles, and would feed intercept information to the Allies continuously. His achievements probably helped to change the course of the war in North Africa. For his services to the Allies he would be awarded the Legion of Merit. He would relocate from North Africa and work in Scotland on training initiatives as Chief of the Polish Infantry Training Centre. Poland would also award him high military honours for his services during the war. See *North Africa*.

Spirella factory workers under BTM. A listing is given here of some of those female workers who assembled Bombe codebreaking machine components under the direction of BTM in Letchworth during the war, but at the converted Spirella factory:

Mary Triplow; Peggy Topham; Alice Haynes; Deanne Wallace; Cissie Smith; Helen Wilbraham; Win Hodder; Sheila Jennings; Doris Hoffman; Barbara Hathley; John Johnson; Mrs Day (Union leader); Mrs Blumfield; Mrs Crowe (Salvation Army); Mrs Buttle; Mrs Killen; Connie Cain.

These women would have had to sign the Official Secrets Act before commencing their wartime duties at the factory, and it is likely they would have lived in Letchworth, or possibly in the surrounding villages. BTM took over the Spirella factory to expand the Bombe-making operation, and the Spirella corset factory had to relocate to London for the duration of the war. The Bombe components would be wires, cables and connectors to make up specific parts of the Bombe. It is unlikely that the women would have been told what exactly they were constructing, for reasons of secrecy. The Spirella building was on the edge of the city and not that far from the main BTM factory. Other locations would have existed for component assembly prior to the parts being sent across to the main BTM factory for final assembly of the codebreaking machines. This listing of Spirella/BTM personnel has been obtained from the Garden City Collection Museum at Letchworth, Herts. See *Spirella*. See *BTM*. See *Letchworth*.

Stalin Josef (1878–1953). Premier and leader of the Soviet state during the Second World War. Russia became an ally of Britain and the West when the Nazis attacked Russia under Operation Barbarossa. Enormous resources were supplied to Russia during the war by the USA, and Britain played its part too, running dangerous shipping convoys in the Baltic Sea. Stalin was fed certain information on enemy intelligence by the British and probably the Americans too, but the sources of the intelligence were protected. Stalin didn't know about the Bombe or Robinson or Colossus codebreaking machines, and this was done on purpose for reasons of security. If the Nazis had discovered that their communication messages were being intercepted by Allied codebreaking machines, then they would have put measures into place to prevent it or make it much more difficult.

When Roosevelt, Churchill and Stalin met at a conference in Tehran to discuss the progress of the war, there seemed to be little trust between the parties. Stalin wished for a second front in the West, but this was not going to be possible for some time and that frustrated him. Bletchley Park was instrumental in decoding enemy intelligence from the Germans that indicated they would attack the Russians at Kursk, and this probably saved many lives as a result. After the war, with the Russians having overrun Poland and Germany, they would have discovered the Nazi Lorenz advanced machines and probably used them for secret communication. They would not have been aware of Colossus, the British decoding invention at Bletchley Park. Churchill did not want the Russians to get their hands on our cryptographic decoding machines and gave the instruction after the war to dismantle and destroy them. That was probably a bit rash, but it was driven by fear. See *Russia*. See *Churchill.*

Stewart Mortimer (Captain). A signals officer from Texas in the US Army, who worked initially at Outstation Stanmore and later at Outstation Eastcote, being part of the 6812th Signals. He was responsible for around 200 men who operated Bombe codebreaking machines at Eastcote during the war. They concentrated on U-boat cipher work via the Bombes. Training was carried out by the Wrens at Eastcote. The Americans were very successful in their operation of Bombe machines and data processing to identify message settings. The complement of American signals personnel was part of the ETOUSA agreement for joint co-operation between Britain and the USA during wartime. Stewart was a former IBM employee in the USA. See *OSE Outstation Eastcote*.

Swaffield, John (Dr). Physicist and engineer who worked on a variety of equipment for the Post Office Engineering Station at Dollis Hill. He was instrumental in the successful development of the vocoder and worked on improved use of submarine cables. Post-war he was involved with the Joint Speech Research Unit (JSRU) at Eastcote. The JSRU amalgamated with a speech research group at Royal Signals and Radar Establishment (RSRE, part of the MoD) and formed a speech research unit. The main vocoder research was post-war from 1958 to 1984. Swaffield worked in conjunction with John N. Holmes. See *Dollis Hill*. See *PORES*.

Tester Ralph (1902–1998). The establishment of a specialist codebreaking section by Ralph Tester at Bletchley Park, the Testery, would transform the cryptographic approach to challenging the Nazi secret writer advanced encoding machines. This was one of two sections that, added together, would speed up the processing of the teleprinter encoded intelligence messages. The Testery would be the second stage, with manpower to use hand and manual methods to crack Lorenz and the secret writer machines. Several women also worked in the Testery, some being Wrens. They would be using semi-processed data from punched tapes processed on the Robinson and later the Colossus codebreaking machines. There was little communication at first with the stage one section called the Newmanry, but management memoranda required better communication between the sections and people to talk to one another to improve communication and the chance of success. Things improved considerably over time. The combination of the two sections was greater than the sum of the individual parts, and particularly with the later codebreaking machines enemy intelligence was being read on a regular basis.

There were those who worked in the Testery who considered they were not given the proper recognition for their codebreaking activities and services. Their work would be both challenging and extremely stressful at the time, and their perception was that all the credit in codebreaking went to either Alan Turing or to those in the machine-section of codebreaking advanced machines, known as the Newmanry, at Bletchley Park. The two sections had to complement each other to obtain a meaningful result. In theory, the Testery could have possibly worked without machines to support them but would have been much slower and fewer messages would have been broken. On the other hand, the machine section, the Newmanry, relied on those personnel in the Testery to finish the job and obtain the decrypted messages using the information from the initial stage of machine processing.

Tiltman John (Brigadier) (1894–1982). A codebreaker at Bletchley Park who was the first to manually decipher the Lorenz advanced 'Fish' intelligence machine, prior to machine decoding being used. He had learned about ciphers from his experiences in the 1920s in the Indian Army, and manual methods of analysing messages and deciphering were used at this time. This put him in a good position when engaged at Bletchley Park within GC&CS, even though he had not been to university. In 1944, Tiltman was made deputy Director of GC&CS, a significant level of responsibility, but reflecting his knowledge and teamwork with others. He was instrumental in cooperation with the Americans, working closely with the US intelligence services and sharing information on enemy ciphers. His contribution to help in solving the German advanced Tunny ciphers was significant at the time. After the war, he was at GCHQ from 1954 to 1964. He would later become a consultant to the NSA. Tiltman was formally posthumously recognised and honoured by the NSA in 2004 for his contribution in cryptographic techniques and international cooperation in intelligence and security. He remains the only foreign person to be honoured by the NSA/CSS Cryptologic Hall of Honor. His nickname was 'the Brig' and he will go down in codebreaking history as an influential and exceptionally talented codebreaker, analyser of ciphers, and first-class communicator with others. He was a person who touched both sides of the Atlantic with his knowledge and expertise in a most positive way, earning him justified recognition. Tiltman gave sixty years of service to signals intelligence. See *Bletchley Park*.

Timms Geoffrey (1903–82). He joined Bletchley Park in 1944 as a codebreaker. Timms worked in the Newmanry, on Tunny intercept decoding. Towards the end of the war he wrote a general report on Tunny with Donald Michie and Jack Good. He remained with GCHQ after the war and applied computer techniques to codebreaking at the time. Prior to the war, he studied at Cambridge and lectured in mathematics at St Andrews. He was president of the Edinburgh mathematical society in 1941–42. Timms, a PhD in mathematics, worked for the Foreign Office until 1968.

Travis Edward W.H. (1888–1956). Commander Travis became the head of GCHQ, being the successor to the Government Code and Cypher School or GC&CS. At Bletchley Park, he succeeded Denniston in 1942, to be Head of GC&CS, as Deputy Director. Travis modernised the establishment in terms of numbers and categories of personnel, and improved systems of codebreaking. He would be in charge when the advanced decoding machines would come into being, to attack the Lorenz and secret writer Nazi machines. With his organisational skills and determination, he would oversee the setting up of specialist sections including the Newmanry and Testery, which would be run by Max Newman and Frank Tester, in order to attack the latest Nazi machines and decode messages.

Mathematicians at Bletchley such as Turing recognised the important changes made in administration and systems management by Travis. He would arrange for BTM in Letchworth to manufacture the codebreaking Bombe machine, which was the brainchild of Turing and Gordon Welchman.[40] Without Travis's development of Hut 6 at Bletchley Park in 1939, and assembling cryptanalysts and mathematicians, it is arguable that Britain would not have been prepared for the decoding of Nazi intelligence in the early years of the war.[41] Travis sent a letter of congratulations to H. Keen at BTM in Letchworth on 24 May 1945 after the war in Europe had ended, congratulating him and his team for his efforts with Bombe manufacturing and modifications.

He would leave GCHQ in April 1952, having made a significant contribution to codebreaking and intelligence processing both during wartime and post-war. His work on international cooperation with America in 1943 and 1946 became the foundation for the basis of sharing of key intelligence and information between the NSA and GCHQ. Travis was awarded a CBE and became KCMG, as well as receiving a special award for a Briton by the USA, after the war.

Truman Harry S. (1884–1972). Truman became the President of the United States on 12 April 1945 after Roosevelt died. He was to be the thirty-third President. Truman was previously vice president, but Roosevelt had not kept him informed on several crucial matters, including the development of the atomic bomb and ongoing issues with Russia. Churchill would communicate with Truman in 1945 on the Atlantic telephone line and associated SIGSALY encoding system, designed and built by the Americans. The longest phone call on the SIGSALY encoding system was held between the two allied nations for two hours. This was a telephone conference in 1945 to discuss the terms acceptable for a German surrender, as the war was coming to an end in Europe.

Truman's background included the investigation of corruption and waste in America's bureaucracy, and he saved millions, if not billions, of dollars of taxpayers' money. He had fought in the First World War in France as a captain in the artillery. His most important action during his presidential career was to authorise the dropping of atomic bombs on Japan at Nagasaki and Hiroshima, ending the war in the east. This would be the first time a weapon of mass destruction had been used in war. Several scientists had been researching electronic-counting technology to progress the weapon, and monitoring of its effects, and studied research papers on both sides of the Atlantic.

Truman would witness the United Nations Charter being signed after the war ended. In 1948, he would organise a substantial airlift operation to the western sectors of Berlin following a blockade by the Russians. The airlift successfully supplied food, fuel, vehicles, materials and medicine. Truman would be instrumental in the establishment of the North Atlantic Treaty Organisation (NATO). See *Roosevelt*. See *USA*.

Turing Alan Mathison (1912–1954). Often attributed as the 'father of computing', Turing made his most significant contribution during the Second World War at Bletchley Park as a mathematician and codebreaker. Turing was an academic recruited from King's College, Cambridge. He had studied at Sherbourne school in 1926–31, and was recognised early on for his academic ability, winning several prizes. Turing became particularly interested in codes back in 1937 and was at Princeton studying for a PhD. He feared there could be conflicts in years to come between Britain and other countries. He would design a multiplying machine and used relays, the system using binary numbers. He had an offer to remain in America but decided to return to England and to King's College. Turing had many ideas and concepts about machine learning and intelligent machines to assist mankind, releasing man from tedious work tasks where numbers and logic was involved. It is arguable that Turing was ahead of his time in his visionary, unorthodox approach. His greatest contribution during the war, arguably, was to design and develop the Bombe codebreaking machine (with assistance from others) to challenge the Nazi 'Enigma' encoding machine. This pioneering work, fraught with difficulties and some considerable concern by his bosses and those funding the project, enabled the message settings of Enigma to be stripped of the many millions of permutations down to a more manageable level. He worked alongside Gordon Welchman, another brilliant mathematician, but also one with a good engineering mind, and who made certain technical improvements to Turing's design.

Note that Turing did not actually build the Bombe himself, as he was not an engineer. He needed a great deal of assistance for that. His concepts and ideas had to be interpreted by engineers and some of those were at BTM in Letchworth, Hertfordshire, where they constructed the machines from scratch. He would visit the factory periodically to monitor progress, make suggestions for improvements and report back to his bosses at Bletchley. Turing's close colleague, Welchman, played his part in the design, too. Turing had written many papers on machines and mathematical ideas, machine learning, and gelled with colleagues like Donald Michie, playing chess with him frequently, and discussing their common ideas together.

Not always easy to get on with, Turing continued to play his part on developing equipment, methods and systems to help defeat the enemy at Bletchley Park. He would sometimes ride his bicycle to work with his gas mark on, even if there were no sirens warning of air raids. He would also chain his mug to the radiator pipework so it would not go missing. In 1936 Turing had issued a paper on the Universal computing machine. During the war, in 1942, he went to the USA to discuss matters of Bombes and intelligence with his opposite number and colleagues but was surprised to find the Americans refused the offer of one of his Bombe machines. This was due to them designing and building their own improved version of the Bombe, and he visited the National Cash Register Company in Dayton, Ohio, where he discussed the design of the new four-rotor-based American Bombe machines.[42] He also gave some advice at Bell Laboratories in the USA on the design of the advanced, complex voice-encoding SIGSALY machine, eventually used by Churchill for international calls with the American President in Washington. Turing was most interested in speech-encoding and speech-scrambling technology, and how it could benefit the security of private Allied conversations.

He met Joan Clarke, a codebreaker and linguist at Bletchley, and they became engaged but Turing broke it off. This was because he was homosexual and realised that marriage to a woman was not what he really wanted. They remained good friends. Turing would develop important techniques and systems in cryptography such as 'Banburismus', used on Nazi *Kriegsmarine* messages in Hut 8 at Bletchley Park, to save much time in deciphering the messages. That method was derived from a Polish cryptographer's approach, which had been studied at length by Turing and adapted. This technique was adopted widely and improved the success rate of deciphering enemy messages. Turing worked on early computer designs after the war and continued to write papers, prepare articles on machine learning and research his area of interests in early computing and machines. In 1948 he published an essay titled Intelligent Machinery. This attempted to demonstrate how machines could emulate the human mind with logic circuits and processes. Turing travelled to GCHQ Eastcote in Middlesex as a consultant for a brief period, and his friend and ex-fiancée Joan Clarke also went there for a short time.

Post-war, Turing worked at the National Physical Laboratory, and also at Manchester University in the Computing Machine Laboratory with his old colleague Max Newman. Turing's ACE computer at the NPL would be shelved for a time due to management disagreements. This would frustrate him, which triggered his move to Manchester University, accepting Newman's offer. ACE was eventually restarted at NPL and operated in 1950. It was quite advanced for the time, and with relatively high-speed processing of around 1MHz. Versions of it were built for both defence and commercial uses, and it was arguably the first real basis for a future 'supercomputer', outclassing the competition until America leapt ahead in later years. Turing was made an OBE for his services during wartime, and was elected a Fellow of the Royal Society in 1951.[43]

Turing was convicted of gross indecency in 1952 after being arrested due to his relationship with a younger man, and was chemically castrated as an alternative to prison. He died of cyanide poisoning in 1954, which may have been suicide. In January 2019, Turing was voted by BBC viewers as the winner of the *Icon* TV series about inventors, discoverers and achievers in the twentieth century. Turing's achievements are so broad and wide, impacting so many parts of modern technology, it is impossible to write just a few pages on his life and to do him justice. The numerous academic papers and essays he wrote over his career were largely groundbreaking and would form the basis for further development and research by others. Alongside Donald Michie, Turing realised that Artificial Intelligence was what the world needed, and was achievable, given time and resources. Few understood this. But he was most certainly ahead of his time and needed the world to catch up in inventing and discovering new materials, methods and techniques. It is sad that he felt the need to take his own life, challenged by prejudice and a judgemental society, when the post-war world and particularly post-war Britain needed innovators such as him to help us move forward with science and technology. The severe restrictions imposed by the Official Secrets Act at the time did not help the situation.

Turing has his picture on an English £50 note, which was first issued on 23 June 2021 as recognition for his tremendous achievements in computing, codebreaking and developments arising from his ideas. The range of technical papers and notes that Turing produced over his career as a mathematician is quite staggering. A brief table listing some of his academic papers is given in the appendices. Turing was granted a posthumous Royal Pardon in 2013 by Queen Elizabeth II. See *Bletchley Park*. See *Gordon Welchman*. See *Appendices and Turing Papers*.

Tutte William Thomas (Bill) (1917–2002). A young, brilliant mathematician who worked at Bletchley Park, although he may not have been taken on but for the persistence of one of the staff. With codebreakers frustrated with analysing the new enemy Non-Morse messages, Tutte was given a task to 'have a go', almost as a last resort, as the codebreakers could not resolve the structure of the advanced encoding 'Tunny' machine. Bletchley Park could not challenge the new Nazi encoding machine until they understood the its structure and configuration. They assumed it had wheels and rotors, but no one had ever seen one. Compare this to Enigma, which had been seen and studied by the British, the Poles and French. Over many days and weeks, Tutte worked quietly at Bletchley Park, on his own, trying out systems and using pencil and paper to try different solutions. He would lay sheets of paper over other sheets and check where information overlapped. Eventually, after several weeks, he succeeded, to the astonishment of the senior mathematicians and cryptographers at Bletchley. Tutte, without ever seeing the Lorenz advanced encoding teleprinter Nazi machine, had mathematically calculated the arrangement and configuration of rotor wheels and other aspects of it to work out the settings. To do that nowadays with an advanced personal computer would be a major achievement. To do this with no computer and just intellect, trial and error and logic, was truly astonishing. As a direct result of Tutte's work, Bletchley was able to facilitate the design and building of specialist decoding machines, to eliminate the many millions of permutations of the message settings. Turing's Bombe's were not compatible with the advanced machines due to the configuration of Enigma being different to Lorenz, so that new machines had to be invented, built and tested. See *Bletchley Park*.

Twinn Peter Frank G. (1916–2004). Mathematician and codebreaker. He applied to join GC&CS in 1939 and became head of *Abwehr* section at Bletchley Park in 1942. Initially, when joining GC&CS he worked under Dilly Knox, and progressed rapidly. Knox solved the *Abwehr* Enigma in 1941, opening the door for mass intelligence intercept decrypts of messages. Twinn was a professionally qualified mathematician.

Valentine Jean (1924–2019). Born in Perth, Scotland. A Wren who worked on codebreaking activities during the war. Her initial training was at Tullichewan Castle in Dumbartonshire. After two weeks she was posted to Outstation Eastcote in Middlesex to operate the Bombe codebreaking machines. She was later posted to Adstock, a country house with a much smaller number of Bombes. She had a spell of duties at Bletchley Park and experienced the mix of civilians and military personnel. She recalled there was a very different atmosphere to Eastcote and Adstock, which were run as naval bases with saluting and other naval rituals. Later, in 1944, she went initially to Bombay in India, then on to Ceylon, and worked on intelligence against the Japanese. She probed the Japanese meteorological codes and passed on to those that could make a difference in the war with such intelligence. Valentine recalled the times at the outstations and the relentless, continuous noise of the Bombe machines, clicking away like knitting needles, and the oil sprayed onto her shirt cuffs. This was noticed by her mother when she went home on leave, but she was unable to tell her parents to what work she was assigned. Jean gave talks and lectures at Bletchley Park some years after the war, when it was established as a codebreaking museum. See *OSE Outstation Eastcote*.

Von Rundstedt Karl (1875–1953). Given the rank of field marshal in the German Army in 1940. He had been involved in the invasion of Poland in 1939 as a high-ranking officer, and also had experience later in the Soviet Union, attacking Kiev. He was made commander in chief in the West in 1942. The Allies needed to understand the order of battle and strategic issues in France, which revolved around von Rundstedt, as he was issued instructions through the High Command structure via advanced encoding machines such as Lorenz. This was via one of several 'Fish' communication links, i.e. with fish names given to each link. The link of great interest to the British, from Berlin, was 'Jellyfish' and communication along this route came to von Rundstedt in Paris. Therefore, the Allies had to intercept strategic High Command messages as well as others and used the listening stations in Kent at Knockholt to record the non-Morse high-speed teleprinter and radio wave transmissions. The decoding process took place at Bletchley Park with punched tape and using a combination of manual processes and advanced codebreaking machines built largely by the Post Office Engineering department in Dollis Hill, north London.

Von Rundstedt failed to block the advance of the Allies in Normandy, partly due to a deception operation, and was removed by Hitler, only to be reinstated later as Commander in Chief. Von Rundstedt directed operations in September 1944 at the Battle of the Bulge in the Ardennes, and caused serious problems for the Allies, delaying their progress for a time. He was charged with war crimes after the war but did not stand trial. See *Germany*. See *Hitler.*

Welchman William Gordon (1906–1965). Mathematician and codebreaker, who worked alongside Alan Turing at Bletchley Park, and played a significant part in developing the Bombe codebreaking machines. Known as Gordon, he arrived at Bletchley on 4 September 1939. He had attended a short course organised by his boss, Denniston, on codebreaking, before he commenced work. During development of the Bombe, Welchman realised that the machine processing could be made more efficient by developing an electrical circuit, 'the diagonal board'. Turing was pleased that the Bombe was becoming more efficient but probably annoyed that he did not think of this simple circuit before Welchman did. Welchman quickly recognised and pushed for the expansion of the cryptographic section of Bletchley Park in order to meet the rapidly growing Enigma threat. Additionally, Welchman combined signals intelligence and cryptography for greater efficiency. This was achieved by reviewing the work the Poles had done earlier on Enigma and codebreaking. The volume of messages being intercepted by listening stations were increasing and they had limited resources to deal with it. He was made a leader and key person within the organisation and headed a group that would analyse and decode close to a million enemy Enigma messages.

By 1943 Welchman would have even more responsibility and become more involved in machine development at the park, even though the machines were constructed elsewhere. He became a liaison person to establish what needed to be done and others would then design and build the machines. At least that was the theory. In later years when advanced machines were at Bletchley, including the unreliable 'Robinson' used to crack Lorenz message settings, Welchman fell out with Post Office engineer Tommy Flowers. This was the same engineer who designed and built the Colossus machine, with input from Max Newman at Bletchley. Perhaps it was the class division between them, as Flowers was traditional working class.

When the war ended, in 1948 Welchman went off to America, spent time working for MIT and in the 1960s joined the MITRE corporation, involved in defence and technology. He became involved in computers and giving advice, helping to develop systems. He was effectively working for the security services, with a high security clearance. Welchman decided to write a book, *The Hut Six Story*, which caused great concern both in America and England, when certain chapters were analysed by the authorities. His home was raided by security staff from the NSA and agents interviewed Welchman several times about the book and its contents. He was fortunate not have been charged with breaching the Official Secrets Act, as others, including some at GCHQ, thought he had overstretched the mark and revealed secrets about the approach to analysing enemy intelligence and codebreaking techniques, which could become very useful to enemy states like Russia. President Ronald Reagan became involved and contacted Margaret Thatcher, the UK Prime Minister. They agreed that the book needed to be quashed, and subsequently, Welchman was given a stern warning not to promote or to publicise his book. He became a broken man from then on, according to his family. He felt he had done nothing wrong, and was a scapegoat for the authorities. He had his security clearances withdrawn and could no longer work for the American security agencies.

The book was eventually republished a couple of times in later years, and a chapter or two removed and replaced with other text. However, discussions between the author of this glossary and a subsequent publisher confirmed the amendments made were not because of any official Government pressure or direction, and that there was just some new information for readers and for the publishers to refresh a later edition.[44] According to that publisher no copies of the original were destroyed, or the book banned; it was principally a quash by the American and British governments on the promotion and marketing of the book, that killed it.[45]

It is the case that some of the approaches to analysing enemy intelligence used and developed at Bletchley Park still hold valid today in modern times, and may be applied by many world states to protect themselves from enemies. The machines and computers may have leapt ahead, but the principles behind the analysis remain sound. See *Turing*. See *Newman*. See *Bletchley Park*.

Wenger Joseph N. (1901–1970). Wenger was a rear admiral in the US Navy who became Deputy Director of the Armed Forces Security Agency. In 1942 Wenger would head up a new department within OP-20-G under Communications, being decryption and translation. He would push for the funding and production of a US-built four-wheel-based Bombe machine using advanced electrical contacts. It would be a heavily modified version of the Turing/Welchman Bombe, and Joseph Desch, engineer and inventor, would work on it at the NCR site in Ohio, in a heavily guarded building for secrecy, built by mainly volunteer women (WAVES). Alan Turing found out about the intention of the Americans to build a four-wheel Naval Bombe. Wenger met Turing at NCR in December 1943 and shared some of the design features of the American machine with him. The completed Naval Bombes would be transported and used in Washington, on a secure site within Nebraska Avenue. There would be two different versions of the machine. The Armed Forces Security Agency would be the seed to grow and develop into the later NSA, or National Security Agency of today. Wenger would hold a senior role in that agency in the early 1950s. See *J. Desch*.

Wingate Kathleen, Audrey (nee Wakeman). A member of the ATS during the Second World War, and a Y-station operator at the Forest Moor Army listening station. Kay worked there from 1944 to 1946 as a service Intercept Operator under 'B' Watch. A veteran of codebreaking support activities and on the official Bletchley Park role of honour. She attended the Bletchley Park Veterans day in September 2022 and was able to discuss her radio-traffic interception wartime experiences with other veterans from a variety of different backgrounds, and to do this without fear of prosecution under the Official Secrets Act.[46] See *Y-stations*.

Wynn-Williams Charles E. (1903–1979). Welsh-born scientist and physicist. During the war he worked on radio detection, instrumentation and electronics at TRE in Malvern. This was later known as the Royal Radar Establishment. He worked on high-speed Bombe codebreaking machines, cooperating closely with BTM in Letchworth who built them and contributing to their design and efficiency. Bombe registers[47] recording the dates of manufacture, issue to sites, and modification of Bombes have some entries referring to the high-speed machines and Wynn-Williams. He designed the Cobra attachments that were to modify the Bombes and were used at Outstation Stanmore and Outstation Eastcote. These would have very thick and many hundreds of multiple wires to form thick cables attaching the devices to the main machines. They were extremely noisy and created much dust. The Cobra machines were not liked by the operating Wrens, and they took up a great deal of space next to the Bombes. Wynn-Williams also contributed to the advanced Robinson machine that was used at Bletchley Park to help crack the advanced Nazi teleprinter machines, before the Colossus computer could be designed and built by others.

Following his wartime contribution, Wynn-Williams lectured at Imperial College and read physics. He worked on electronic-counter technology, which was recognised for its contribution to modern computing, after the war ended. His papers and research would be read widely by others and influenced Josef Desch in the USA in respect of valve-based thermionic counting instrumentation. Desch was an engineer and inventor who would go on to develop electronic calculators, and was a key person in the development of the American version of the British codebreaking Bombe machine for the US Navy. See *Josef Desch*.

Yoxall Leslie A. (1914–2005). Mathematician and codebreaker at Bletchley Park. Developed systems and techniques of analysing enemy codes and ciphers, called 'Yoxallismus'. He had been recruited from Cambridge by Gordon Welchman and joined Bletchley in 1941 to assist the team of cryptographers. In late 1942 he would join Hut 7 to work on the Japanese ciphers and deconstruct them. This would have been using the Enigma known as 'Purple' that was used by the Japanese. 'Purple' was also attacked by the Americans. Later, he would move to the United States and provide a liaison role during the Cold War, when intelligence again had a high priority. This was a period where GCHQ was developing further in Britain and would need to share information with the NSA and other similar intelligence organisations across the Atlantic. Yoxall had made an important contribution to the area of codebreaking and cipher analysis in his career. See *Bletchley Park*.

Zhukov Georgy (Marshal) (1896–1974). Russian senior officer who was assisted in battle by intelligence gleaned from Russian codebreakers. Zhukov was nicknamed 'Marshal of Victory'. He would go on to help repel the Nazis in the battle to take Moscow. See *Russia*.

Zuse Konrad (1910–1995). German civil engineer. Zuse worked on aircraft design and applied mathematics on aircraft structures. He was also instrumental in developing equipment that had computer-based logic. Heavy bombing in 1945 by the Allies brought his research to a halt. Indeed, in 1943 and 1944 he had his work and workshops destroyed by Allied bombing raids when he was developing pioneering computer-based equipment. He had produced some work and equipment for the German military to aid calculations. His colleague, Schreyer, had suggested he consider using valve tubes as switches, but Zuse initially had thought this not viable. He preferred relays and used many of them. Eventually he did use valves, similar to Tommy Flowers, who used them as digital switches on the advanced Colossus machine. After the war he set up several companies and built early computers. He had, with Schreyer, tried earlier to make equation-calculating machines that could use a degree of repetition and use binary code. It appears that it was a combination of resistance and lack of belief in Zuse by Nazi leaders, together with relentless bombing of his laboratories and workshops, that prevented him from leading the way in early computer development. Resources and materials would be severely limited as regards availability during the war. Hitler would only support and resource developments in weapons of mass destruction, such as the V2 rocket, as the war developed in later years. A sophisticated calculating machine was not seen as relevant to the Nazi objectives. How wrong they were.

Many inventors experience a disbelief of their ideas and concepts by people in command or control, who fail to understand the importance of their inventions and then prioritise other activities over them. They may only realise their mistake some years later, when it is too late to make a difference. Invention is fraught with risk, on both sides, and wartime may put an additional complexity on such matters when resources are scarce.

Arguably, there were some similarities in concepts between Zuse, Schreyer, Turing, Michie, and even Tommy Flowers. Each individual had a mindset where they could see a different method and approach to solving challenging problems, but would encounter resistance in convincing others of their ground-breaking methodology and radical ideas.

Zygalski Henryk (1908–1978). Polish cryptologist and mathematician. As part of a team of Polish cryptographers, he analysed and deduced the wiring for the early Enigma machine, and this information was passed on to others, including Britain, which was able to use it to establish systems to decode message settings by hand. A civilian in the Polish Cipher Bureau, in 1938, along with Marian Rejewski and Jerzy Rozycki, the team had built a codebreaking machine to decipher the settings, named Bomba.[48] The development of such a machine meant that as Enigma became more secure and sophisticated over time, other decoding machines were designed and built by the British, called Bombes. It is said the Turing–Welchman-designed Bombe worked differently to the Bomba, and the only similarity was in the name. Indeed, the name Bombe, applied to Turing's concept of a rotary-based decoding machine, may have come from the Polish machine.

Even though the Bomba soon became technically obsolete as Enigma developed and became more secure, the principles developed were crucial to the breaking of the cipher. Zygalski developed a special system using twenty-six perforated sheets called Zygalski sheets to aid analysing encoded messages and help towards identifying Enigma rotor positions. These would be used initially by the Polish Cipher Bureau. A different version of them, but using physical perforation machines, was later developed at Bletchley Park and termed Jeffreys sheets. See *Poland*.

Commentary on People

One may ask: 'Who was the most influential person or persons during the Second World War within the area of military intelligence, deception, and codebreaking?' The answer probably depends on a large number of factors. Who made a difference to saving countless potential lives and ending the war? Who had the intellect to design and build innovative equipment and machines? Who made concepts and discoveries that were to go on and shape our world post-war and into the twenty-first century? Many would answer but one name: Alan Turing. He is the individual on which there have been numerous books, articles, lectures, documentaries, and even a film made with him as the principal character. But we can see from the previous chapter on people the range and diversity of many individuals who had an influence somewhere along the road, and who made contributions in their own way. Sometimes it was as individuals working alone, at other times as part of a substantial team. The film *The Imitation Game* was only able to portray certain aspects of the approach to penetrating enemy intelligence and codebreaking. I do not recall it including the Wrens operating the Bombe machines. Nor was there any mention of there being many Bombe machines, not just one, and that there were modified versions of them, too.[1] No mention of the influence of Polish codebreakers. The film was made for entertainment purposes, and if the viewing public learned a few things about Turing, Enigma and codebreaking during the war, then that was a bonus. I didn't envy the director one bit. Obtaining a balanced view of those events in a limited time for a cinema audience of different generations was always going to be a challenge.

International Effort

This glossary on wartime codebreaking rightly includes many individuals who were not British. It includes Americans, Poles, Russians, Germans, Italians, and so on. Some Wren personnel were transferred to Ceylon, now Sri Lanka, to help take the intelligence fight to Japan and the east.[2] After all, we are considering and evaluating the whole of the Second World War, and its influences. Also, it includes an eclectic mix of military personnel and civilians, such as at Bletchley Park.

For many academics employed as codebreakers, their fight against the enemy was at a distance, in a draughty old hut, but may have had a more significant impact on shortening the war than killing a few of the enemy would as a soldier on the battlefield. However, there would have been tremendous frustration too, with long periods of no, or little progress, such as when trying to crack U-boat Enigma messages, which saw no progress for around nine months and concerned everyone, including Churchill. It was the U-boats, and their impact on shipping convoys supplying essential resources to Britain, that really concerned and frightened the Prime Minister. They had to be stopped, or at the very least contained. Those in management circles at the Park had to also deal with the advanced German encoding machines and their messages, a system that was separate to Enigma, and yet required more resources in terms of men, women, money and equipment to challenge it. A young mathematician, Bill Tutte, eventually made a difference there, while also significant was the setting up of discrete departments to analyse and process the messages received from the Y-stations and the advanced listening stations. These departments grew over time to include many people including civilians, Wrens and others, all with specific tasks and skills. As one might reflect, the whole was greater than the sum of the parts. Working as individuals was necessary at times, but others had to work as team players to make a difference. Collecting and analysing message data, even pure trivia, may be of use when pieced together with other trivia to make an important discovery about a German officer or his movements. Hundreds of people, many of them women, would work in long shifts to help gather assemble and recover those bits of messages and trivia. Most of them would never realise how important and game-changing their contribution would be in the bigger picture of things.

Lever and Bletchley

Mavis Lever worked at Bletchley Park and while there she identified a message from the Italians that ended up giving the British fleet in the Mediterranean a huge advantage in surprise. She liaised on the analysis of the message with a mathematician colleague, who she later married, Keith Batey. Lever later then spent a bit of time at Eastcote after the war ended when it became GCHQ.

There was room for a certain degree of individualism as well as a team player to get the job done. Lever was fortunate at having a boss, Dilly Knox, who gave opportunities to women within his codebreaking team, when others in his senior position at the Park might not have been so welcoming and trusting and have issued females work of lesser importance. Knox was just keen on using whosoever it took to get the job done and done efficiently. His enthusiasm and trust in his pupils improved morale and resulted in relatively high yields and outputs in codebreaking performance at Bletchley. It is sad that he died from illness before the end of the war.

Decisions at the top in wartime

With Churchill responding positively to a letter from four of the Bletchley Park codebreakers for urgent resources, one wonders whether any of our modern Prime

Ministers would have done the same in the situation he found himself in? Few, if any, would have stated 'Action this Day', and gone along with the codebreakers' request. Churchill was so astute, he realised that the resources for Bletchley Park were critical to its potential success against Enigma and the Nazis. That is what true leadership is about, separating the wheat from the chaff, knowing what is important and what is not. He understood that if the interception and analysis of enemy intelligence failed due to lack of resources, Britain and its allies would be at a major disadvantage and could lose the war. Hitler was ploughing all the resources he had at his disposal into the Nazi war machine, and supplementing these from occupied countries in terms of labour, fuel and materials. The United Kingdom had to use its limited resources and skilled experts effectively, to gain any chance of success.

The female contribution in wartime codebreaking

The vast amount of female personnel employed to help with processing enemy intelligence, both home and abroad, is quite astonishing. These were civilians, Wrens, ATS, and others, but mostly Wrens, who operated most of the Bombe machines, and the later more advanced decoding machines such as Robinson and Colossus. Their initial training at Mill Hill, Scotland, or elsewhere would not have incorporated 'Special X' duties training, as one had to be selected for aptitude and discipline among other attributes, and this happened after basic training. The on-site training at outstations or at Bletchley would have been more specific on the operation and setting up of the Bombe machines, usually by more experienced Wrens who had earned their data-processing spurs over many shifts, weeks, months, and even years. The term 'data processing' is used here, as that is what most of the Wrens did at the outstations – process data for Bletchley Park to eliminate most of the many millions and millions of permutations of the Enigma machine settings.

Transfers between Bletchley and other outstations were common, so some had operational experience at different sites. The country houses would have been more laid back in operation, being smaller and having fewer machines, but the *Pembroke V* sites were run as naval ships, with all the associated terminology and routines. But it wasn't just about the Wrens. They needed support from armed Royal Marine guards, maintenance personnel, gardeners, drivers, GPO engineers, RAF personnel, cooks, etc. The author worked out the structure and the organisation at Outstations Eastcote and at Stanmore and was surprised how many people were present. The shift system used on sites would have allowed for staff leave, sickness, transfers to other sites, training time, promotion tests, and so on. The locals providing shops and amenities would have seen all these personnel, mostly in uniform, come and go, but have no idea what exactly it was they were doing. Of course, the staff could not divulge their activities to anyone outside the base as they had signed the Official Secrets Act before commencing duties. Not even their close family knew what they did. It was just too important to prevent a leak, which might be picked up by careless talk by an enemy agent and expose Britain in a way that might result in success for the Axis powers. Even personnel on the same base but not involved in codebreaking or setting up the Bombes were curious about what went on in other blocks and huts, but they received no clues, even when making casual conversation with Bombe-operating Wrens. HQ would have had numerous Typex machine operators, being a key stage after the settings were transmitted or conveyed back to Bletchley from the outstations. Some would include ATS female personnel. Operating Typex for hours at a time could be bruising on the fingers or nails, so the staff had various tricks to make their work easier.[3]

The despatch riders, or military couriers of documents from outstations and Y-stations to Bletchley Park and elsewhere, were crucial to success of the entire codebreaking operation. These were mostly women, often Wrens or ATS personnel (with some civilian Post Office couriers), and they would travel up and down roads and lanes during day or night in all weathers to deliver their packages and goods. These packages would include the Y-station log sheets with the encoded letters on many sheets of paper, which the operators had taken down from their radio receiver. Gordon Welchman, one of the codebreakers at Bletchley Park, commented on the inadequacy of the teleprinter machines in the early years in terms of coping with the volume of messages coming in.[4]

Roll of Honour

Surprisingly, many books and articles on the Second World War codebreaking and intelligence never mention anything about the factory that designed and built the Bombe machines in Letchworth or the advanced machines in Dollis Hill, or that large quantities of Wrens, thousands of personnel, operated most of the codebreaking machines. It is as though the support services to Bletchley Park were entirely insignificant, which is untrue and disingenuous. Ex-Wrens have written to me in the past and stated they had been largely forgotten about and have become frustrated when there are articles in the media about events during wartime, omitting to mention the significant support role they took on. The Roll of Honour at Bletchley Park goes some way to changing this state of affairs, but not all Wrens who served in intelligence or codebreaking are on that roll.[5] Most members of the public don't even know it exists. If the reader was previously unaware there were essential codebreaking outstations in existence, managed and run by female staff and have now learned of their relevance, then that is progress. There would be over two hundred machines, most of them on other sites away from Bletchley Park.[6] These were operated mainly by female personnel.

Intellectual academics and chess

Playing chess with your colleagues was one way of concentrating on something other than Enigma or Lorenz, and there would be some championship-standard players at Bletchley. Playing chess in the breaks at Bletchley was a social event, and although everyone would be competitive in spirit to win the game, it gave the players and participants the opportunity to discuss concepts, ideas, thoughts, and bounce ideas off one another, sometimes on matters such as artificial intelligence and machine learning. Some of those chess players turned out to be chess champions and prize winners, and of extremely high intellect. A very few might have 'genius' attached to their names when historians look back as to what they achieved in their careers. Chess players at Bletchley included Turing, Michie, Alexander, Golombek and Milner-Barry.

Common Links

While chess was certainly one of several common links between people as a form of relaxation between stressful work on breaking ciphers and codes, Alan Turing was considering the mathematical possibilities of permutations of the game. Indeed, he wrote a paper on another sophisticated game, Go. Could a machine learn from playing numerous games of chess or Go? What would be the permutations of all the possible moves mathematically? In modern times, super-computers have been constructed to beat human masters at these games. These have succeeded through the process of machine learning, just the sort of subject that interested Turing and a few others. A topic that was common between Turing and Donald Michie, another codebreaker at Bletchley Park, was Artificial Intelligence. Machine learning is but one aspect of AI, but Michie later went on to chair boards and committees on the subject. Sadly, both died far too young.

Both the Poles and the British investigated machines to break Enigma message settings, but the Poles got a head start on building the first of them. The Bomba, and the Bombe, while very different in design and construction, had a common link of using machines to help crack Enigma. The enemy, the Nazis and Axis powers, also had a common aim in trying to produce an encoding system that would be secure for sending and receiving messages. Despite many different variations of Enigma, different rotors and increasing from three rotors to four, and different code books, the Allies were able to crack the message settings. Even the more advanced Nazi encoding machines were broken by Bletchley Park decoders and cryptoanalysts.

Listening stations were used by both sides, but perhaps the Allies had a more comprehensive system overall, spanning across America, the British Empire, parts of Africa, the Mediterranean, and even across the Pacific. Where the Allies differed from the Axis powers was that while the latter wished to occupy and control vast areas of land, other countries and populations, the Allies wished to stop Nazi expansion in its tracks and eliminate it once and for all to ensure peace longer term. Common to both sides would be the pulling together of countries and 'teams' to fight the enemy and achieve victory. But Hitler had been tracking other countries and nations for some years before the war commenced, trying to influence Russia, Italy, even Great Britain. It was a bit of a shock to him then when Britain declared war on Germany for invading Poland in 1939. That was not in Hitler's plans.

He even respected Britain for establishing the British Empire, so to have it as an enemy was a great disappointment, and one that would take up a great deal of Nazi resources. The First World War had been a precursor to the next war, but perhaps the Allies had not been sufficiently prepared for a Nazi fascist uprising, at least not at the speed that it became formidable.

Links may be also considered between people, engineers, scientists, mathematicians and cryptoanalysts that worked on both sides of the fence during wartime, but who were not connected, other than through their radical new ideas. Zuse, Schreyer, Turing, Michie and Flowers all had various concepts and ideas to move the world into the digital age, with varying degrees of success. If they had all been in one room, and particularly during peacetime, even more discoveries may have been made.

There is evidence that some individual Germans had the idea of a valve-based digital 'computing' machine during the war, but senior officers supporting Hitler would not fund such a wild idea. However, we must remain thankful how things turned out; technological advances by the Nazis could have extended the war by many years.

Process

One might analyse the processing of operations such that it was largely a six-tier system for dealing with Enigma via a Bombe machine:

Stage One: Collect enemy transmissions sent by radio using Morse code, with the numerous Y-stations listening in. Transfer that back to Bletchley Park by despatch rider or via teleprinter.

Stage Two: Bletchley to consider which messages were going to be analysed there and which were to be sent to an outstation. Their mathematicians to design the instructions, called a Menu, to be used with the Bombe machines.

Stage Three: Outstations receive the Menus of instructions/encoded messages and data processing is carried out by people who know nothing of Enigma, mostly Wrens, but who must follow strict instructions to determine the Enigma settings.

Stage Four: Successful data processing, checked via a checking machine, conveyed back to Bletchley Park and a layer of female personnel using Typex machines uses those calculated settings to test the message.

Stage Five: The message is translated from German into English by translators.

Stage Six: The message is cross-referenced with other data, categorised, prioritised and passed on to relevant military commanders and the Prime Minister, where pertinent. Churchill would also receive a summary of intelligence regularly.

The above is a highly simplified summary of the process of tackling the Enigma messages and there would also be checking machines incorporated at Bletchley Park and the outstations to check the readings after Bombe machine runs.[7] This system worked like clockwork in the main. There would have been problems, failures, mishaps, incomplete messages, poor reception and atmospherics playing havoc with messages over the radio, people going off sick at a crucial time, or having to rush off to a close relative's funeral, having died in a Luftwaffe bombing raid. But overall, the system worked, and worked remarkably well. Add in the Americans too, who operated some of the equipment, and were trained by Wrens. Add in the GPO and RAF engineers and the factory personnel building the Bombes and modifying them. Add in the design modifications suggested by a host of different people from Bletchley, from TRE in Malvern, from Dollis Hill, from Letchworth, and one can begin to acknowledge how complex this was, and how many different people took part. People of both genders, different backgrounds, different social classes. These were military people, civilians and medical support personnel. The list is almost endless. While some would be talented mathematicians and engineers, others would be valued for their incredible discipline and perseverance in getting a task done, no matter how long it took.

Parallel systems of encoding and decoding

What makes this even more astonishing to the author is the parallel encoding/decoding systems that had to be coped with, when the Germans introduced the advanced encoding machines such as SZ40 Lorenz and others. Not only were the Enigma messages coming through daily thick and fast, and had to be processed quickly, initially by hand or by Bombe machine, but the new challenge meant the Bombe was impotent against Lorenz. New analysis and systems had to be established, and quickly. A race against time. However, not everything is within your control. You sometimes have no option but to seek external assistance from your allies, but some of your allies are already stretched.

Taking risks

One must possess vision to make those decisions and take risks. Churchill took risks as a leader and didn't get everything right. He put forward a commando raid on France which failed miserably. But few leaders get everything right. Max Newman and Thomas Flowers, working on the solution of Colossus took big risks, but achieved success in the end. It could have all gone very wrong, and Colossus might never have been designed or built. We need to thank Alan Turing for introducing Max Newman to Thomas Flowers, the GPO engineer. That was a crucial meeting and introduction. But don't just dwell on the brilliant minds at the time, do please give credibility to the many thousands of men and women who worked behind the scenes, those who were not in the limelight. These did not receive recognition for their efforts, even after the war had ended, even though they were crucially important within the overall picture of intelligence gathering, analysis and codebreaking.

Frustration post-war

Thomas Flowers was clearly frustrated after the war ended at not being allowed to build even more advanced versions of the Colossus machine. Secrecy in Britain after the war was iron-clad and restricted British innovation to a degree. Post-war, America and other nations would leap ahead in electronic technology, partly due to the Official Secrets Act tying the hands of the British. There will always be differences of opinion between engineers and computer experts as to who achieved which specific electronic innovation first. The development of the modern transistor in 1947 and 1948 and the introduction of solid-state technology by the Americans would change electronics across the whole world and aid mass production and reliability of components.[8] Even the definition of what is a computer has been challenged, and whether a machine without a stored programme can be considered as a computer.

Polish contribution to codebreaking

The Poles, led by Henryk Zygalski, enabled Bletchley Park to make progress in attacking Enigma and developing important and useful systems and techniques using their mathematicians and cryptographers, much faster than otherwise would have been the case. Sharing of information at cryptographic conferences and meetings between France, Britain and Poland would prove to be essential in those early years just before the war, and in 1939 particularly. The Poles appeared to have an aptitude for cryptographic work, and with the need to eavesdrop on its neighbours that became extremely useful at a time of rapid change and uncertainty. They had intercepted thousands of German Enigma messages in France, also processing radio intercepts relevant to the Norwegian occupation by the Nazis. While Enigma was further modified by the Nazis and adapted over time to make it more secure, the pioneering work done by the three Polish mathematicians gave Bletchley Park a head start with the encoding machine, and the ability to break into its settings and codes.

Successes, failures and mistakes

The Italians had their successes in cryptography and acquiring Allied code books and documents by all manner of means. In studying the historical background to those involved in intelligence in the last war, mistakes were certainly made on both sides. Ciphers were left wide open at times, for the enemy to attack and read with some ease. Sometimes it was just leaving drawers or safes open for an opportunist to wander in and photograph the documents with a small camera. Eventually, the loopholes would be closed, but not until sensitive intelligence information had been passed to the enemy, who always made good use of it. The reason for this happening at all is complex. Some of it is down to carelessness of individuals and human failings. Failing to follow the protocols and systems such as changing the settings regularly, in accordance with the orders, rules, and instructions. Much of this may have been down to fatigue. Most of those serving were excessively tired and worried, with their minds on other things such as close family members fighting elsewhere, or not having enough food and being hungry. Some would be worried about their home being bombed. There was a lack of trust and disagreements between the Germans and the Italians. They were allies, and the major part of the Axis powers in Europe, but they did not always agree on the systems and procedures imposed on one another. That situation can lead to errors and mistakes. In any war on such a large scale and time, there will be errors, But the key is to not allow them to significantly impact on the outcome of the war. If intelligence errors by the Allies had given away the D-Day plan, then that would have been a disaster and led to probable failure. Ironically, the Allies took a risk with introducing the Fortitude South operation, and major deception of the enemy. This was even to the degree of having a double agent transmit a message to the enemy in the early hours of D-Day saying that ships were setting off from the British coast and an invasion was happening. But that deception appeared to work.

A considerable number of Enigma codes were never broken, partly due to the high volume of them, bearing in mind the substantial quantity of Enigma machines used by the enemy. One specific encoded Nazi message eluded most cryptographers after the war, until an amateur cryptographer, Stefan Krah, along with the assistance of forty-five other amateurs, in 2006 managed to crack the settings. It transpired that a U-boat commander had been under attack by enemy depth charges and gave the last known position of the enemy as well as weather conditions and visibility. This was on 25 November 1942. Krah had used or written a computer programme, which he called M4, and then used the computer power of his colleagues in a powerful, combined network to persevere and eliminate the Enigma settings that were of no use, leaving only the final correct settings relevant to encoding and decoding the message. It was an attack effectively using mere brute force against the Enigma encoded system, and just took time. The authenticity of this message was later proved as valid according to the Second World War German naval records. It had taken over sixty years to crack this message, and ironically, the cryptographer who achieved this was German.[9]

A Spanish gift to Britain and the Allies

Garbo, or Juan Pujol, was a unique individual, a Spaniard who hated the Nazis and wanted to work for the British as an agent. He made several attempts but was turned down repeatedly, the British being somewhat suspicious as to his motives. Eventually he was taken on by MI5 and assigned a controller or handler. Pujol goes down in history as probably the most successful double agent during the

Second World War. His false network of agents and spies was created through his imagination, as though he was writing and arranging a play for a theatrical performance. In one way, it was almost a theatrical performance, but one with enormous risks. If he had been caught as a spy he surely would have been tortured and executed by the Nazis. The early years of him being abroad as an agent for the Nazis gave him a degree of credibility when he relocated to Britain and England. He could now see and locate actual British and Allied shipping, report on troop movements, and give seemingly valuable information to the enemy. But all this was in a controlled way. When you are involved in deception against another party, one must introduce some elements of factual information to make your reports credible. With the support of MI5, he achieved this, and became important and highly valued by the Nazis, having his reports read in Berlin by the German High Command and even Hitler. His piece de resistance, perhaps, was the transmitted call he made in the early hours of D-Day, 6 June 1944, advising about significant movements of shipping from ports in England. He also indicated that the First US Army Group (FUSAG) was still in place in Kent. His messages over the next few days following D-Day had to reinforce the illusion that FUSAG was still in southern England waiting to come over the Pas-de-Calais with what was probably the main armed assault on France. A map of Britain obtained post-war from the Nazis showed the FUSAG forces clearly marked on that map.

Pujol, together with Britain and the Allies, created a grand illusion. They were like magicians, each playing a small but crucial part in the overall master plan. The prize for making the illusion work was to impact significantly on the outcome of the war and world history. Deception in wartime is still relevant today.

The US Naval Bombe

Josef Desch was an inventor and American engineer, and although his background was not in codebreaking or cryptography he managed to organise the design and production of the US Naval Bombe codebreaking machines, based on four-wheel Enigma machines. His work at NCR and after the war brought him recognition and awards for technical brilliance and innovation. He would study the research of British physicist Charles Wynn-Williams and develop counting instrumentation using thermionic valves. Scientists and engineers interact with other peers in their scientific fields, reading papers, attending conferences, meeting and discussing theories and experiments. Alan Turing was concerned when he discovered the Americans were building their own version of the British Bombe. As it turned out the US Naval Bombe was reportedly more efficient than the British equivalent.[10] Britain could also benefit from their operation when they were sent to Washington. Indeed, there were connections to Bletchley Park from many of the machines. It is interesting to note that, of the total of British and American Bombes overall, Bletchley Park had a relatively small proportion of them on site, the vast majority being located at outstations and in Washington. Few people outside the detailed technical subject of codebreaking seem to be aware of this fact.

Turing

If previously, you had been told, or had the understanding or perception that it was 'all done by Alan Turing', with a small amount of assistance from a few colleagues at Bletchley Park during the last world war, then this glossary should have dispelled that illusion at least. This is not to take anything away from Turing, who was a brilliant mathematician, cryptographer, and a true visionary in technology and systems, who was only held back by the Official Secrets Act after the war, and by society's prejudice about his personal life. Some consider him a genius. It is right that we should celebrate Turing's exceptional achievements both during the war and afterwards. In post-war British society there were various hurdles and barriers to deflect Turing from capitalising on his specialist knowledge and skills, and we are all the poorer for that. His Royal Pardon sadly was only granted many years after his premature death. However, we can look at his archived notes, papers, lectures, and agree he was an individual who was significantly ahead of his time.

Hollerith and data processing

Who could have foreseen that the statistician Herman Hollerith, the son of a German immigrant to the US, would develop and invent a data-processing machine, the Hollerith Pin-box tabulator, which would support the Allies and Bletchley Park in keeping tabs on millions of bits of information gathered from the listening station messages intercepted? That it would help experts piece together small, seemingly trivial information and pair it with other data to provide useful intelligence. Intelligence data was transferred to hundreds of thousands, even millions, of punched cards. The Hollerith machines could carry out sorting of the punched cards, based upon basic instructions provided. In wartime there was a difference of opinion at Bletchley Park as to how the Hollerith Section manager, Frederick Freeborn, should operate his section. Freeborn stuck to his guns and provided an efficient service to Bletchley. His largely female staff had little time off for relaxation due to the volume of punched cards needing to be processed and stored. Requests would come in from Bletchley and expect a speedy turnaround. None of this would have happened, at least not at the rate achieved of data processing, without the American Hollerith tabulators.

It was BTM that had those Hollerith machines under contractual licence, selling them around the world, and understood how they worked. While the Bombe was not an expanded Hollerith machine, and built to a completely different design and objective, there would be benefits in BTM having had experience in data processing, particularly with their involvement in census processing and counting-machine technology over the years.

Education and Engineering

Thomas Flowers, the Post Office engineer, had never been to university. He had gone to evening school to study engineering. Yet he designed and led the team to construct the world's first semi-programmable computer during the war, for

Bletchley Park. A machine that may have, arguably, helped to shorten the war by up to two years and save many lives. This was possible due to his knowledge and interest in using tube valves as digital switches and having done some work in the past on this, but on a much smaller scale than with the Colossus codebreaking machine. Very few others were also keen on this approach in other countries, but funding was really the barrier at the time. Valves were expensive to produce and buy. What a coincidence that Alan Turing should have met Flowers and introduced him to Max Newman, and that their discussions would prove to be beneficial to GC&CS at Bletchley. Life is full of chance meetings and coincidences – some good, some bad – but they may be considered as opportunities. Some of those chance meetings can often change world history.

Wrens, Bombes and resourcing in wartime

Edith Blagrove, Superintendent of the WRNS or Wrens during wartime, had an enormous responsibility to ensure that all her women in uniform upheld the highest standards in the Royal Navy. Simultaneously, she had to ensure her female team performed such that they were able to support Bletchley Park both effectively and efficiently in codebreaking data analysis, across a variety of sites. In a world where technology was only just starting to become important and making a difference, Blagrove must have wondered if these man-made noisy and smelly Bombe machines were really worth all the effort of setting them up, running them and monitoring them by her Wrens? Couldn't there be something more worthwhile for them to do? Something perhaps more productive for the war effort? Maybe she did realise the importance and significance of their efforts, and the crucial enemy intelligence that was deciphered to help defeat the Axis powers. She would also have been aware that as the war in Europe ended, there would be a need for Wrens in places like Ceylon and the east, to help defeat the Japanese, miles away from England. How would her Wrens cope in countries with mosquitoes, snakes, spiders and creepy-crawlies, not to mention the intense heat and humidity? Very well, as it turned out.

Across the British Empire and beyond

Canadians, Australians, New Zealanders, Indians, Russians, French, Poles, and many other allied nations across the world, came together to defeat the enemy, whether they were the Nazis, the Japanese, or Italians. The arrival of VE day in 1945 was a major turning point in the war, but those forces in the east would still have to deal with Japan and wonder how much longer the war would last. If one studies the entries within the 'Places' part of the glossary in the next section, it is possible, at least to a degree, to appreciate the complex interaction between bases across the world sharing intelligence and information in the war. Australia communicating with Hawaii in the Pacific, Canada communicating with the US, England and Europe, India communicating with the eastern forces, and aided by the British. Listening stations around the world. Any one individual encoded message could make the difference of helping to shorten the war, or even prolong it, if missed by the radio listening operator. It is difficult to equate the enormous level of cooperation at the time between nations, and between individuals within those allied nations, with modern times. Back then they had no computers, no social media, to support them. Records were kept on cards, and later punched cards. Many communication links were crude. Fax transmissions were in their very early days, and it was Knockholt in Kent that became the first listening station to intercept an enemy facsimile transmission.

Perhaps the existence of the British Empire helped cooperation at the time, and acted as a sort of glue, where Britain's influence was still significant in different continents around the world. We can be sure that the cooperation of nations was largely due to the alternative being unthinkable: a world dominated by the Nazis and the Japanese, oppressing freedom and taking away liberty from most of us.

Measures and countermeasures

Dr R.V. Jones was arguably the father of electronic warfare and used science and physics to help defeat the enemy, who were using technology to aid their armed services. Items such as 'chaff' (strips of metal jettisoned by aircraft to confuse enemy air-to-air missile tracking) are still used today by air forces around the world, even the US President's Air Force One plane. The area of countermeasures has grown exponentially since the end of the Second World War, and forms part of a nation's tools to disrupt the enemy in conflict. There is a synergy between detecting enemy secrets, analysing them and using them to your advantage, alongside designing and applying scientific countermeasures. One must use all the tricks one can to defeat the enemy. Intercepted intelligence via Morse code and Enigma would have been extremely valuable to the Allies to understand where or when the Luftwaffe were planning to align their navigation beams. The presence of a new and unfamiliar German name or phrase in an Allied decoded report might give a clue as to a new piece of equipment or technology being tested by the Nazis. There would be a clear advantage in seeking out other reports with similar references to pull together parts of the jigsaw puzzle in an effort to understand the nature and scale of the threat. This was the case with the development of weapons of mass destruction, such as the V2 missiles, and the processing of 'heavy water' for the development of an atomic bomb.

Lesser-known people who made a difference

I decided to include the names of some of the factory workers who worked in Letchworth under the direction of BTM in the Spirella building. These were women from a variety of backgrounds, including someone from the Salvation Army. Then, there was a union official to ensure the conditions were reasonable in the factory, at a time when health and safety did not count for much and accidents might occur. Some might have changed from making women's corsets to assembling components for Bombe machines. Many would have close relatives fighting in France, North

Africa, Italy, or training in the armed services. Alternatively, they were part of vulnerable convoys in the Atlantic, North Sea, or the Mediterranean. But working as part of a team, these women continued day after day, cutting and fitting cables, wires, connectors and relays and screwing various parts together to be inspected for quality control. Then, the components were transported to the main BTM building down the road for final assembly on the framework of the codebreaking machines. The final stage after quality checks and testing would be to deliver them to Bletchley Park, or to one of the five codebreaking outstations in England. The robustness and reliability of those Bombe machines was dependent not only upon the material quality of components, and the design, but also the accuracy of work by those women workers back at Letchworth at their workstations, awaiting with trepidation the next enemy air raids.

Y-stations across the world

The interception of enemy intelligence across the worldwide listening stations, the processing of it by cryptographic experts and the use of linguists to decode them would have to be efficient, and shared with selected allies, to make a difference. The UK did not trust the Soviet Union, but then the feeling was mutual, and they didn't really trust the West. Britain also had to be careful with 'neutral' countries, particularly the Swiss. But we were very interested in what was going on politically and financially in Switzerland, as were the Nazis on the opposing side. Knowing about transactions in the financial world in detail would help greatly to understand about the movement of materials, resources and items that are essential to running a war. The Swiss would be targeted for the 'bugging' of their telephone lines and security systems by both sides. Indeed, the Swiss would even have some Enigma machines, too.

Achievements and post-war careers

We know from our individual experiences that people can be vulnerable at times, be unsure of themselves, have doubts, be open to manipulation, or be put down by others who may not have the vision that others have. There can be differences of opinion as who is best to tackle a problem, and arguments and disagreements behind the scenes. But out of this can also come the positive side of mankind: innovation, creativity, cooperation, sharing ideas and troubleshooting. It seems there were many who excelled themselves and after the war went on to even greater things in their careers in astronomy, anatomy and medical science, Artificial Intelligence and computing. Whether they were cryptographers, Y-station listening radio operators, translators, despatch riders/couriers, Hollerith machine tabulators, physicists, or others, many would achieve extraordinary things in wartime, and under intense pressure. Let us celebrate those people, and what they achieved. The next part of this glossary puts much of this into context, as people need locations and places to do whatever they are tasked with. It should now be possible to better understand the links and connections between many of the people and places mentioned.

Places

Abbots Cliff House, Capel-le-Ferne, Kent. A listening Y-station not far from Dover that could intercept non-Morse advanced Nazi radio transmissions from Tunny encoding machines. Around sixty German-speaking linguists would be based there. There were a limited number of listening stations that could cope with interception of non-Morse messages. Others included Denmark Hill, in south London; Sandridge near St Albans; and Knockholt in Kent. The latter was a major interception station that expanded greatly in area and personnel and equipment as the war progressed. See *Ivy Farm* and *Knockholt*.

Africa While North Africa may have dominated wartime action in the Second World War on this continent, it is prudent to state that Allied intelligence and listening bases were also established further south, such as near Mombasa in Kenya. Wrens operated receiving equipment, but later the unit was transferred to HMS *Anderson* in Ceylon[1] and expanded considerably as a listening 'ear' for the East and Pacific fleet area. Three Poles, all mathematicians and cryptographers, who had been instrumental in cracking the early Enigma machines, had gone to France from Poland, but as the Nazis progressed they would travel to Algiers and collect and decrypt enemy intelligence from North Africa.

Polish Intelligence officer Major Mieczyslaw 'Rygor' Slowikowski was awarded an American medal, the Legion of Merit, for his contribution to the Allied North African Campaign in 1944. His work and that of others assisted the British in Operation Torch, the landings in North Africa in 1942. He was awarded an OBE in 1944 by the British for his intelligence services.

America – See **United States of America**

Arizona, USA. As in both New Mexico and Utah, the Navajo Native American tribe that occupied parts of this state for generations contributed greatly to the subject of coding and encoding messages for the US Army during the Second World War. The Navajos spoke a strange language and dialect that was apparently impenetrable to outsiders. When this was realised, it was proposed to use members of the tribe to encode and decode military messages across the battlefields in the Pacific. This was not an easy task as initially one needed to locate English-speaking Navajo people who were familiar with the terminology as well as their own dialect. Tests were carried out and some additional military words added to aid communication. An initial group of twenty-nine trained Navajo soldiers were trained up to work in pairs, to encode and decode transmitted orders and messages. Two were held back in the USA to train more Navajo recruits, with the majority allocated to four regiments in the Pacific on active service. Finding and training the appropriate Navajo people with the level of education and other qualities required was problematical and took time and resources. After certain teething problems on test transmissions and decodes, which had to be ironed out, they went into action in their allocated regiments. They were extremely successful, blocking out the Japanese enemy from penetrating the transmissions and none could be unravelled by them. But there was some initial confusion, and experienced US signals officers intercepting these strange dialects thought the Japanese had taken over the Army radio frequencies. This was promptly rectified, and they began to earn their reputation in encoding and decoding instructions and reports across the Pacific islands to divisions and platoons. It was soon apparent that Navajo messages could never be faked due to the unique language structure, and were completely reliable. Additional words were introduced to help communication in military reports but had to be disguised carefully so as not to form a crib or clue for the enemy.

At the latter part of 1943, there would be a formal request for eighty-three more Navajo personnel. At the end of the war there would be a total of 420 Navajo code-speakers who had acted either as trainers or in battle in the Pacific doing their specialist work. The vast majority of these would be in the thick of the fighting, where it was bloody and intense, the Japanese not surrendering even when the odds were stacked against them. It is the case that in the early days of the scheme there needed to be sufficient Navajo trained speakers available, as if one was injured or killed at one end of the communication chain, unless another was there to take his place immediately the entire communication link and system would fail. It was like having two Enigma machines set up configured for encoding and decoding and the soldiers at both ends when one of the bases is destroyed. The controller for the Enigma messages about to be sent would then need to await another machine to be located at the end of the chain to replace the one destroyed. That needed to be set up using code books and the correct configuration, and the trained personnel, usually two or three men, made available to operate it. However, it was far worse if one of the Navajo specialists was lost. One could make many Enigma machines, and there were thousands of those, but it was not easy to identify and train the Navajos to become language, communication and military specialists in their own right. They had to be taught about the US, Japanese and German armies, the phrases and words used in military reports, and those converted to Navajo dialect. There was also limited use of other Native American dialects, including Comanche, Hopi and Menominee languages, by US armed forces in 1941–45.

One American general later commented that if it wasn't for the Navajo encoders and decoders, Iwo Jima would not have been taken in the Pacific. Although their work was highly classified for security reasons, many years after the war had ended they were recognised for their exceptional contribution in signals communication for the US Army. They were especially honoured at a ceremony in the US in August 1982. The selection of which language and which parts of the tribe to be used was a complex one, and the people and tribe finally chosen were one of the few that had not had German student researchers study their dialect at the time. This assisted the security aspect considerably. One might even consider that if there had been sufficient and very large numbers of Navajo-trained code speakers available, there would have been less need for British and Allied communication devices and establishing encoding/decoding machines for communication. In practice there was a need for both solutions. One wonders if a modern high-speed computer, combined with bespoke specialist software developed by a cryptographer and language expert, might be able to penetrate the Navajo dialect. See *USA*.

Arlington Hall, Virginia, USA. During the Second World War this was a base for female codebreakers and cryptanalysts for the US Army. It would be at the Arlington Hall Junior College for Women. There, the Japanese 'Purple' encoding machine would be decrypted. Purple was a form of Enigma-type encoding machine but set up specifically for the Japanese. Diplomatic codes were intercepted and later Japanese army codes, too. This would be one of two main cryptographic bases for the US and the work was top secret. Post-war the base would concentrate on Russian intelligence leading into the Cold War era.

Australia. Allies of the Western world during the Second World War and supplier of troops to fight in Singapore, Burma, the Philippines, and the Far East against the Japanese enemy. They would have listening stations, or Y-stations, across the country to intercept Japanese intelligence Morse code transmissions. Australia and its intelligence services would support codebreaking stations across the world, including those in England, America and India. Melbourne was an important codebreaking base, having sections for cryptography run by Australians and another by Americans. Intelligence in advance of the Battle of Midway was initially intercepted in Melbourne but transferred across to Hawaii. General Douglas MacArthur relocated to Melbourne during the war. Australian codebreakers had a reputation for being effective in the field. They appeared to be more effective than the Americans due to their local knowledge. Codes were broken by Australian units in Brisbane. Some units supported American troops with intelligence. Japanese High Command codes were broken in Brisbane as well. Intercepted coded transmissions from the jungle in New Guinea and the Philippines were sent to Brisbane for analysis and decryption. Sydney encoded Allied signals to London or Washington with intelligence for analysis by places such as Bletchley Park. The Japanese changed their codes about every six months, according to the Australians. There was a five-digit number for each syllable or word and a random five-digit code from a code book to make the item suitable for transmission. Intelligence officers would be used out in the field, e.g., jungles, farms, villages, depots, rice fields, open country, etc.

Indigenous Aboriginal persons supporting the army were used for a form of encoded language for certain transmissions, and these would have confused the

Japanese if listening to the radio. Central Bureau was the principal Australian codebreaking service, and that organisation managed to successfully attack the Japanese water transport codes, as well as those of the Japanese Army and Air force.

Baker Street, London. Not only is this the location for Sherlock Holmes, with his statue opposite the station, but in wartime it was a hive of activity, with many different buildings in the vicinity being used for war work and the sharing of intelligence. Close to Baker Street Station, at No. 64, is a blue plaque on a wall under a large glass canopied entrance, commemorating SOE. It marks the specific building that was used by the Norwegian section of SOE for the planning of the daring Telemark raid in Norway to significantly disrupt and destroy the production of heavy water, which might be used in the creation of nuclear weapons by the Nazis. The wireless operator was Donald Hunter, who worked on various Norwegian ships during the war. The commando raids took place between 1942 and 1944 and the Norse Hydro production plant at Vemork in Norway was severely damaged, and a ferry containing rail wagons carrying heavy water sunk with a planted bomb in 1944 on Lake Tinnsjå. Further Allied heavy bombing prevented the Nazis restarting heavy water production to any large scale. It was a multi-phased SOE commando operation, and was not without its failures and challenges, but it caused severe problems for the enemy and arguably delayed the introduction of nuclear weapons by the Nazis. A film was eventually made and released in 1965 called *The Heroes of Telemark*, which brought the story to a wider audience. While it was not entirely factual as portrayed, it did provide the basic outline of events, including the final sinking of the ferry on the lake with the wagons of processed heavy water on board. Heavy water was used by the Germans instead of graphite and acted as a 'moderator', to slow down and help sustain a chain reaction in an atomic bomb. It was essential to prevent a vital component from reaching German scientists to manufacture such a weapon. The operation would have been supported by collected intelligence from the area, including from agents and radio traffic. The film has a specific scene of direction-finding Nazi mobile operator units trying to locate Allied agent radio transmissions, a risk that all agents and resistance fighters were up against.

Baltic Sea. An area of high activity during the Second World War, and a place where more than 200 German ships and boats were scuttled in May 1945 after the Nazi surrender. In 2020, an archaeological team looking for old fishing nets discovered something that appeared to be an old typewriter covered in barnacles. This, in fact, was an Enigma machine from the war, with still some of its labelled keys visible through the crustaceans. The area it was discovered in was Gelting Bay, near Flensberg, off the Danish coast. The archaeologist who discovered it was Florian Huber, part of a team of archaeologists. When examined by experts it was stated that the model of Enigma discovered was more commonly used on German warships. The Enigma has been donated to the Gottorf Castle Archaeology Museum. It is likely there are many more decaying Enigma machines on the seabed, but the find is of significant interest. Several countries were vying for control of the Baltic Sea during the war, or using it for transporting armaments, fuel, materials and men, including Poland, Finland, Germany, Britain, and also with input from Sweden. Many areas were heavily mined around ports, including near Tallin, the Estonian capital.

Baltic States. A trilogy of countries, Estonia, Latvia and Lithuania, most bordering Russia, and a politically unstable area even prior to the Second World War. There would be some common ground between Finland and the Baltic States, particularly with Estonia, its nearest neighbour of the three across the Baltic Sea. Intelligence gathering in the area would be ongoing, and shared where practically possible, to determine what Russia's plans and political aims were after the Russian Revolution and the expansion of communism. The Nazis would make a secret agreement with Russia in the early years of the war, the Molotov–Ribbentrop Pact of 1939, effectively a non-aggression agreement that provided that Russia could take over and occupy the Baltics. The Nazis would occupy the Baltic States from July 1941 until 1944 and considered many people in the Baltics were closer to the ideal Aryan race, which the Nazis wished to expand as part of their European domination. SS divisions of Estonian soldiers were recruited and trained by the Nazis. Most of these would be used against Russia as part of Operation Barbarossa and the planned occupation of that country by the Nazis. Post-war, after a lengthy period of occupation by communist Russia and oppression, the Baltic States became free independent nations on 6 September 1991.[2] This was recognised formally by Russia. The intelligence of this volatile region would be monitored constantly by Britain, Finland, Sweden, and other countries before, during and after the Second World War. The Cold War period would put a different emphasis and need for intelligence of the geographical area for the West. In October 1948, the Russians changed their cipher systems, an event known by the West as 'Black Friday'. A serious intelligence blackout on Russian intelligence intercepts for the NSA and the West gave rise to considerable concern at the time. Even today, it is likely that the Russian President, President Putin, has his eye on the Baltic States, with their close proximity to Russia and access to the Baltic Sea. The NATO alliance provides a limited deterrent to Russian occupation, with British and other NATO troops providing a presence in Estonia at the time of writing.

Battle of Britain House, Ruislip. Now demolished due to it falling into disrepair, and with just some remaining foundations and evidence of its existence, this site was used during wartime to train American SOE agents to drop behind enemy lines into occupied territory. The site was within Copse Wood in Ruislip and was concealed with surrounding trees and vegetation. The American military would plan operations and assignments including espionage and acts of sabotage against the Nazis. Although unconfirmed, it is likely that their timing of the air drops into France, Belgium, Holland and Germany would be based on intelligence gathered from Bletchley Park through the Y-stations listening in across the country, and abroad, and most likely from other agents in occupied countries. The house was built in 1905 by Joseph Conn. It was leased by a wealthy businessman and shipping

PLACES

magnate in 1920, Meyer Franklin Kline. It was then named Franklin House, after the new owner. In later years, it was used as an RAF memorial for those personnel lost in the Battle of Britain. The house was officially renamed Battle of Britain House on 1 March 1949 by Air Chief Marshal Sir James Robb. The house was destroyed by fire in 1984 and demolished afterwards. Guided tours are given of the site, and there is a website that gives some of the history. It is situated close to Ruislip Lido within the London Borough of Hillingdon. Much of the site and remains are overgrown with vegetation, but some masonry is still visible, including an adjacent pond structure. The guide who also runs the website has much information on the history of the site, its uses and various photographs and maps.

Barnet, north London. The collection point for the Radio Security Service (RSS) using Voluntary Interceptors or VIs to listen in via radio to track frequencies and hopefully identify enemy agents or enemy transmissions during the Second World War. A Post Office Box Number (PO Box 25 Barnet) was allocated for VIs to send their findings from listening sessions back to the centre and await further instructions. This was at Arkley View, Barnet. This site was previously used as an intercept station by the Post Office. Sometimes they would be issued with new radio frequencies to target, and at other times to keep listening on frequencies they had done before and obtain interesting results. VIs would not be able to tell their family what they were listening for, or that they had been recruited by the government. The Radio Society of Great Britain played their part in helping to coordinate their members to help the voluntary teams to obtain the necessary equipment to listen into foreign radio transmissions. Some would build or modify their existing radios, whereas others would be allocated radios. Around 1,700 radio amateurs were recruited as VIs in this specialist work across Britain. Although initially they were incorporated into the Royal Observer Corps, many later came into the RSS, and were engaged as uniformed, professional radio listeners.[3] The RSS would relocate to Arkley View in Barnet in October 1940. Earlier on, it was the evaluation of some of the log sheets at Wormwood Scrubs prison in West London, used by MI5, where certain messages of interest were being scrutinised. Wormwood Scrubs was used in part as a quasi-military censorship station under GC&CS during wartime. It would not have been suspected as such by the enemy or enemy agents, being within a secure prison. Analysis of the messages indicated that enemy *Abwehr* intelligence was being identified through radio listening and had to be expanded to a wider network of monitoring stations. It would take some time to set up the organisation, but formal listening stations such as Hanslope Park would become important as they were established to gather more enemy intelligence. See also *Hanslope Park*.

Beaumanor Hall. Located not far from Loughborough, Leicestershire, a top-secret listening station or Y-station of some importance. A large country house and grounds, it was requested by the MoD in October 1941. The station was manned by a combination of military and civilian personnel, with ATS staff. Some reports say there was no heating provided in the huts on the site. Many of the huts would have been camouflaged for secrecy. Forms were filled out by listening operators including date, time, radio frequency and operator's number. A copy was transmitted to Bletchley Park and the actual handwritten form in red ink may have been couriered across, in addition. It was the Army's main intercept station and staff were allocated radio wavebands to listen out for Morse code transmissions. It was also crucial to intercept non-Morse German High Command messages. The official title or name for Beaumanor was WOYG or War Office Y-Group. Protection was provided for the base by the Military Police, guard dogs, and the local Home Guard. By the end of the war, it had a complement of 900–1,200 ATS plus 300 male civilian wireless operators. Post-war it became 'War Office Civilian Wireless Station', or WOCWS.

Bentley Priory An RAF Fighter Command base in Stanmore, Middlesex, RAF Headquarters, and not far from the codebreaking Outstation Stanmore (OSS). Bentley Priory had many female intelligence plotters below ground level to track enemy activities in the air to help direct British aircraft to intercept them. It narrowly escaped a German V2 rocket in January 1945, which came quite close to the base. King George VI and Queen Elizabeth visited Bentley Priory in September 1941, accompanied by Air Chief Marshal Sir Hugh Dowding. The Bentley Priory site was sold for luxury housing some years ago, but the listed building still remains as an RAF museum, open to the public. The author has given several talks on codebreaking and intelligence at the museum. Within the museum is an exhibit of a letter to Douglas Bader's parents to inform them that his artificial legs were dropped to him in a prisoner of war camp in Germany following his capture. Some magnificent artefacts, awards and paintings exist at the museum, and it holds talks regularly on military history. The stained glass within the entrance is also magnificent, depicting Second World War aircraft. The 'filter room' was created during wartime to filter intelligence from listening stations, before being passed through to the operations room. This has been recreated as the actual filter room was installed in a bunker just before the Battle of Britain commenced in 1940 to protect staff from bombing.[4]

Berkeley Street, London. Home to the Diplomatic Section of GC&CS, it was located in Flats 8 and 9 Berkeley Street. There, four floors would provide office accommodation for up to seventy-five staff. Adjoining property would be used to incorporate an expanded Japanese section as the war escalated.[5]

Berlin. Capital of Germany and the place where Hitler committed suicide in 1945 as the Russians and Allies occupied the city, destroying the Nazi war machine. Post-war, large areas of Germany and the capital were split between the Russians, Americans, British and French. Attempts by Russia to blockade the western parts of Berlin failed, due to a massive Allied airlift bringing in supplies for the starving Berlin population. Phone-tapping espionage would play its part on both sides but the Operation Gold phone tapping and tunnelling operation by the Americans in 1955–56, with some British assistance, would surprise the Russians and East Germans.

PLACES

It would become an embarrassment for the Americans when it was exposed by British agent George Blake, working for the Russians as a spy. The Berlin Wall would prevent a mass exodus of East Germans to the West, but many ingenious ways of escape were used over several years. Berlin would become renowned for its exchanges of spies between the West and East, and as a source of intelligence for both sides. See *Post Office Research Establishment.* See *George Blake.*

Bletchley Park. Initially purchased in 1882 by Sir Herbert Leon, a businessman and entrepreneur. The main building was then extended substantially, with work completed in the 1920s. Acquired in 1938 by Hugh Sinclair for the sum of £6,000 just before the Second World War, Bletchley Park was a large mansion house surrounded by acres of grounds and landscaping, complete with a large lake. It was surrounded by some 580 acres of farmland and countryside.

Bletchley Park was established as the Government Code and Cypher School (GC&CS), a site that had developed from intelligence specialists working at Room 40 (Old Buildings) at the Admiralty in London, and MO5b, later known as MI1b. GC&CS was formed for intelligence purposes in 1919 after the First World War. This was some twenty years prior to Bletchley Park becoming active and developing into a major headquarters for processing signals from a wide range of countries and sources. In 1922, the administration was taken over by the Foreign Office and was then under the Secret Intelligence Service (SIS). In 1939 various SIS communications transmitters and receivers were installed and operated at Bletchley. Section 'D' of SIS specialising in sabotage, explosives and clandestine methods came to the site in 1939. SIS was now separate from GC&CS but shared some of the site until war broke out, when it was transferred back to London. Early on, the smaller security side of the organisation was the preparation of British code books and enciphering tables. These were printed in Oxford. Bletchley Park would commence as a series of wooden huts around the estate, and the mansion house, but later have brick-built permanent buildings. Some of the neighbouring properties were taken over, including cottages, that would be used by codebreakers and mathematicians at Bletchley. For a period, in 1942, diplomatic and civil targets would be dealt with in London, with Bletchley concentrating on military intelligence and communications. During wartime, the key objectives in intelligence processing and decrypts would be against enemy states including Germany, Italy and Japan. There would also be interest in neutral states such as Switzerland, and other countries sympathetic to the Nazi ideology. As countries became occupied, such as France, Belgium, Holland, Norway, those too would be of interest and intelligence gathered across Europe and elsewhere. Russia would be spied upon in some detail, before the war and prior to its entry into the war. However, this ceased for a brief period when it became Britain's ally when invaded by Germany. *The Daily Telegraph*, in 1941, would publish a crossword competition based upon a request from those involved with Bletchley Park, and would then go on to contact those who did exceptionally well as potential candidates for a career in codebreaking. Both men and women applied.

Bletchley Park would become 'Station X' for secrecy in its codebreaking activities, although from late 1942 Wrens were formally instructed to drop that name completely and Bletchley would be termed HMS *Pembroke V*, along with other codebreaking sites.[6] From July 1942, the code word Ultra would be substituted for 'Special' when referring to intelligence decrypts, and its use would continue throughout the war.[7] The codebreaking and cryptographic staff and personnel at Bletchley were assembled from a range of academics, many from Oxford and Cambridge, being mathematicians, physicists, and lecturers in classics. The purpose of GC&CS was to provide an intelligence and cryptographic section to support the Government and the military, to find out what suspect states in Europe and elsewhere were planning. Most countries used some form of intelligence encoded message, and it was the objective of GC&CS to identify the system used and break the codes to read the intelligence.

Bletchley Park grew over the years to become the headquarters of analysing intercepted enemy intelligence, using methods by hand as well as by complex machines. There was a mix of military personnel and civilians, so rather different from RAF, Army or Navy bases. Not everyone would be in uniform. This was a top-secret base. It was essential that other countries, particularly potential enemies, did not identify Bletchley Park as a codebreaking base, or even that it existed at all. It would have numerous huts built to house different groups of personnel and carry out different tasks. Alastair Denniston would establish the base initially, until Commander Travis took it over. Notable codebreakers at Bletchley included Alan Turing, Gordon Welchman, Bill Tutte, Jerry Roberts, Hugh Alexander and John Tiltman. Turing had the idea of mechanising the codebreaking process to tackle the Nazi Enigma machine. This was at a time when all work was done by hand, a slow process. The Bombe machine was designed and built up in Letchworth, Hertfordshire, and would be sent to Bletchley Park as well as to five codebreaking outstations, which would have the lion's share of the machines. These would be operated by women from the WRNS, or Wrens. Not only did Bletchley have the headache of intercepting and decoding Enigma messages, and a large volume of them, but another system would require substantial resources, the advanced German Tunny machines such as the Lorenz teleprinter, which was far more complex than Enigma. Turing's Bombe machines would be impotent against the new non-Morse messages being intercepted. Specialist sections would be established to tackle the messages, and these were the Newmanry and the Testery, each of them headed up and managed by an experienced codebreaker.

Starting initially with around 150 people back in 1939, the base grew in numbers of skilled staff, and those in a support role too. A substantial proportion of the personnel at Bletchley Park were women. Some WRNS and ATS personnel were actual codebreakers at Bletchley Park, and accordingly they may have worked on the advanced Tunny or Fish intelligence, collected from Knockholt in Kent, Sandridge near St Albans, and elsewhere. A select number of Post Office research station engineers worked on Robinson or Colossus machines, and many others supported Bletchley Park on the technology side.[8]

PLACES

In 1935 GC&CS formed the FECB, or Far East Combine Bureau in Hong Kong, which was later to become essential to intercepting Japanese signals and intelligence. An intercept SIGINT base was later established at HMS *Anderson* in Ceylon for this purpose. They would share intelligence with an Allied network ranging from America to Australia, also with Hut 7 at Bletchley Park, which focussed on Japanese intercepts.

Around 10,000 personnel worked at Bletchley Park at the peak of activities, with three quarters of them women. This high proportion of women was probably because men were needed to both train and fight in the armed services, leaving a large gap in labour resources. The WRNS, ATS and other female military organisations would have both skilled and semi-skilled people to do everything from complex technical jobs to typing and administration. Wrens and ATS would work in the data Hollerith card indexing section either at Bletchley Park, or later at Drayton Parslow a few miles away.[9] Some of them would be used as cryptographers at Bletchley in the Huts and learn on the job. Not everyone at Bletchley would be a codebreaker, but those who worked there would make a contribution to helping end the war.

The German Triton Enigma *Kriegsmarine* communications would be known as 'Shark', and were of particular interest due to the effect of U-boat activity in the Atlantic on convoys. There would be lengthy periods of frustration intercepting Shark, with large gaps in breaking the Enigma codes and huge shipping losses. Morale at Bletchley in the naval codebreaking huts must have been at an all-time low at times. But progress was made, with the codebreakers determined to meet the challenge.

Bletchley Park was an important stage for the metamorphosis into GCHQ, and there is some evidence that this title or name was planned for the base back in 1940.[10] Elements of the US Army 6813th Signals Unit Detachment were based at Bletchley during the war, part of the ETOUSA agreement for joint co-operation between allied nations.[11]

Although considered as potentially risky, due to their visibility from the air, several aerials were established at Bletchley Park during the war, and a hut designated for listening for enemy intercepts. This would effectively become a Y-station to supplement the numerous main such stations. For some reason the management initially considered Wrens as signals operators but then opposed the idea and had male signals operators in the hut. This is rather strange as Wrens were used at some of the other Y-stations and were operating Bombe codebreaking machines across Buckinghamshire and Middlesex. Due to the size of the aerials the station was relocated to Whaddon Hall to ensure Bletchley was not seen as a potential target by the Luftwaffe.

Radio receiving aerials were also erected at Bletchley Park for the D-Day invasion, from May 1944, using personnel from Scarborough listening station. Around twenty-four staff were allocated to the listening operation at Bletchley, and speeded up the transmission of intercepts, although the other purpose-made listening Y-stations around the country were also utilised.[12]

Bletchley Park could not have made real progress without input from many different sites, organisations and personnel, both men and women. The outstations were a crucial part of the success, as were BTM, the factory in Letchworth, TRE in Malvern, and Dollis Hill, where the Post Office Research Establishment was based. Bletchley Park also helped to manage the allocation of codebreaking machines and resources across the outstations, including high-speed machines, which are also clearly mentioned in the Bombe records. High-speed Bombes went to Gayhurst, Wavendon, Stanmore and Hut 11.[13]

After the war, Bletchley Park was gradually closed down and the core purpose transferred to GCHQ at Eastcote in Middlesex, at least for a few years. Most of the machines were destroyed on Winston Churchill's instructions. A few survived at Eastcote and later at Cheltenham, but by the mid-1960s all had been destroyed or dismantled.

A Roll of Honour at Bletchley lists many of the individuals who contributed to intelligence, codebreaking and support and this can be viewed and searched online. Bletchley Park is now a substantial and important museum on codebreaking and intelligence and provides educational facilities to learn about the wartime period. From time to time, new information on codebreaking activities during the war is passed onto the media and BBC. Various documentaries have been produced about Bletchley Park, and it featured in two major films, *Enigma*, and *The Imitation Game*. The latter film is largely about Alan Turing's time at Bletchley Park and in the author's opinion does not give the viewing public a properly balanced view of the overall teamwork and organisation that was necessary to collect and process the enemy intelligence. For example, it does not give any indication that much of the data processing was done by the Wrens, or of the vast array of listening stations, or of the despatch riders and couriers needed. It does not mention the factory that designed and built the Bombe machine at all, and the impression gained by less informed people could be that everything was done at Bletchley Park, using one Bombe machine, and they were all built there, which would be misleading. However, it was entertainment, and had certain factual information on Turing and his life at Bletchley, including his brush with the law for being a homosexual, which was illegal at the time.

The Bletchley Park Museum has been enlarged recently to incorporate new and modern educational facilities aimed at people of all ages, but particularly young people, who may wish to learn more about codebreaking and the history of the area.

Bletchley Park is adjacent to the National Museum of Computing (TNMOC), which has a replica Bombe. It also has a working replica of the Colossus codebreaking machine, the first computer, which was built by Tony Sale with a team of enthusiastic volunteers. TNMOC is now a separate trust to the main Bletchley Park museum. The site is quite substantial, and beautifully landscaped around the large lake and mansion. It captures key moments in British and world history in the twentieth century, and is an educational experience.

Errors were made at Bletchley, such as refusing to fund the Colossus codebreaking machine designed and built by the Post Office Engineering team at Dollis Hill. Thankfully, the Post Office management and Flowers funded the work themselves. If they had not, then the outcome of the war might possibly have been different.

PLACES

Block C, Bletchley Park. A hut that contained Hollerith tabulating punched-card machinery and worked on the processing of punched cards. This was managed by the head of the Hollerith section via BTM, Frederick Freeborn. The punched cards processed, filtered and sorted data and intelligence as well as information relevant to the Bombe codebreaking machines for Bletchley Park. Prior to being contained within Block C, the equipment and punched-card activities were located in Hut 7 until November 1942. A further relocation was eventually arranged of the entire Hollerith punched card section to Drayton Parslow, a few miles from Bletchley Park. The reason for the relocation was that Bletchley Park needed the space occupied by both the machinery and vast volume of punched cards, which would be in the high hundred thousands, and even millions. The cards would be an aid to record-keeping, cryptanalysis and intelligence reporting, with data flowing back and forth between Block C or Drayton Parslow and Bletchley Park.

Block D, Bletchley Park. A brick-built building that eventually housed the personnel of Huts 3, 6 and 8. Hut 8 was established to deal with the Nazi naval Enigma traffic, such as U-boats and similar. It was cryptanalysts in Hut 6 that would convince management that codebreaking machines, Bombes, would save much time in the decoding process. These used an electro-mechanical system that would be 'programmed' by plugging in lengthy connecting wires at the rear of the machine and using rotating wheels to simulate Enigma wheeled rotors. The term Ultra was used to identify and categorise intelligence decrypts from Hut 6, and from Hut 8 initially. Welchman would devise the phrase 'Hut 6 Ultra' to differentiate it from other hut decrypted output.[14] Churchill would receive a summary of the important Ultra decrypted messages.

Broadway Buildings, London. Within the area of Westminster, this was a base for the Secret Intelligence Service and GC&CS some years after the end of the First World War. It was established in 1926 and the proper address was No. 54 Broadway. It was situated close to St James' Park underground station. While GC&CS relocated to Bletchley Park just prior to the Second World War, SIS remained at 54 Broadway. These buildings have been used by London Underground and TFL plus their associated administration after the site was vacated by SIS in 1964.

BTM. The British Tabulating Machine Company was based in Letchworth, Hertfordshire, and designed and manufactured codebreaking machines for Bletchley Park and the five codebreaking outstations. It also licensed the use of Hollerith tabulator machines for data processing, and these would also be used at Bletchley Park and nearby Drayton Parslow. The factory would be in different parts across Letchworth but with one main, imposing, long factory building for final assembly of the various components and modules of the machines. The project was designated Cantab, and was top secret during the war. The reference code for the Cantab contract for BTM in Letchworth to make the Bombe machines was 6/6502. Relevant documents would then refer to this code. BTM would also take over the

Spirella building in the town as the war progressed to secure supplementary space for assembly of Bombe components. A listing of some of the workers, mostly women, who worked in the Spirella factory during the war under BTM's direction, making and assembling Bombe components is appropriate, and the reader is referred to the 'People' section of the glossary under 'Spirella factory workers under BTM'. A substantial workforce of both men and women would assemble and manufacture the Bombe machines, which were largely the concept of Alan Turing and colleague Gordon Welchman. Turing, Welchman and others from Bletchley Park would visit the factory periodically to check and monitor progress and to suggest and test certain modifications. The first Bombe was delivered to Bletchley Park in early 1941. It was named 'Victory'. Most would go elsewhere as they were manufactured.

A 'super-Bombe' machine was built at the factory but found to be too large to transport and was used on site for a time before it was dismantled into individual Bombe machines, which were then allocated to outstations and Bletchley Park.[15] Harold Keen was the chief engineer at BTM and would be instrumental in making modifications and improvements of the codebreaking machines as the war progressed. Two hundred and eleven Bombe machines were built at BTM in total. Almost a third of the main factory building was taken up at the peak for the manufacture of codebreaking machines. Initially the output of the first machines would take just six weeks to construct, then two or three per month during 1941 and 1942. By mid-1942, thirty machines had been delivered to Bletchley and the country house outstations. By 1945 there would be over 9,000 staff working at BTM across various sites. The Ascot Government training factory in Letchworth, a 20,000 sq ft storage space acquired by BTM from the Government, was used to further expand production.[16] The US Navy would commission their own version of Bombes and build them in America using WAVES, female volunteers. BTM had a track record of using calculating machines before the war. Post-war it would jointly build computers with GEC and others, such as the model 1301.[17] There is a close link to the IBM company in the USA with the development of BTM and its metamorphosis post-war. See *Spirella*. See *Letchworth*.

Cabinet War Rooms, Westminster, London. (Redesignated as the Churchill War Rooms). Constructed in 1938 as a command centre for the British Government with military support from the Chiefs of Staff. Churchill would meet regularly at the Cabinet War Rooms to discuss progress, strategy and options with his military advisers and certain ministers involved in wartime matters. The centre became fully operational at the end of August 1939, just prior to the Second World War. It would have extensive communication cabling, ventilation, extensive power supplies and associated controls. Churchill would have his own bedroom there for late nights attending meetings. The rooms were underground and had multiple telephone lines and an operations room with maps, including a formal map room, which would have had restricted access. The Chiefs of Staff would meet Churchill and provide reports, often requiring strategic decisions. Thick, reinforced concrete slabs provided a degree of protection from bombing, but it was not bomb-proof from larger ordnance.

One advantage of the Cabinet War Rooms was that it was relatively close to Parliament, so easy for Churchill to access. Advanced communication links connected Churchill with US President Roosevelt across the Atlantic using the SIGSALY voice-encoding system. Known as 'the Green Hornet', it was a game-changer for international security during wartime. Prior to the installation of this American system, the enemy had intercepted several of the transatlantic messages from listening stations in Holland. DRP, a non-military organisation in Germany, a telephone intercept bureau, also penetrated the earlier insecure messages. With SIGSALY installed, the security breaches ceased. Churchill was advised not to use the less-secure scrambler telephones. Churchill would use the War Rooms for meetings to monitor the Army withdrawal from Dunkirk in the early years of the war. It would be touch and go as to the numbers of British forces that could be saved from constant German air attacks and the advancement of the Panzers. The decision to assemble multiple civilian ships and craft to cross the English Channel to help rescue soldiers on the Dunkirk beaches would help save many. There would be many discussions, differences of opinion, and difficult decisions made by Churchill and his advisers at this location.

A back-up plan to use the Paddock in Dollis Hill, Willesden, near the Post Office Research Establishment, in case the War Rooms were bombed, was established, but Churchill did not enjoy using the damp, underground rooms there, preferring the rooms at Westminster and the associated facilities.

More than one hundred meetings would be held by Churchill here, the command centre being in operation twenty-four hours a day. It would cover times both good and bad, from the Blitz to the penetration of German defences at Normandy at D-Day, and beyond. The rooms were used until 16 August 1945. The War Rooms are now an important and popular museum, run by the Imperial War Museum. A special exhibition outlines the life of Churchill, and this contains many artefacts and documents relevant to the great British leader. The site is now formally known as the Churchill War Rooms, the name having been changed in 2010.

Cambridge, England. The university city that was the source of many mathematicians, classicists, linguists and others recruited by the Government to work on codebreaking and support services at Bletchley Park and elsewhere during the war. Alan Turing was but one of the many Cambridge graduates selected to work at Bletchley. Several returned after the war to teach or contribute to the university but would not be permitted to speak of their codebreaking activities in order to protect the state. The Archive at King's College contains many examples of Turing's notes, papers and documents.

Canada. One of many of Britain's allies in the Second World War. It was considered as a safe refuge for the King in exile should the Nazis have overrun and occupied Britain. In 1942 the Canadian Intelligence Corps was established. Many of the personnel were seconded to both British and American forces on a variety of duties and activities. Canadian linguists assisted the United States Intelligence agencies in translating and decoding enemy German, Italian and Japanese intercepts in Washington. Exchange of intelligence personnel, training and refresher training would be common between Canadians and British intelligence officers. By 1943, the Canadian Intelligence staff would be much more proficient than previously was the case, and there was less need for British support on training courses. Postwar, the organisation was reorganised as the Canadian Forces Security Branch, and Signals Intelligence.

The Canadian Examination Unit (XU), in Ottawa, was an intelligence and cryptographic organisation. A French section was providing codebreaking and translators against the Japanese enemy. A Military Discrimination Unit then later combined to form the Joint Discrimination Unit (JDU) in 1946. Two months later there would be a further organisational change, forming the Communications Branch National Research Council, or CBNRC.

It is of interest that GCHQ in England has awarded commemorative badges to those who worked in Britain and around the world on signals intelligence, codebreaking and support to codebreaking. A total of 127 commemorative GCHQ badges have been issued to Canadians for their services in wartime out of 3,379 in total, almost 4 per cent.[18] One such veteran is Sonja Morawetz Sinclair, who originally came from Czechoslovakia. She escaped from the Nazis and went to Canada during the war to work as a codebreaker and a translator in the Examination Unit. In 2017, aged 96, Sonja was awarded recognition of the Bletchley Park commemorative medal in Ottawa.

Y-stations and direction finding would be established at St Hubert in Quebec; Hartlen Point, Nova Scotia; and Esquimalt at Vancouver Island, British Columbia. Canadian Forces Base Esquimalt (CFB Esquimalt) is now a major military coastal naval base. It is the home port of Maritime Forces Pacific, and Joint Task Force Pacific Headquarters. It is on the southern tip of Vancouver Island and covers thousands of acres.[19] Some disagreements occurred between GC&CS and Canadian codebreakers during the war, such as when Bletchley Park's Alastair Denniston asked Canada to concentrate on dealing with Japanese intercepts. However, the head of the Canadian Examination Unit stated that their work was for Canada and not for Britain. Some meeting of minds was later achieved to help avoid duplication of effort in the complex organisation of coordinating with many different nations and allied countries across the world.

Ceylon. Now known as Sri Lanka, Ceylon was a base for Wrens and other military personnel from England to work on intelligence gathering and codebreaking on Japanese-occupied countries. After VE day there would be a winding down of personnel in the United Kingdom but there was an urgent need to provide support for intelligence services for the east. For many of the Wrens it would be their first trip overseas, and a change was needed to acclimatise to the humidity, heat and insects. Colombo would be one of the bases to set up Typex machine sections

PLACES

for decoding enemy messages. The Japanese would use a version of Enigma designated 'Purple'. Wrens would come under the command of COISEF, or the Chief of Intelligence Staff Eastern Fleet. One of the bases in Colombo was HMS *Anderson*, a shore-based naval station. It would link up with Washington, Pearl Harbor in Hawaii, and Melbourne in Australia. Islands in the Pacific would form part of the expanded communications link, as the war progressed in the Allies' favour. There would be specialist equipment to operate, including American combined cipher machines. A team of Wrens had relocated to Colombo from Mombasa in Kenya. The Colombo set-up was far more sophisticated and had more equipment and personnel. Interception of intelligence from Burma became a high priority for the listening station. Some reports indicated that the personnel at HMS *Anderson* peaked at around 2,000, but this needs confirmation. Either way, this was a considerable number of military personnel, including many Wrens, from what was a small undertaking initially.

Channel Islands. The islands which were, and still are British territories, and the only British territory in Europe that was formally occupied by the Nazis during the Second World War. The proximity of the islands to France made this occupation possible. Jersey, Guernsey, Alderney, Sark and Brechou, made up these islands in the English Channel, the largest being Jersey with St Helier as its capital. Illegal radios would be made and constructed by British islanders during occupation to listen to the BBC and find out progress on the war, with heavy penalties if caught using them. Both St Helier and St Peter Port, Guernsey's capital, were bombed by Luftwaffe Heinkels just prior to occupation, as an incentive for the islands to concede to the Nazis. Forty-four civilians would die as a result of that bombing. The islands were occupied from 30 June 1940 to 6 May 1945. They would be heavily fortified with reinforced concrete lookout towers and bunkers, many built with forced labour from Russia and elsewhere, under terrible conditions. Many still remain today, although in a state of deterioration. Some are open today as museums, and a substantial underground hospital was built in a hillside. Listening posts would be established on the islands by the Nazis, and part of their work would be to use direction-finding equipment to target those in the population who might be British enemy agents or those working for the Islands' or French resistance, transmitting troop movements back to England. Enigma machines would most likely be used on the islands by the Nazis for communication between military sections and colleagues in France and Belgium, particularly between islands and between the Channel Islands and the French mainland. The quantity of Enigmas that were used is unknown.

A railway was built on Jersey using forced labour, opening in July 1942 using locomotives and wagons sent over from France, but it was demolished after the war. Organisation Todt would carry out all the construction during wartime, with enforced labour working under poor conditions. There are records indicating that Jersey hairdressers refused to cut the hair of those in Organisation Todt, although that may have been unfair as they had little choice but to work for the Nazis.

The Nazis wanted Jersey and Guernsey to pay for the electricity and power that they were consuming as part of the military occupation, and there was formal objection to this, but the Germans ruled the islands.

Hitler wished for the Channel Islands to be turned into an impregnable fortress. When D-Day came in June 1944, it bypassed the Channel Islands, and the islanders were not freed from oppression by the Nazis until May 1945, around a year later. The German troops occupying the islands were probably relieved that the D-Day assault avoided the islands, giving them some breathing space. However, they were on high alert, as they would not know if forces falsely reported to be in Kent would split off to attack the islands when the main force came across the Pas-de-Calais.

Documents and references were encoded for Organisation Todt, with Jersey named 'Jakob', Guernsey 'Gustav' and Alderney 'Adolf'. Such references would be meaningless to the local population. Bunkers with signals engineers were established across the islands to support artillery commanders. Nazi rangefinders were installed on the coast by the Germans, some being of humungous proportions, to track and range enemy shipping within their sights. Some were later replaced with underground concrete lookout posts, many blending in with the rough cliffside landscape. At the end of the war, the rangefinders were dismantled and thrown down the cliffs to destroy them. The perimeter coastline was graded for its topography, geography and potential use by the enemy. As an example, areas at the end of St Aubin's Bay on Jersey, known as Noirmont Batterie, included searchlight stations, generators for electrical power, gun emplacements, personnel bunkers, naval direction-finding equipment, range-finder battery commander post, ammunition bunkers, Flak anti-aircraft gun emplacements, and so on. This information would be of interest to British Intelligence, but as there was no plan to occupy the islands until the end of the war, it had lower priority than other areas. The positioning, type and range of German guns on the islands' coast would have been of interest, however, to keep clear margins for shipping around D-day and supporting supplies. Anti-tank constructions, ditches, and similar obstructions were positioned along parts of the coast to buy time for the Germans if invaded by the Allies. D/F or direction-finding structures and equipment were built around the islands such as near St Brelade in Jersey in 1941. It was built to resemble a house, to fool the local population and aircraft, and was coded M10. Part of the structure still remains today, but without its roof.

Oberst Friedrich Knackfuss was the *Feldkommandant* of Jersey for the bulk of the war, from 4 October 1941 to 29 February 1944. He then moved to operate in France, but was later captured by the Allies and died a prisoner-of-war in Yugoslavia in late 1945.

Some of the remaining concrete bunkers and lookout posts can be visited today, and give a good idea of how life for the German soldiers would be as regards sleeping accommodation, food, discipline, rules and regulations, armaments and supplies. The military museum at St Ouen in Jersey is one example of the Atlantic wall lookout bunkers.[20] The occupying troops would have been scanning the horizon with field glasses from their fortified positions, some of which remain today on the islands.

PLACES

Château des Fouzes, Uzès, Provence, France. Used by three Polish mathematicians and cryptographers, and supported by the French Resistance during the war. The three Poles at the château were Marian Rejewski, Henryk Zygalski, and Jerzy Rozycki. They had escaped from France when it was being occupied in 1939 by the Nazis, and gone to Algeria, only to return in 1940 to collect and analyse enemy intelligence from North Africa to assist the Allies. They would work here until 1942, in Vichy France, and had to move when the Nazis occupied the region in late 1942. The risk of working on Enigma intelligence under Nazi occupation would have been too great. If found out, they could have compromised the operation at Bletchley Park. A plaque outside the château commemorates the site for the valued contribution of the men carrying out codebreaking during the war and the men and women of the French Resistance. The code name for the base was Cadix. See *Poland.* See *Rejewski, Zygalski, Rozycki.*

Cheltenham, Gloucestershire. The base for GCHQ, or the Government Communications Headquarters, and the main coordinating intelligence agency for the United Kingdom. While the origins of GCHQ were in GC&CS in London as far back as 1919, it developed over time via Watergate House and Bletchley Park, to be established as GCHQ Eastcote in April 1946, prior to moving to Cheltenham in the 1950s. The transfer to Cheltenham from Eastcote took place between 1952 and 1954. A bank account had been opened for GCHQ at Eastcote on 1 April 1946.

There is evidence that Bletchley Park was sometimes referred to as GCHQ during the war, but perhaps initially in an unofficial capacity.[21] Offices in Northwood Hills, Middlesex, provided some support for GCHQ Cheltenham up until the 1980s before being closed down. Cheltenham, the base for the modern GCHQ, now has a large doughnut-shaped building to house its thousands of staff, and to help protect the UK from terrorism, to prevent major hacking of computer networks, to monitor enemies and potential enemies, and to share crucial intelligence with specific allied countries' intelligence agencies. It also provides advice and assistance on languages and technical terminology, advice on cryptography and the protection of information. GCHQ was the first intelligence agency in the world to open a Twitter account to share certain limited information with the public, and to encourage co-operation. It also has an Instagram account. The UK-USA post-war formal agreement, which was expanded to other specific countries, is relevant here. See *World powers of co-operation (UK–USA Agreement).*

Chesterfield Street, London. A civilian outstation for GCHQ in an office block in the central of the capital. Others included listening posts in Northern Ireland such as Gilnahirk, overseas listening stations concealed within British embassies, and Knockholt listening station. Operated between 1944 to 1953 supporting GCHQ in Cold War operations.

Chicksands. The site known as Chicksands Priory was purchased by the Crown Commissioners in 1936. A key Y-station during the war, it was taken over by the

RAF from the Royal Navy and operated as a SIGINT listening station. It opened in 1941 with male staff and operators. Thereafter, WAAF personnel supported the station. Around 1943 there would be four key intercept sites, Chicksands, Beaumanor, Chatham in Kent and Shaftesbury, Dorset. The station commander, Wing Commander Shepherd, would liaise with Bletchley Park on intercepts and intelligence from Chicksands. Weak signals would be picked up from as far away as Russia and Africa. After the war, in 1950, the US Air Force occupied part of the site and worked on Cold War intercepts of intelligence. In 1987, it would be the only RAF station in England leased to the United States Air Force, but for technical reasons still required an RAF squadron leader. In 1996, the British Intelligence Corps took over the site. See *Y-stations*.

China. Opponents of the Japanese in the last war, the country assisted America with decrypted Japanese radio transmissions via the Communist Party of China, or the CPC. It also assisted the Americans with the establishment of meteorological weather stations and listening stations in Yan'an and other areas in China from 1944. This gave the Americans a series of forward listening bases in the east, not too far away from Japan. This made a significant difference to American pilots, who would as a consequence have much improved intelligence during bombing raids against Japan. Observers from the US Army learned a great deal of Japanese intentions near the border with China.

Earlier in the war, a Chinese official learned by accident that in May 1941 Germany was about to attack Russia under Operation Barbarossa. This information was quickly communicated to the Russians, but the Chinese were not believed at the time. The information proved to be accurate, however, and later Stalin sent a telegram of thanks to the Chinese Communist Party. Some reports from the CPC indicated that the Japanese attack on Pearl Harbor in Hawaii had been identified and decrypted by the Chinese codebreaker Chi Buzhou, and passed on as a warning immediately to President Roosevelt in the United States. However, it appears that this has not been confirmed by Western sources. Those who agree that the intelligence was passed across to the Americans before the attack state that the actual date of the raid was not provided, only the intention for Japan to attack, and that it was not taken seriously by the Americans.

Admiral Yamamoto of Japan was on an inspection tour of the South Pacific when his plane was attacked and shot down by American aircraft. China claimed that it was due to an intercepted Japanese encoded radio message, again decrypted by Chi Buzhou and passed on to American intelligence forces, that gave details of the route of his inspection, and led to Yamamoto's death.

Chopmist Hill, Scituate, Rhode Island, USA. One of thirteen listening stations commissioned and built in the US during the Second World War. The Federal Communications Commission (FCC) surveyed sites across America for the most useful locations. One was Chopmist Hill in Scituate, where a farm of 138 acres existed. This site proved to be the most sensitive and efficient listening station during wartime, and even intercepted certain German High Command communications from North Africa. Two principal large antennae had 16 miles of cabling wire erected, and it would be used for identifying frequencies and direction finding of signal output from the east, across the North Atlantic. It would make use of compass bearings of intercepted signals, and work with other stations nearby. Adjustment of antennae masts would be needed from time to time to ensure sensitivity was maintained.[22] Nazi weather forecasts were received in Scituate and forwarded to the European Command HQ. In 1942 a listener at Chopmist Hill detected conversations in German and recorded them on to disc. These were passed across to naval command. It became clear that these were orders from German High Command in North Africa sending instructions to their tank commanders. Such intelligence would be extremely valuable and was communicated to Allied forces in that region.

When Rommel intended to encircle the British 8th Army at El Alamein, intelligence received at Chopmist Hill would thwart his plans, and Montgomery would be waiting for him with his troops forewarned in good time. The British ship *Queen Mary* was saved from going to the bottom of the Atlantic by the listening base picking up and intercepting messages from German spies advising U-boats of the planned route of the great vessel. It would be carrying 14,000 troops across the Atlantic, potentially at risk from the enemy. Thankfully, *Queen Mary* was spared U-boat torpedoes by using a secret alternative sea route, helped by the station's careful listening on the airwaves and its organisation and communication. Ironically, *Queen Mary* is now a tourist attraction in Long Beach, California.

At times, Japanese balloons would be loaded with high explosive and sent off at high altitude towards America but these were intercepted early on by the base. It would also play its part in intercepting U-boats along with surface vessels and aircraft, coordinating the information towards an effective outcome. The group of thirteen listening stations was so effective during the war that no German spy network could go undetected when transmitting across the USA. Any attempts by German agents were quickly closed down and arrests made. Reports that Chopmist Hill sensitivity and success in receiving distant radio signals was due to the specific geology of the area has been dismissed by a geological expert as being highly unlikely.

Churchill Rooms, Westminster, London. The current name for the Cabinet War Rooms where Churchill managed his wartime affairs and met senior politicians and armed services commanders in the war. Now open to the general public as a museum. An alternative meeting base was in Dollis Hill, north London, but was used infrequently. See *Cabinet War Rooms*. See *Selfridges*.

Dayton, Ohio. The base for the National Cash Register Company, which built the American version of the Bombe codebreaking machine during the war. It was built within the United States Naval Computing Machine Laboratory, within Building 26. These would be four-wheeled Bombe machines to attack German naval codes and ciphers. The Bombes were ready in 1943 and then went into major production, with well in excess of a hundred machines assembled.

Alan Turing visited the USA on 21 December 1943, and was initially concerned that the Americans did not accept a British Bombe he offered them from Bletchley Park. He quickly established they were to build their own version. Turing was able to obtain some detailed information on the American-designed Bombe, and noted there were some marked differences in approach, particularly with regard to the wheel rotor configuration. His visit was based on a meeting at NCR with Commander Wenger, Lieutenant Commander Engstrom, Lieutenant Commander Meader, Lieutenant Eachus and Major Stevens. Wenger was generally in charge and drove the project forward. Turing later made a detailed report of his visit for Bletchley Park.

Construction of the American Bombes was largely carried out by Women Accepted for Volunteer Emergency Service (WAVES). Effectively, they were the equivalent of the BTM British engineers and assemblers at Letchworth. They needed to be trained for the operation, and to follow the blueprints and diagrams. Some civilians and navy engineers also worked on the production. The Americans claimed their version of the Bombe was more efficient and faster than the British equivalent. They were shipped to Washington and used to analyse naval enemy intelligence and to identify the Enigma settings of four-wheeled machines. Machine code references were the N-530 and later improved N-1530 four-wheel Bombes. According to an NSA report in 2015, History of the Cryptanalytic Bombe, approximately 55 per cent of the machines were used to attack Nazi Naval Enigma keys, the remainder on non-naval keys. Joseph Desch was in charge of the design and production at NCR, and he was an inventor with many patents granted over his career. He was awarded a Medal of Merit by President Truman for his services to America during wartime. Building 26 at NCR in Dayton was the United States Naval Computing Machine Laboratory (NCML). See *Desch*.

Denmark Hill. The site of a police station in south London with a listening station above. It detected high-speed non-morse messages one day and informed Bletchley Park these were unusual transmissions. Bletchley confirmed it was not traditional Morse code and after investigation established it was a different encoding machine being used by the enemy, of advanced type. It was a teleprinter attachment at high speed. As a result, a special listening station was established at Knockholt in Kent, at a place called Ivy Farm. The site was acquired from the farmer and engineers then installed and fitted with several large radio masts and aerials to collect the messages transmitted over the airwaves. The personnel grew to large numbers and specialised in listening and recording the data on reels of punched tape, sent to Bletchley Park. Advanced codebreaking machines had to be designed and constructed to crack the message settings and read the messages. However, even with new machines, much work had to be done with manual codebreaking input at Bletchley, in a new section called the Testery. A young mathematician, Bill Tutte, at Bletchley had analysed the data and worked out the number of rotor wheels and configuration of the Nazi teleprinter attachment. Considering that no one in Britain had seen or come across a Lorenz teleprinter attachment machine before, this was a considerable achievement. Knockholt listening station was also used for recording facsimile messages from Europe, received over the radio waves. See *Ivy Farm* and *Knockholt*.

Derby House, Liverpool. Home of the Western Approaches Tactical Unit (WATU). This was a training establishment and war gaming centre to evolve methods to defeat the success of German U-boats attacking Allied convoys. Initially, senior commanders were sceptical of the war games using convoys and U-boats marked on the floor, but the progress made eventually identified weaknesses in the attacking system. The result was that when these new methods were employed in the Atlantic, U-boats were more easily detected and targeted, considerably reducing losses of shipping.

The system involved using a ship with ASDIC, or sonar, capability within the convoy area and support frigates driving the U-boats to a smaller geographical pocket. The U-boats were then depth-charged, or forced to the surface and attacked. Interception of Enigma messages would be used where appropriate, bearing in mind that for several months in 1942 and 1943, Bletchley Park was not able to crack the *Kriegsmarine* codes, which tended to use a more advanced version of Enigma and additional rotor wheels. It was in that period that U-boat successes were most prolific and caused great consternation for the Allies. Bletchley Park benefited from the capture of enemy Enigma code books in March 1943, which helped staff to penetrate the Enigma settings once again and listen in to U-boat messages. WATU was heavily staffed with Wrens, and they were trained up in the operation of the tactical system. The system devised against U-boats at WATU was termed 'Raspberry', and assumed to be based upon 'blowing a raspberry' to Hitler.

Dollis Hill. A suburb of north-west London that housed the Post Office Research Station (which worked on codebreaking equipment during wartime). It also had alternative Cabinet War Rooms known as the Paddock, used occasionally by Churchill, but not favoured by him. He preferred the main facility in Westminster. The Paddock was also known as CWR2, or cabinet war rooms 2, and were constructed from 1939 and completed by June 1940, at a cost of approximately £250,000. No sleeping accommodation was available there, so Churchill requested being allocated flats in the nearby Neville Court. The roof of the Paddock was relatively bombproof with a five feet thick concrete roof in two layers. There had been plans to relocate the Government to an out-of-town alternative site as far back as 1937. The name 'Paddock; is probably from Willesden Paddocks or stables. The entrance to the Paddock was not obvious at ground level. Use was limited, and after the war used by the Post Office, who were on the adjacent site. The Post Office Research Engineering Station (PORES) was opened formally on 23 October 1933 by Prime Minister Ramsay MacDonald. Engineering staff were not permitted to access the Paddock at any time. The Post Office Research Station is famous for the work done by Tommy Flowers and his team of engineers on designing and building the Colossus semi-programmable valve-based computer, to help decrypt the enemy non-Morse high-speed messages. These were messages intended for Hitler and his generals. PORES acquired a factory to ensure recording machines and recorders would be supplied to government agencies for clandestine methods of recovering intelligence.

The research station had a large brick building for research, together with supporting workshops. It was here that the world's first semi-programmable computer machine, Colossus, was designed and built by Flowers, Head of Systems, and his team. They also constructed equipment for part of the Robinson codebreaking machine. By April 1944 there would be sixty-eight staff in Flower's laboratory working on constructing Colossus and Tunny machines for Bletchley Park. The use of valve technology as digital switches was quite unusual and used for the advanced codebreaking machines in large quantities, often to the concern of Bletchley Park as to their reliability. However, Colossus worked as it was designed to do, and a high-speed version, the Mk 2, contained 2,400 glowing valves and was built here. Shortly after VE day in 1945, Alan Turing spent the summer at the Post Office Research Establishment. He would discuss with Flowers his concepts and design for the voice-encoding system he had been working on, along with others at Hanslope Park. It might have been considered for commercial use if funding could be obtained, but it was seen as low priority by the authorities as the war in Europe had ended.

Prior to the start of the war the centre at Dollis Hill was used for radio and telecommunications research. As the war went on it was increasingly used for supporting MI5, MI6 and MI9 (i.e. signals intelligence). For example, installing and testing bugging devices. These would be used to listen in to conversations between prisoners of war, defectors and suspect persons, by installing listening devices into telephones, ceiling roses and other fittings. This work was done in conjunction with the Radio Corporation of America (RCA), which supplied much of the equipment. PORES worked closely in support of CSDIC in this specialist clandestine field of operations.

Post-war, it was the base for conversion to automated digital telephone exchanges. This was also the site that produced the National Savings premium Bond computer ERNIE, which was designed by Flowers. The Post Office Speaking Clock was also designed here by a man called Speight, and he worked closely with a young engineer, Gill Hayward, who would later work alongside Flowers on building Tunny machines for Bletchley Park. The buildings were in an elevated location, not far from Willesden.

The main building used by the Post Office during the war is now residential flats. Dollis Hill, Eastcote and Stanmore are three (overground) tube stations that have codebreaking links to their geographical areas during the war. TFL were unaware of this until the author pointed it out.

Dollis Hill was also where a British team of engineers designed a vertical tunnelling shield and chamber for a secret tunnel built in Berlin in 1955. This was a long-term project organised by the Americans, but with British assistance for some critical sections. The tunnel was constructed for the British engineers to secretly tap into East German and Russian telephone lines, from a lengthy underground tunnel organised and built by the Americans. The final stage after the horizontal tunnel had been built was for the British engineers from Dollis Hill to go in and create the final vertical excavation and tunnel shield, and make connections to the fragile Russian telephone lines under the road. This was a potentially risky venture for those engineers, who would have been either imprisoned or shot if they had been caught by the enemy. The telephone cable insulation found was of very poor condition, flaking away from the wires, and could have easily triggered a warning to the Russians if handled incorrectly. This project was Operation Gold, or as the CIA called it, PBJOINTLY. When discovered by the East Germans, the tunnel and equipment became an acute embarrassment for the USA. The site was established as an underground museum and became a popular East Berlin tourist attraction. The British came out rather well in the escapade, and much useful intelligence was obtained from the Russians over several months, from May 1955 to April 1956. But the embarrassment of the exposed tunnel was pointed directly at the Americans, who had gone to great lengths in acquiring a special building in Berlin, excavating it and digging the tunnel across enemy boundary lines close to telephone lines, then installing amplifiers, underground tape recorders and associated specialist equipment. The project was only approved due to British success in tunnelling and tapping cables elsewhere in Germany, but on a much smaller scale. Taking wartime and post-war activities into account, the Post Office site at Dollis Hill had a significant impact on enemy intelligence gathering and decoding it, with assistance from others, whether that was Bletchley Park, the NSA, or other intelligence organisations.

The author hopes that TFL reconsider its policy on informing and educating the public as to the history of the areas relevant to their network of stations, as it might otherwise be considered a lost opportunity. See also *Post Office Research Engineering Station.* See *Flowers.* See *Hayward.*

Dorset. This county housed the original Telecommunications Research Establishment (TRE), which later moved to Malvern College in Worcestershire to be less exposed and more secure in the English countryside, away from potential Luftwaffe raids. TRE was a radar research establishment and had access to a German *Wurzburg* radar that had been captured in a commando raid at Bruneval in France. This was a gun-laying advanced radar used by the German Army and Luftwaffe. The original base at Worth Matravers was near Corfe Castle, a few miles from Swanage. A small airfield at Christchurch was used to test the prototypes and test equipment that would assist RAF planes with radar development, bombing accuracy and aircraft tracking, among other innovations. Many technical and professional engineers and scientists would be involved, including Bernard Lovell, who later became significant in technical developments within astronomy and radio telescopes. OBO, H2S and GEE were but three innovations developed by TRE in Dorset, and were most likely further improved in their new base in Malvern, along with other innovative systems.

In early 1942, the equipment, personnel and everything that comprised the site was relocated to Malvern. Around 800 staff would relocate to Malvern College, a boys' public school. The boys would be relocated to Harrow School for the remainder of the war, which was a considerable upheaval. The TRE new site at Malvern would expand further over time, both in the area occupied and the staffing, as well as infrastructure. TRE would provide expertise to the Post Office Research Establishment, BTM and Bletchley Park, and to others in helping to develop parts of codebreaking machines, and particularly relating to the Robinson and other advanced machines. The complement of staff at TRE would be specialists in their own field, and produce numerous innovative systems and equipment for the wartime effort. Locals who would see many men wandering around the locality dressed in civilian clothes would ponder why they were not in uniform, but the activities on the base were kept top secret.

Drayton Parslow. The village that housed the Hollerith punched-card section, which was set up originally at Bletchley Park but relocated later some miles away. This was with equipment supplied by BTM in Letchworth, who sold and hired out Hollerith tabulating machines. Frederick V. Freeborn was made head of Hollerith tabulation machinery operations supporting Bletchley Park. It was staffed with both men and numerous female personnel, including Wrens, ATS and civilians.

Cards were punched out on a machine. A room with twenty to thirty machines were contained in the Punch Room. The main room had the much larger, noisy Hollerith machines, which were sorters and tabulators. These could read the punched cards and filter them according to the operator's requirements. Some machines were for collating the cards. It operated day and night, with long shifts. There was little respite even on Christmas Day, when the staff could go only home for Christmas dinner in the late afternoon. Many thousands of messages were processed here, and links made between different categories of message to identify a useful bit of information. Freeborn had some interference from Bletchley Park management as to how he should run the place, but resisted.

Storage of the punched cards was a big problem at Bletchley when the division had the Hollerith machines there, but there was more space at Drayton Parslow. The complement of staff grew to around five hundred, and data was fed back and forth to and from Bletchley, to aid the codebreaking analysis of information.[23] Female clerks would cross-reference information that was intercepted and went through Bletchley Park. These included items such as the names of girlfriends of German generals and officers, code words, details of radio transmitting stations, fuel reserves, artillery ranging figures and similar data, etc. A great deal of trivia was collected and indexed as it could be added to other information that may expose a useful link, perhaps giving an indication of a troop movement, fuel resources issue, or planned operation by the enemy.

Information would be punched by the women on to special cards, which could then be 'read' or sorted by the Hollerith machines. Storage and processing included stages such as the Collator and a Reproducer, terms that would have to be learned and understood as to their specific functions. Linguists would be involved in the analysis of the data, looking for certain clues. One needs to appreciate that the volume of data and of punched cards was huge, and had to be organised like a military operation to be of any use. Bletchley Park would be requesting information from Drayton Parslow, and a response would need to be prompt. The whole team would be under extreme pressure.

Marjorie Halcrow, a university graduate from Scotland, was recruited for the section by Freeborn. She recalled the extreme noise the machines made in operation. BTM in Letchworth also built many of the codebreaking machines for Bletchley Park and made important modifications. Prior to relocating to Drayton Parslow, Bletchley had its Hollerith section and punched card processing in Hut 7. It was part of the central index. With a card consumption of two million per week, the Hollerith section was the largest punched-card installation in Britain. Consider it as an early semi-manual wartime version of Google perhaps, and with manually programmed sorting of the index cards. The large number of female personnel operating, sorting and tabulating the data was necessary for it to be used in a constructive way, and provide useful connections between seemingly unrelated items of intelligence.

Eastcote, Middlesex. During the last war, Eastcote was to house both the last and the largest codebreaking outstation to support Bletchley Park, which was the codebreaking headquarters. Named Outstation Eastcote, abbreviated as OSE, it was one of five satellite outstations run by the WRNS. The buildings and site no longer exist, being sold in 2007 and built upon for a housing development, but retains the name Pembroke Park, as the codebreaking base was part of *Pembroke V*, Special Duties X operations. It also retains the ancient public footpath that divided the site into two parts, the north part housing Bombe codebreaking machines, the south being for accommodation as barracks and administration.

The base was run as an onshore naval base with naval protocols and procedures. Before it became a codebreaking outstation it was planned to be a military hospital for injured servicemen and women as it was assumed there would be a second front in years to come after D-Day. This didn't occur, however. Many American servicemen attended the outstation during wartime and an even greater number post-war. The Americans supported the Wrens in codebreaking on several Bombe machines at Eastcote, with much success. With post-war activities and the need to reorganise and rebuild large parts of Europe, American military personnel worked on the base on administration. They also provided security for various embassies, including the American Embassy in Grosvenor Square, London. Personnel who worked at GCHQ after the war ended would have lived in the surrounding areas such as Ruislip, Pinner, Eastcote, Northwood and similar. There is a history society, Ruislip Northwood Eastcote Local History Society (RNELHS), which has some archived papers on the site and area prepared by local historian Susan Toms. The name 'Eastcote' means 'Eastern Cottages', according to the author's research of historic local names. Eastcote was not mentioned in the Domesday book, but nearby Ruislip was. A map of 1672 shows Eastcote as 'Ascote'.

The site was transformed into GCHQ in April 1946 after the war, until it moved over the period 1952–54 due to limitations in the size of the available site. Over time it became part of RAF West Ruislip (hence the designation RAF Eastcote) and was used extensively by US Marines Corps Security Force, as well as the Naval Criminal Investigation Service (NCIS). Eastcote, like many parts of England, was bombed during the war, but only one incendiary bomb hit the outstation and it caused relatively minor damage, affecting a hut and damaging some plumbing and water supplies. The fire was put out relatively quickly as the main incendiary bomb did not fully ignite due to a malfunction. A bombing map of the area has been studied by the author, showing it before the base was operational. Ruislip, adjacent to Eastcote, was also heavily bombed. Post-war the site, which was occupied by many Americans, also had on site the British Price Commission, under the Department of Trade, Industry, Prices and Consumer Protection.[24] The Property Services Agency also was based there, as were research facilities for the Post office. See *OSE Outstation Eastcote*.

Eastcote, GCHQ. Records show that GCHQ was established formally on 1 April 1946 and a bank account set up for the organisation by Barclays Bank in Eastcote. The locals, i.e. the general public, at Eastcote would have heard the new name mentioned, but had no idea of the purpose of that organisation. In 1952 Eric Jones became director of GCHQ, and therefore took over from Commander Travis. GCHQ relocated to Cheltenham in the early 1950s. A remote rented office in Northwood Hills would provide some support for GCHQ Eastcote not far away, until 1978, when it was closed down and redeveloped for housing. That would have been the Services Communications Development Unit (SCDU).

Eastcote had installed an Elliot 405 computer after the war, which used first-generation thermionic valve technology. The GPO may have used the computer for some of the time to analyse parcel weights and distribution, or it may have used other computers on the site. Two Colossus Mk 2 computers had been transferred to Eastcote post-war from Bletchley Park, prior to that base closing down for cryptographic work. It is thought that the computers were used after the war ended to help decipher encoded Russian transmissions, which may have been using confiscated Nazi teleprinter attachments. The vibration of some of the printing and teleprinting machines in the rooms housing Colossus was such that the Wrens had to lash them down with rope, using various naval knots. Knots can be useful at times, but it is unlikely that their training course tutors would have envisaged the need for Wrens to lash a printer with strong rope to the world's first semi-programmable computer, a computer that had not even been invented at the time of their training course.[25] GCHQ used Block 2 at Eastcote and some spurs in Block 3 prior to their relocation to Cheltenham between 1952 and 1954, which was phased over a couple of years.[26]

In the post-war years a great deal of work was done at Eastcote to analyse data on the Venona project, which was an international investigation into spies and security breaches across the Western countries, but also included Australia, where suspect information was first identified. This would be crucial interception of Soviet espionage intelligence. Funding was eventually found to enable Eastcote to go back over thousands of old radio intercepts, to piece together links where there had been Cold War activities against the West. Americans called it Venona and the British 'Bride'.

GCHQ at Eastcote was divided into six main groups:

Technical (Interception & Communications)
Traffic Analysis
Cryptographic Exploitation
Cryptographic Research
Intelligence
Cipher Security

It is important to emphasise that the wartime role of the outstation at Eastcote was quite different from that of GCHQ Eastcote in 1946. The common ground is that they were both involved in analysing enemy intelligence, although the former was really a base for data processing using codebreaking machines, and was but one key stage in a complex process of decoding enemy messages, which ultimately was carried out to completion at Bletchley Park, HQ. In comparison, GCHQ was the equivalent of Bletchley Park but modernised to a degree, and with much closer links to the NSA, CIA and Western European intelligence agencies to tackle challenging post-war threats in a new nuclear age.

The author has seen several historical books, and articles that seemed to imply that either Eastcote never existed, or that GCHQ evolved from Bletchley Park directly into GCHQ Cheltenham without the transition stage in the post-war period via GCHQ Eastcote. Also, some captions to photographs seen of the site are possibly misleading. Not intentionally so, but nevertheless, misleading. Photos of Bombe equipment at Eastcote would be from the wartime period in Outstation Eastcote generally (and therefore should be captioned as such), as the author knows of no known genuine photos of Bombes post-war at Eastcote, or at GCHQ Eastcote, even though some codebreaking Bombes were retained there after the war ended, some operational and others put into storage. There exists a photograph at GCHQ Eastcote of three directors, Travis, Jones and Clive Loehnis, with Josh Cooper and Hugh Foss at a formal lunch.

The London Communications Development Unit (SCDU) was part of a restructuring of the London Communications Security Agency (LCSA) in 1965. Offices were rented in nearby Northwood Hills at the east corner of the junction of Tolcarne Drive and Chamberlain Way to assist and support the Cheltenham GCHQ until 1977–78, when all GCHQ staff were then at Cheltenham. The Communications Electronics Security Department (CESD), previously known as the LCSA, remained at Eastcote for a time until GCHQ was better established to accept the staff and department.[27] This can be seen as a time of difficult transition, to reorganise departments, restructure them and plan for the future intelligence organisation in order to meet the challenges of the post-war period and the Cold War.

Few books and articles recognise that Eastcote became the first officially named GCHQ after the war had ended. While Bletchley Park had sometimes used the name GCHQ, it was in an unofficial capacity at the time, and was principally known as GC&CS. The author has seen envelopes marked GCHQ that were sent to Bletchley Park, so there is no doubt that on occasions that terminology was used unofficially.[28] The modern GCHQ in Cheltenham owes a great deal to its post-war metamorphosis and development from the establishment of Bletchley Park and via GCHQ Eastcote.

Although actual dates are unclear, the Americans occupied Blocks 1, 2 and 4 post-war on a tenanted basis, and a computer section was established in Block 3 at Eastcote.[29] That block may have contained the Elliot computer, advanced for its time. In 1963 it was replaced by LEO 3, even more technically advanced, although by then the Americans were overtaking the British in computing technology on a large scale. *See Outstation Eastcote.*

English Channel. The Channel gave British Fighter Command some brief warning of attacking Luftwaffe enemy aircraft in order to allow aircraft to be scrambled to meet the foe. A complex but effective warning system was established in England, involving the Observer Corps, radar, listening stations, underground control bunkers and a coordinated military approach to manage air defences. The Luftwaffe's failure to destroy the RAF during the Battle of Britain was a major blow for Hitler in 1940. Operation Sealion, the invasion of Britain, was cancelled, or at least, postponed indefinitely. The intelligence sought by the British and its Allies included penetrating Enigma and other coded messages to German command posts. Methods to put off the Luftwaffe bombing raids crossing the Channel from France included applying the technology developed by physicist Dr R.V. Jones to distort enemy tracking radio beams (in German, *Knickebein*) and convincing the Luftwaffe aircraft they needed to fly a much farther distance than the actual targets they had been issued with. This resulted in some bombs dropping clear of cities and major conurbations, although they still caused damage and losses. Aircraft containing S27 ham radios detected the German radio beams and passed this information on position and frequency to ground receivers. Three separate enemy radio beam systems were identified and effective countermeasures applied successfully against them in the form of interference beams.

The Channel would become both a setting off point and route to Normandy in France for D-Day in June 1944. The planning for D-Day was as much about the coordination of the massive quantities of ships across the Channel to arrive safely at Normandy, as it was the actual assault of troops and guns on the Normandy beaches. The route itself had to be established, marked on naval maps and aligned with precision, such that mined areas were identified and avoided. U-boats and E-boats were kept away by a combination of aircraft and naval vessels.[30] This all had to be communicated to the commanders in time for 6 June. Shipping would depart from several different locations in Devon, Dorset, Hampshire, Kent and Essex. The timing of the departures would be critical. The Germans would await the supposed main force coming over the Straits of Dover and the Pas-de-Calais, but it would never arrive. British agents and double agents would weave a web of espionage and false information to buy the Allies time at Normandy.[31] Bletchley Park would play its part in providing essential intelligence to the top brass about the instructions given to Field Marshal von Rundstedt from Berlin on the *Jellyfish* communication link, intercepted at Knockholt listening station and advanced non-Morse listening stations in England.

Estonia. One of three Baltic States, which would be occupied by the Russians, the Nazis, then the Russians again, during and after the war. In 1940, the Russians occupied the Baltic States under the Molotov–Ribbentrop Pact, a secret agreement between Russia and Nazi Germany. Germany occupied Estonia commencing July 1941 and ending in 1944, when Russia reoccupied the Baltic States. Initially, many Estonian locals preferred the Germans in occupation as they were permitted to maintain their cultural roots, flag, and heritage, whereas the Russians preferred to rewrite the Baltic States' history by destroying books and publications, and imprisoning academics. A British signals engineer, William Green Swanborough, a radio operator, went to Estonia before the war and monitored Russian intelligence, also training Estonians before he left so that information could be passed back to Britain. Britain was interested in Russian intelligence and planning many years before the war as this area was potentially politically unstable. Swanborough would train them in the principles of military signals intelligence against military targets. Unusually, he was authorised to provide the Estonians with UK intelligence relevant to the area, which would benefit the Baltic states. This continued after Swanborough had left Estonia for Britain, and returned home.

Post-war, after a lengthy period of occupation by Russia, the Baltic States including Estonia became independent nations on 6 September 1991.[32] The British Army are at the time of writing present as part of a NATO force in Estonia to help discourage a Russian incursion into the Baltic States. The geographical area remains like a tinder box, with the Ukraine situation giving Estonians, Latvians and Lithuanians cause for concern.

Étretat, northern France. A Nazi listening station on the coast to listen for and collect radio transmissions across the Channel. This signals intelligence network of stations was established by the *Abwehr*. Although there were many listening stations, four key ones concentrated on British radio transmissions. This was one of the four.

Finland. Finland's principal enemy was Russia, even before the war, and it would collect intelligence either alone or combined with the Baltic States, particularly with Estonia, which was relatively close geographically. Finland became an independent country in 1918 after a war with the Soviets. Finland had a border with Russia of thousands of miles, and eventually had to concede certain territories to it following long, drawn-out conflicts. The Estonian military intelligence organisation would work closely with the equivalent Finish Intelligence Service before and during the Second World War. There would also be Finnish communications with Japan against Russia, which was not well-known at the time but invaluable information was obtained.

The Finnish radio intelligence service was established by a Finn, Reino Hallamaa, who set up a signals communications agency in 1927. Divided into separate sections, the intercept section was known as RTK or *Radiotiedustlukeskus*. Finland also compromised the intelligence of various non-Axis countries during the war, to remain well informed and be aware of imminent changes in Europe. In 1939, when the Soviets attacked Finland, the intelligence interception section was able to attack several Russian ciphers and codes. There would be up to around 100 cryptanalysts working on Russian codes at its peak, as the war progressed. Such intelligence would aid the Finnish army to be aware of Russian troop and tank movements, supplies and logistics. At the time of writing, Finland is considering joining NATO due to events in eastern Europe, a potential move and change that will greatly unsettle Russia if it is implemented. Sweden, once independent and neutral, has also considered joining NATO. The picture in Europe and the balance of power is changing, and will continue to change in our lifetime and beyond.

Flowerdown. As HMS *Flowerdown*, an Admiralty base, it would operate from 1939 to 1945 intercepting intelligence from Italian naval and Japanese enemy sources. Additionally, it would listen in to German, French and Russian high-frequency Morse messages. This would be an important listening station or Y-station during the war. Records indicate there was provision for ninety-eight radio receivers, and an extensive rhomboid aerial network and masts. There would be sixteen omni-directional rhomboid aerials for reception of Japanese traffic. The layout of the receiving room and aerial array would be revised following the attack on the Americans at Pearl Harbor, and Japanese entry into the war. This was to make it more efficient as a listening station from early 1942. Post-war it would be taken over by GCHQ Composite Signals Organisation (CSO) and used as an advanced listening station during the Cold War period.

Fort Meade, Maryland, USA. Home of the National Cryptologic Museum, located next to NSA headquarters. The museum was originally planned to house NSA artefacts, but has expanded considerably over the years with items of Second World War codebreaking equipment and associated items of interest.

France. Occupied by Nazi forces via the Blitzkrieg, commencing on 9 May 1940, France soon came under occupation save for an area of Vichy France in the south, which had some temporary breathing space for a time. In November 1938, Alastair Denniston of Bletchley Park wrote to Hugh Sinclair to obtain advice on how to best deal with the French, as they had provided Britain with many useful documents and photographs, together with extensive information on the German Y-Service and telegrams. This exploration of liaison was largely about the objective to crack the Enigma encoding machine. The subsequent meeting of minds in Paris in January

1939 included Poles and British representatives from Bletchley Park. The Poles were initially reluctant to share too much information with the French and British, but a later meeting in Warsaw made more progress.

The British, Canadians and Commonwealth military support armies to France crumbled at Dunkirk, with a complex and messy withdrawal. By the end of June 1939, an armistice had been signed between France and Germany. Belgium, Luxembourg and the Netherlands were also tied into the occupation web by the Nazis. Polish cryptographers worked in the south of France and had considerable success with cracking Enigma messages until they had to move to Algiers when the Germans occupied the area.

The ciphers and intelligence of the French state were easily broken by the Germans before the war in the 1930s, and they failed to change their ciphers. It was a system that was termed a 'finite addition cipher'. This made easy pickings for the Germans, who were able to read the messages through their intelligence section, OKW-Chi. In February 1940, thousands of messages from the French Army were intercepted and read by the enemy. Of even more concern was the intelligence gained through the codebreaking about the British Expeditionary Force (BEF), which was assisting their French ally on a large scale. The Germans established that fuel resources for Allied aircraft were very limited. Also, they discovered that the BEF would be prepared to evacuate France if necessary. Even the French High Command codes were compromised, and easily read. Effectively, the Germans could find out all the intelligence they needed by reading the French codes and ciphers at will. After France fell Britain could only look on from across the Channel while the Nazi fortified wall was built around the French coast, largely using slave labour. As regards codebreaking and intelligence, a network of French Resistance listened in to radio transmissions from Britain and overseas, when the penalty for such activities was death. Intelligence came back to Britain via radio transmissions, agents, carrier pigeon and other means.

In the town of Uzès, in Provence, a secret decoding intelligence château largely operated by Poles would intercept Enigma messages from North Africa before the area was overrun by the Nazis. These would be the same trio of Poles who had initially cracked the early Enigma machine and had built a codebreaking machine back in Poland before the war commenced.[33]

It was thanks to the French that Polish mathematicians had access to certain German code books on Enigma and a manual of operation at the beginning of the war or just prior to it. But it was not just the Nazis that Britain and France were interested in. Apparently, the British had exchanged key information on Russian ciphers with the French since 1933. This was via the Deuxieme Bureau. Paris was the core of intelligence gathering and much information on Enigma was collected in the early years by the French. The use of a disgruntled German agent, Hans-Thilo Schmidt, with bribery as a vehicle of opportunity resulted in extensive numbers of secret German documents making their way to the French and eventually the British. In excess of some three hundred German documents were obtained in this way, with some of it on workings of the Enigma encoding machine. This information was also used by the Poles, and detailed analysis provided them with methods of penetrating Enigma, helped by access to some recent German code books for the machine settings. At a conference in 1939, the Poles would give an explanation of the way into Enigma, both by manual methods and by machine.

The D-Day landings in 1944 to regain French territory and crush the Nazis were supported with both the cracking of Enigma intelligence, strategic intelligence using the Fish high command links, and advanced codebreaking machines. The process in the background was highly risky and very complex. It relied upon creating an illusion in Britain with help from the Allied forces to convince the Germans that the main attack force would come across the Pas-de-Calais. The intelligence obtained aided by double agents at the time was that these tactics appeared to have fooled the German high command, and was highly successful in buying time for the Allied forces penetrating Normandy in June and July 1944. Bletchley Park was in a position to share the intelligence with those in command of the Allied forces in Britain, and give some comfort that certain German armoured divisions would be held back awaiting the assault across the Channel. An assault that never actually came. It was one of the most successful confidence tricks under Operation Fortitude, split into Fortitude North and Fortitude South, the latter being the Allied deception of the enemy affecting the actual D-Day operations. This probably saved many lives and gave a better chance of success for the huge armed assault on 6 June 1944. These were the largest amphibious landings the world had ever seen.

France was also where the Baudot code was invented in the nineteenth century by Emile Baudot, using a system that was in effect a digital way of communicating using crosses and dots. That was adapted by the Nazis during wartime for non-Morse message transmission for the Tunny advanced teleprinter-based encoding machines. It used punched paper tape and was a relatively efficient system, avoiding the errors of using an Enigma machine. See *Emile Baudot*.

Frankfurt Am Main, Germany. The birthplace of inventor Arthur Scherbius, who devised the Enigma encoding machine. Enigma was in appearance similar to a typewriter, but without a printing facility and with illuminated letters to indicate encoded message letters. While initially Enigma was used for finance houses and banks for confidential and secure communication, it was later established as a useful tool for military communication and well over 100,000 Enigmas were produced, used by the Germans, Swiss and Italians, among others. See *Arthur Scherbius*.

GCHQ See *Eastcote GCHQ*. See *Cheltenham*.

Germany The European country, led by Hitler, that started the Second World War with its initial invasion of Poland in 1939.[34] Germany would conquer large parts of Europe and try to conquer North Africa, and later Russia, but ultimately failed in its objectives. However, the devastation caused was vast in respect of human losses, with the Holocaust involving the mass extermination of Jews and other minority groups. Germany was reading and decoding enciphered messages from

Britain, Italy and France as early as 1932. They would agree with General Franco in Spain to establish intelligence bases for surveillance, to scan the Atlantic and Mediterranean for Allied shipping.

Clearly, Hitler overstretched his armed forces and resources, failing to listen to his generals and commanders, and putting unrealistic goals as objectives. Once Hitler invaded Russia, after misleading Stalin with non-aggression-pacts and treaties, the balance of power for Hitler and Germany changed considerably. Another significant turning point would be the involvement of the Americans in the war, who had the men, materials, funding and resources to make a huge difference to the outcome. The war would end in May 1945, after the Allies, including Britain, USA, Canada, Russia and the Commonwealth countries, gained substantial ground in Germany and finished off its armed forces. Hitler committed suicide in Berlin as the Allies came closer. Germany and Berlin were then split among the Allies, with East Germany becoming communist.

Although at the start of the war, Russia invaded Poland two weeks after Adolf Hitler, it is curious that Britain did not declare war on Russia. That risk was seen as a step too far by Neville Chamberlain, Britain's Prime Minister at the time. Hitler relied initially for his secret communications on the Enigma encoding machine. The development of the machine over time made it more secure when compared to the original. However, Hitler insisted on an even more secure system to communicate with his generals and his High Command. No one had considered these advanced systems could be broken by the Allies. How wrong they were. The breaking of various enemy ciphers was not without failures and challenges, but ultimately the perseverance and considerable teamwork by the Allies was able to penetrate the breadth of Nazi German communications, and leave them weak and exposed. Hitler and his generals had no idea this was the case. Add this to the deception techniques used by the Allies approaching D-Day and they had an advantage over the enemy. There are those who say Colossus, the British-designed and built decoding computer, shortened the war by at least two years, saving many millions of lives.

Germany was also the manufacturing base for millions of weapons and components such as electrical relays manufactured by Siemens. These were superior in design and operation to the British relays used in the codebreaking Bombes and were copied by the British, breaching the copyright of the Siemens design at the time. They worked more efficiently in the Bombes once installed.[35]

Gibraltar A British territory in the northern Mediterranean, adjacent to and linked to Spain. Gibraltar became an important intelligence monitoring site, known as 'the Rock'. Tragically, twenty-one Wrens, who were a combination of wireless officers and cipher officers, were torpedoed by German U-boats in a convoy from England en route to Gibraltar on the SS *Aguila* armed merchant ship. This occurred in August 1941. There is a commemorative memorial at the National Arboretum in England with a sculpture of a Wren on a pedestal and a plaque. Gibraltar was also where in 1941 double agent Garbo was transferred from Lisbon via ship to Gibraltar, and then flown to England to help the intelligence services.

Greece. Reports indicated that the Greeks had located and acquired two cryptographic systems from the Italian Army. Thus, they could initially decipher Italian messages to a large degree. This information is mentioned in Walter Fricke's diary, relevant to the Lauf listening station.

Greenwich, London. This was the base for the Royal Naval College, and trained WRNS officer personnel, or Officer Wrens, for a variety of duties including cipher work. Initially they were based in Queen Anne Court, but in the Second World War relocated to a building now known as Devonport House. Sleeping quarters would be in the Queen Anne Building. Greenwich was heavily bombed during the war due to its proximity to the London docks. More than 8,500 Wrens trained at the college during the war. Many would study meteorology, administration and other topics. The WRNS was disbanded in 1993. The Royal Naval College provided training for 27,000 military personnel (mainly officers and some junior ranks) during the war.

Hanslope Park. The basis of the Radio Security Service during the war. Alan Turing would work there for a time on scrambling voice communication. It is situated near the village of Hanslope, 10 miles north of Bletchley Park. Her Majesty's Government Communication Centre is based there (HMGCC). It was acquired in 1939 by the Foreign Office. From 1941 to 1945 this site became important in the area of intelligence gathering. Radio Security Service operators were voluntary workers on radio, i.e. Voluntary Interceptors (VIs).[36] Other personnel had come from the Post Office, Cable and Wireless, etc. The section had developed into carefully controlled listening stations with target frequencies to listen to and take the Morse messages down for review by others. The Radio Analysis Bureau would target those frequencies of interest. American HRO receivers were established on the site. It would become a full-time listening station and collect a substantial amount of intelligence for Bletchley Park. Alan Turing frequently visited the base and stayed there for a time, looking to develop a voice encryption/encoder system. An engineering section repaired, designed and built specialist electronic equipment. By April 1942 a purpose-built building contained thirty-two banks of listeners, and most had access to two HRO radio receivers each.

Intelligence collected during wartime included transmissions from the *Abwehr*, SD (branch of the SS) and RHSA, the Reich Main Security Office. Direction-finding equipment was used regularly, such as goniometers. Richard 'Dick' Keen was the expert at Hanslope Park on direction finding and was introduced to Turing. A woman called Mary Wilson assisted Keen with mathematical work. Substantial aerial arrays were located in many acres of grounds around Hanslope Lodge. The Radio Security Service and SCU3 had a mix of uniformed and non-uniformed personnel. Staffing changed considerably during Spring 1944, with many engineers and mathematicians joining. The speech encoding project at Hanslope was termed 'Delilah', although the Americans got there first with Bell Laboratories producing the complex SIGSALY machine, used for international confidential telephone calls at the highest level. Turin spent time discussing this American system when he was abroad at Bell Labs.

Hardelot, northern France. A Nazi listening station on the coast to listen for and to collect radio transmissions across the Channel. This signals intelligence network of stations was established by the *Abwehr*. Although there were many listening stations, four key stations concentrated on British radio transmissions. (i.e. the Hague, Étretat, Hardelot and St Malo-Paramé).

Harpenden, Herts. Designated as Army No. 1 Special Group Wireless listening station during the war.

Harrow School. Schoolboys from Malvern in Worcestershire had to be relocated to use part of Harrow school during wartime, as TRE, the radar research base, had relocated from Dorset on the south coast to Malvern boys' college. The boys were relocated initially to a country house, and then later on to Harrow School.[37] The boys were not seen as Harrow pupils, although they shared certain facilities. There may have been some snobbery with the Harrow boys and staff resenting the intrusion, but overall it seemed to work and life got on to provide the education needed in wartime. After the war, TRE enjoyed the site at Malvern so much, which had expanded considerably with staff and buildings, that it had to be actively encouraged to leave, with politicians intervening in the House of Commons to enable the college to take the boys back and to leave the facilities at Harrow School. Malvern College is a private fee-paying boarding school now, and is co-educational.

Hendon, north London. The location of a safe house for double agent Pujol Garcia, code-named Garbo, while he worked for MI5 and intelligence services against the Nazis. He would stay in Crespigny Road, Hendon, and be monitored and instructed on what information to send back to his handler via letters containing secret ink.[38] Garbo established a fictitious list of sub-agents across Britain, and gave reports of their intelligence and spying activities to the Germans.

Highgrove House, Eastcote, Middlesex. The old house, near the Eastcote Road, which was used by Churchill and his new wife, Clementine, in 1908, when he married and had his honeymoon there. Lady Warrender and some of her family were friends with Winston's mother, who suggested it to him for his honeymoon. It was adjacent to large open fields, which would be built upon thirty-five years later to house the Turing–Welchman Bombe codebreaking machines to challenge the Nazi Enigma machines. This would then become Outstation Eastcote or HMS *Pembroke V* in 1943, where Special Duties X activities would be implemented. Part of the adjacent site to the south of Highgrove House is a park that was given to the community by a previous owner. The old public footpath running between Highgrove House and the fields at the time is still in existence, but the outstation was demolished in 2007. Eleanor Warrender, the owner at the time of the Second World War, permitted use of the house by RAF personnel and American soldiers.

Highgrove House was granted grade II listed status in 1975 for its architectural character. It had suffered fires that destroyed parts of the building, including one of catastrophic proportions in 1881, but was rebuilt by Sir Hugh Hume-Campbell. Post-war, it was a social services hostel for the elderly and homeless people, but closed, and was then sold to Westcombe Estates. The building has been renovated and exists today as private, luxury residential flats. Part of the estate was sold in 1935 to the local authority (now the London Borough of Hillingdon), known as Warrender Park.

HMS Anderson. An intelligence onshore naval base and listening station in Colombo, Ceylon, intercepting Japanese radio traffic as part of a vast intelligence network in the east. It also supported GC&CS back in England, and particularly with regard to Hut 7 at Bletchley Park, focussing on Japanese intercepts, containing cryptographic experts and linguists. HMS *Anderson* was part of the Far East Combined Bureau (FECB). By 1944, there would be 1,280 military staff and a few civilians. It was built at the Anderson Golf Links and could accommodate up to 1,700 personnel planned at its peak. The base would also become a direction-finding base for the Royal Navy. Equipment expanded in type and quantity considerably over time, and included a Hollerith tabulating machine and radio receivers with a hundred radio listening bays. Each of the operators would be allocated a discrete Japanese radio channel and frequency to monitor. Hundreds of Wrens on the base would be operating the Hollerith machines, also acting as intelligence analysts, cipher clerks and administrators. RAF personnel would be present on the Navy base to be allocated to shipping as radio listeners to give warnings on incoming enemy air raids. In 1954 the base was relocated after the war to Perkar in Ceylon, based on a GCHQ request for a listening station in the area, and invented a cover story, as a relay station for the replacement listening base. Deception would be required even after the war had ended. See *Ceylon*.

HMS *Pembroke*. Various 'versions' of this existed, but most of the earlier numbered Pembrokes would be for financial accounting purposes within onshore naval bases:

HMS *Pembroke I*:	An accounting base in Chatham, Kent, in 1940–60.
HMS *Pembroke II*:	An accounting base in Chatham in 1940–57.
HMS *Pembroke III*:	An accounting base in Chatham and some outstations, including Outstation Stanmore from 1942 to 1952.
HMS *Pembroke IV*:	An accounting base at the Nore in 1939–61.

HMS *Pembroke V*. The Navy designation for the Special Duties X military bases, used and operated by the WRNS during the Second World War. *Pembroke V* was an administrative designation for the codebreaking outstations for naval personnel,

EN CE LIEU, DU 1ᴱᴿ OCTOBRE 1940 AU 6 NOVEMBRE 1942 DES MATHEMATICIENS ET DES OFFICIERS POLONAIS ONT DÉCHIFFRÉ CLANDESTINEMENT AU BÉNÉFICE DES ALLIÉS AVEC L'AIDE DE RESISTANTS FRANÇAIS ET ESPAGNOLS, DES MILLIERS DE MESSAGES RADIO ALLEMANDS CODÉS AVEC LA MACHINE ENIGMA.

The plaque outside the Chateau des Fouzes, Uzes, Provence, in the South of France commemorating the Polish codebreakers and other allies who risked their lives in decoding messages. *(Courtesy Chateau des Fouzes)*

Wrens in London during wartime. Betty Hollingberry, (Nee Vowles), a codebreaking Wren who worked at one of the Outstations is on the right of the picture.

Wehrmacht Army three-wheel 'Enigma' Machine from a private collection. Note the plugboard or *steckerboard* at the front of the machine. The lift-up hinged metal panel with clear windows near the top is for insertion of the rotor wheels, which could change in sequence according to the codebook instructions. *(Courtesy of Damien Horn, owner of the Channel Islands Military Museum)*

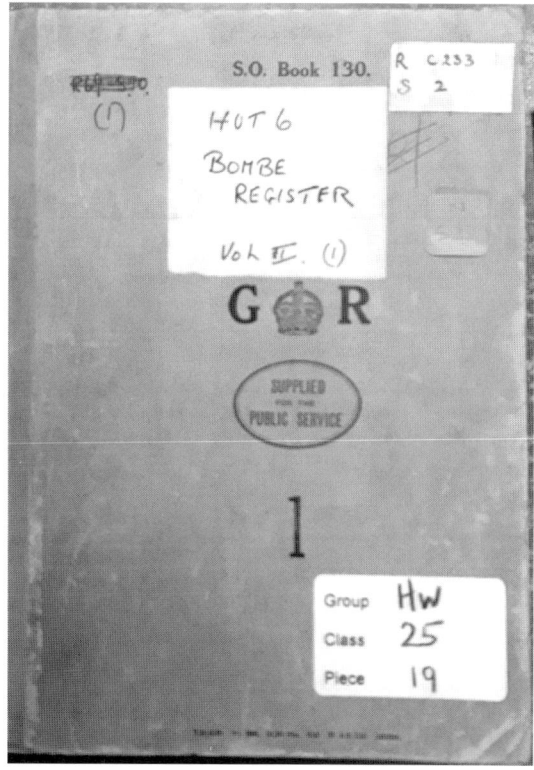

Above: Battery control switching close-up of the three-wheel Enigma. The indicator letters which change according to the key-presses on the machine are visible below. *(Courtesy of Damien Horn, owner of the Channel Islands Military Museum)*

Right: One of the two Bombe Registers on loan to the National Archive which contains the recorded entries for each individual Bombe codebreaking machine as regards numbering, naming, date of manufacture and issue/allocation to various sites from BTM Letchworth. Type and modification of machines is also recorded. Several machines were named and re-named over their life in operation. *(Courtesy National Archives / GCHQ)*

C Watch at Outstation Stanmore, (OSS), comprising Wrens who operated the codebreaking Bombe machines plus RAF personnel. Armed guards were positioned at most of the outstations to deter curious members of the public. (*Courtesy creative commons*)

Above and below: The Spirella Building at Letchworth, Hertfordshire, which made women's corsets and had to be adapted firstly for parachute-making, and then to support BTM in making components for Bombe codebreaking machines. It survives today, having been refurbished at great cost and was opened by HM The Prince of Wales, (later, HM The King). It is now used for commercial purposes housing a variety of companies and organisations. Spirella was originally an American Company. *(Top: Ronald Koorm, Lower: Courtesy of The Garden City Heritage Collection, Letchworth, Hertfordshire)*

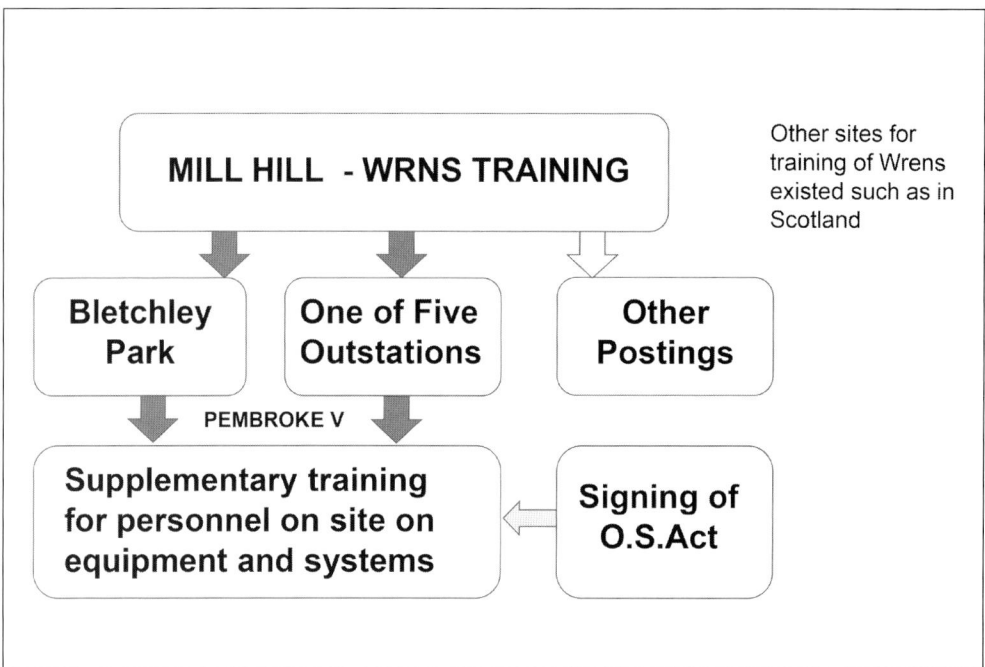

Diagram showing how Wrens (WRNS) at Mill Hill could be allocated to perform on codebreaking or support duties at Outstations or at Bletchley Park, the Headquarters, GC&CS. Wrens were selected and then allocated for 'Special Duties X' work. This name was superseded eventually with *Pembroke V* or *HMS Pembroke V*, for WRNS Naval administration purposes. As the war progressed, some Wrens were posted overseas to work in places such as *HMS Anderson*, Ceylon, now Sri Lanka, to listening stations and codebreaking bases, working for the allies against the Japanese enemy. *(Ronald Koorm)*

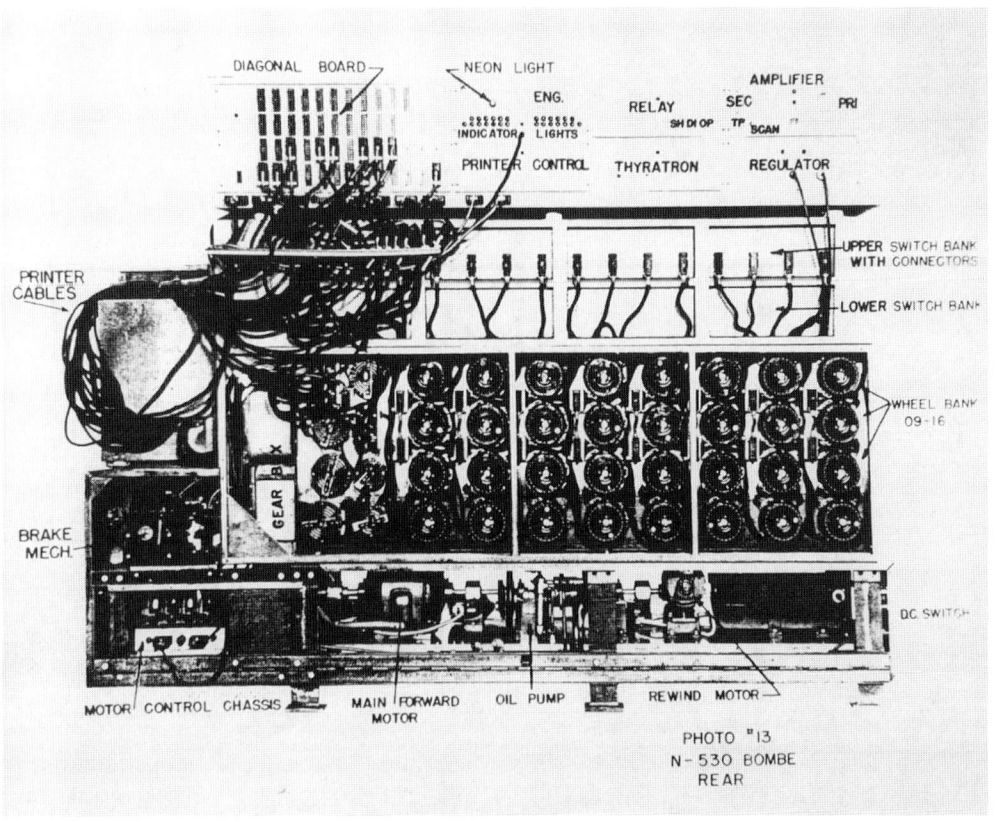

American codebreaking four-wheel (Enigma) Bombe. These were built by the NCR company and shipped across to Washington. They concentrated on German *Kreigsmarine* Naval Enigma messages which were of particular interest due to the U-boat threat in the Atlantic. Alan Turing was aware of these being constructed by the Americans. Reports indicated they were more efficient than the British equivalent Bombe, but one might argue that the Americans had better access to materials and resources at the time.
(Courtesy The National Cryptological Museum, Maryland, USA)

PEMBROKE PARK

Pembroke Park takes its name from the World War II base HMS Pembroke V. From 1943 to 1945 it was an outstation of the Government Code and Cipher School (GC&CS) at Bletchley Park and as such played a significant role in deciphering enemy signals.
The site was home to 800 Wrens who worked on 110 'bombes' (electro-mechanical decoding machines) with the support of 100 RAF technicians.
After the war GC&CS changed its name to Government Communications Headquarters (GCHQ) and moved to this site, where it remained until the relocation of most of its functions to Cheltenham in the early 1950s.
A small unit stayed at Eastcote until the late 1970s.
The names of the roads and some of the buildings in Pembroke Park have been chosen to reflect the history of the site.

Ruislip, Northwood & Eastcote Local History Society, Eastcote Residents' Association, Taylor Wimpey
2014

Plaque at Eastcote in Middlesex adjacent to Pembroke Park housing development to commemorate the existence of the Outstation Eastcote codebreaking base, which would later become GCHQ in 1946 after the war. The plaque is near a pedestrian crossing behind green railings, and was unveiled by the mayor of Hillingdon and with RAF officers present in 2014. The local paper covered the event. At the end of the second world war, there were actually 103 Bombe machines at the site, most were dismantled and destroyed upon Churchill's instructions, but a few escaped that fate, for a time. *(Ronald Koorm)*

Wavendon Manor House, one of the five bases used for codebreaking using Bombe machines. The site was not far from Bletchley Park, being a country house. Three of the outstation sites were country houses with estates. Wren *Betty Hollingberry* was based here for her codebreaking duties and Bombe operational work. Stables and other outbuildings housed the Bombe machines. The site was run by the Wrens, but on a much smaller scale compared to the larger outstations such as Stanmore or Eastcote.

Tommy Flowers, research engineer and designer and builder of the *Colossus* digital computer and valve-based decoding machine at the Post Office Research Engineering Station at Dollis Hill. Flowers worked closely with Max Newman of Bletchley Park, at a time when many were unsupportive of his ideas using valves as digital switches. The engineering part of the Post office would later be acquired and developed by the private organisation, British Telecom, or BT. They have a bronze bust of Flowers at one of their research sites.

No. 39. British Tabulating Co.—Wizards with Wires

'Wizards with Wires'- Production of Bombe components at the Letchworth *Spirella* factory under BTM management and coordination for codebreaking machines. Women also made components and assembled wiring and connectors in outlying villages near to Letchworth, which would be brought together and assembled in the main BTM factory building. *(Courtesy of Letchworth Garden City Heritage Collection, Letchworth, Hertfordshire)*

Commemorative plaque outside Watergate House off the Strand, London, celebrating the centenary of the establishment of the origins of GCHQ, now based in Cheltenham, Gloucestershire. There exists a coded message on the plaque itself. *(Ronald Koorm)*

An office building off Baker Street, London, used during the second world war by the Norwegian branch of SOE to plan a series of raids in Norway against the Nazis, and famous for the *Telemark Raid*. Inset shows close-up of the commemorative plaque fixed on the wall. *(Ronald Koorm)*

Outstation Eastcote with *Larissa*, or 'Bombe' number 20, situated at front of the machines. This was the Greek bay of machines all with names of Greek towns and cities. Each machine represented 36 three-wheel Enigma machines. Wrens (WRNS) operated the Turing / Welchman machines at all the outstations and at Bletchley Park. Each Bombe machine was engineered and built in Letchworth, Hertfordshire, then distributed across to Bletchley or the outstations. *(By the Kind permission of the Director of GCHQ © Crown Copyright)*

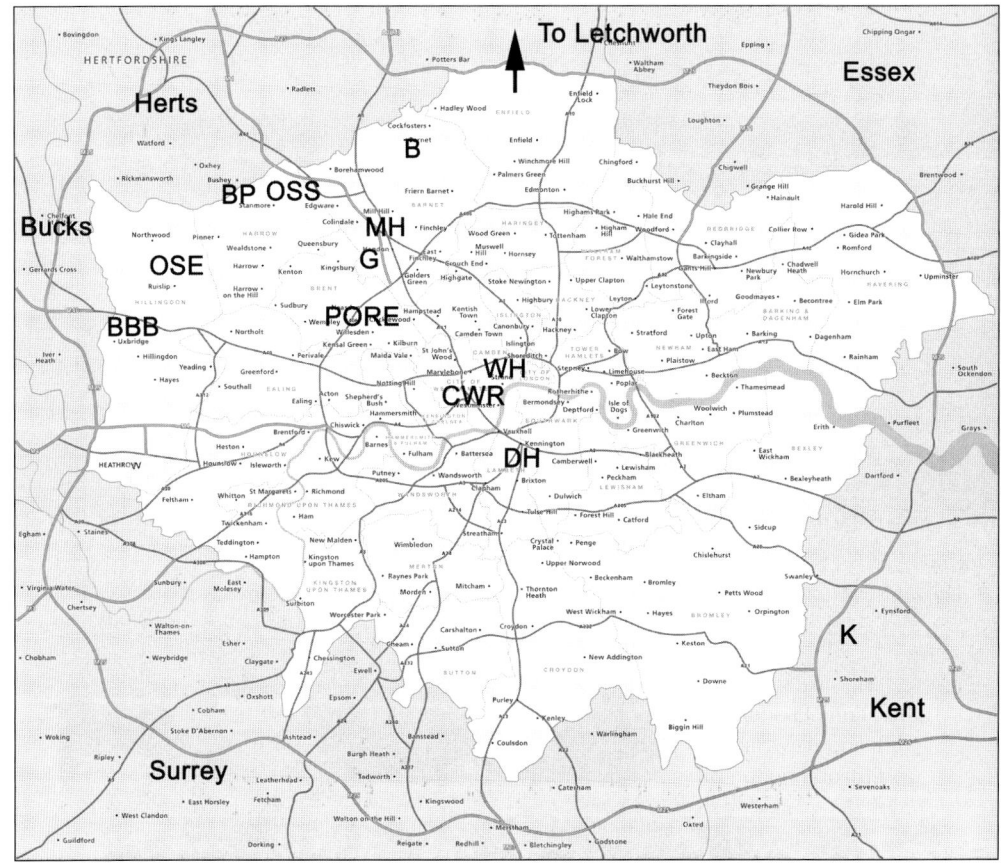

Map of Greater London with locations of points of interest. *(Maproom.net)*

KEY
BP Bentley Priory RAF station
BBB Battle of Britain Bunker at Uxbridge
MH Mill Hill training accommodation for Wrens
OSE Outstation Eastcote
OSS Outstation Stanmore
B Barnet (Location of Voluntary Interceptor PO Box communications)
PORES Post Office Research Engineering Station at Dollis Hill, also home to 'Paddock' for the Prime Minister and cabinet during WW2
WH Watergate House, near the Strand
DH Denmark Hill, Intercept station
CWR Cabinet War Rooms, Westminster (Now known as Churchill Rooms)
XX St James' Street, (XX) Twenty committee
G Agent 'Garbo's' safe house in Hendon
K Knockholt / Ivy Farm in Kent
Letchworth (BTM, off the map to north of London, and in Hertfordshire)

Above left: Arthur Scherbius. Inventor of the Enigma encoding and decoding machine. He sadly did not live to see the impact of his invention used during the second world war.

Above right: Alan Turing. Sometimes referred to as the 'father of modern computing'. *(By the Kind permission of the Director of GCHQ © Crown Copyright)*

U.S. Navy WAVE operating the N-530 BOMBE on the Second Deck, Building 4. Picture dated May 25, 1945. *(Courtesy of The National Cryptological Museum, Maryland, USA)*

Spirella factory workers in a group who were working for BTM on assembling codebreaking component. *(Courtesy of the Letchworth Garden City Heritage Foundation)*

in a support role to Bletchley Park. Instead of being a specific 'place' it was a group designation of naval locations for a specific purpose. That included part of Bletchley Park, when machines were operated by Wrens. See *Pembroke V*.

HMS *Tullichewan*, Balloch, Loch Lomond, Scotland. Tullichewan Castle Camp was a combined operations base during the latter part of the Second World War. WRNS, or Wrens, were trained there, and records indicate that some were sent to Bletchley Park on Station X Special Duties, i.e. codebreaking, or codebreaking support. The base was commissioned 10 March 1945 and decommissioned after the war ended.

Hut 6, Bletchley Park. Arguably. the most famous and significant hut containing codebreaking experts during the war. It was also the subject of a controversial book, *The Hut Six Story*, written by Gordon Welchman after the war. This was not widely publicised as there were threats from the American and British authorities regarding the content that allegedly, according to the authorities, potentially compromised the security of the West.

Hut 6 contained mathematicians, academics and codebreakers such as Alan Turing, Gordon Welchman, Hugh Alexander, James Aitken, Stuart Milner-Barry, Dennis Babbage, David Rees, Mair Russell Jones, John Jeffreys, and many others, who were tasked to break the Nazi Enigma machine codes and enable Britain and its allies to read the German messages, once translated into English. Hut 6 would be established as an idea by Welchman, and run by Jeffreys for a time. Data would come in via listening stations across the country and abroad, and there would initially be hand decryption of the Enigma messages, followed by attacking the settings with the Turing–Welchman Bombe codebreaking machines at Bletchley Park and the outstations. The instructions given to the outstations for setting up the Bombe machines would be based on a 'Menu', a strange diagram with lines linking letters, which was determined by the codebreakers at Bletchley Park, based on their analysis in the huts. The combination of the Menus plus the setting up and running of the rotor-based Bombe codebreaking machines would help determine the settings for the Enigma machine. The aim was to eliminate the permutations of the settings as far as possible to arrive at the correct solution, which could then enable the message to be read once the settings had been programmed in.

Stuart Milner-Barry would succeed Welchman in September 1943 as the head of Hut 6. There would be several hundred people involved in the hut, some carrying out manual codebreaking, others working with data received by Bombe codebreaking machines from other huts and the codebreaking outstations elsewhere. Typex machines at Bletchley, operated mainly by women, would convert the decoded message into German text, ready for translation. There would be liaison with other huts and sections to make all this work effectively. While there would be some teleprinter machines available to communicate messages from Y-stations, the volume of messages outpaced the number of machines.

Despatch riders were heavily relied upon on motorcycles to transfer the encoded messages and data to Bletchley Park. Many of the despatch riders were

Wrens, working in all weathers and travelling to and from the listening stations and the outstations. Listening stations would collect and write down the message data in groups of five letters or 'words', including the preamble the German Enigma operator transmitted prior to the main message, for setting up. It was these forms that would be so crucial to the occupants of the huts at Bletchley Park. They would need to be filtered down and prioritised for decoding and processing. Welchman devised a system to help the efficient prioritisation of certain Enigma-based messages, which were teleprinted to Bletchley for speed. Let us not forget that the purpose of decoding the enemy Enigma and other encoding machines was to establish what the Axis powers were planning, their order of battle, their build-up of resources, requests for supplies and information. The decoded messages would be passed to the Chiefs of Staff and the armed forces, and many were summarised for the Prime Minister, who took great interest in them.

Hut 6 is now formally listed Grade II as reference 1391795 by Heritage England, which reflects its significance in British wartime history and places of particular specific interest, based on their use during the war for codebreaking and associated activities.

Hut 7, Bletchley Park. The hut was constructed in 1940 and used for punched-card data processing as the Hollerith tabulating and records section. This was managed by Freddie Freeborn, an experienced manager from BTM in Letchworth, the company constructing the Bombe codebreaking machines. Information was collected, sorted and processed to support the analysis of enemy messages on a database using punched cards with Hollerith machines. There is relevance here to International Business Machines (IBM), which provided the expertise and design input for the equipment including Hollerith machines, licensed for use in the British Empire via BTM.

In November 1942, the Hollerith and records section was relocated to Block C. Freeborn then set up a new processing section at Drayton Parslow, some miles from Bletchley Park, growing to a substantial operation using hundreds of women personnel. The relocation was necessary due to lack of space for the equipment and punched cards, which escalated into the millions at the peak. Information relevant to Enigma messages and settings together with processed data would be sent from Drayton Parslow to Bletchley and back, based upon requests from the Bletchley cryptographers and experts.

From December 1942 Hut 7 became the cryptographic department of the Naval section. It was later joined by the Japanese section in 1943. A battery room would be constructed in 1943. Wooden structures were demolished between 1948 and 1954, and the battery room modified in the 1950s. One woman, a Canadian, who worked at Bletchley, during the war on Hollerith machines, including in Hut 7 and Block C, was Doris Marshall, née Phillips. She worked very long hours alongside her female colleagues, and lived not far from the site. See *Freeborn*. See *Hollerith*. See *BTM*.

Hut 8, Bletchley Park. Tasked with working on cracking the *Kriegsmarine* (naval) ciphers, Hut 8 would play a significant part in helping to protect British and Allied convoys across the Atlantic and elsewhere. Alan Turing would be in charge of the team at Hut 8 until Hugh Alexander took over from him in 1942. There was a strong link at Bletchley Park with Hut 4, which dealt with translations and analysis of the decrypted messages from Hut 8. A cold, and very basic wooden structure originally, there would later be a combination of people from the huts, including the personnel from Hut 8, relocating to a brick-built structure in February 1943 as Block 'D', where the name was retained as Hut 8.

The codebreakers in Hut 8 would have both successes and failures, particularly during a period of around ten months in 1942, when the additional fourth wheel rotor of the improved naval Enigma machine defied decoding by those at Bletchley Park. This version of Enigma was referred to as Triton. The hut team would also break Luftwaffe ciphered messages as well as naval messages. The personnel codebreakers relied upon firstly the Y-stations, which intercepted and recorded the enciphered Morse code radio messages from the enemy, and the Wrens, who operated all the Bombe codebreaking at the outstations, a small handful of machines being at Bletchley Park itself mostly for training purposes and experimentation. The Americans were successful in intercepting the four-rotor-wheel Naval Enigmas, using their own improved version of the Bombe codebreaking machine, built in Midwest America and moved to Washington for operation.

Hut 8 is now formally listed Grade II as reference 1391796 by Heritage England, which reflects its significance in British wartime history and places of particular specific interest, based on their use during the war for codebreaking activities.

India. New Delhi had the Wireless Experimental Centre (WEC) during the Second World War. This was a form of combined codebreaking section and Y-station. It would receive recruits and personnel from Bletchley Park. It was a large operation, with over a thousand staff, being a mix of Army, RAF, West African and Indian military. Some would be from the Intelligence Corps. Those at Bletchley who had worked on Japanese codes in England would be much sought after for assistance on the base, which was also linked to the Far East Combined Bureau. A few could be spared from England, but probably a limited number. Lieutenant Colonel Peter-Marr Johnson, the head of Section 'C', would ensure formalities would be maintained and military discipline at all times. For this reason, he was not always well liked by everyone, and Bletchley Park would be a much more laid-back base in comparison to WEC. The colonel had previously been trained in cryptography at GC&CS, and spoke fluent Japanese, a clear advantage. Civilians at WEC were conspicuous by their absence.

The site was based around New Delhi University Campus, and the occupied part was the Ramjas College. Progress in cryptographic techniques against the Japanese was made in decrypts. Listening in to Japanese Morse code, intelligence on planning air raids and attacks was fruitful, and gave some added warnings in advance of attack. Decoding Japanese messages gave the British and Indian armies additional time, and an advantage. WEC was considered a successful cryptographic and intelligence base, and had certain information that could have benefited Bletchley

Park codebreakers in terms of maps and local data in the Pacific, particularly around the Pacific islands. WEC had identified the problems the Japanese had with maintaining supplies and rations as they advanced. Codes were then cracked in 1943 by British codebreakers in respect of the resources of Japanese water supplies for their troops, which identified some of the weaknesses of the Japanese army. This was useful intelligence for the general commanding Allied armed forces.[39] India would have around ninety listening posts, and a quantity of mobile stations in addition. Three outstations would also support WEC across the country.

Ireland. A Dublin-based Irish librarian, Richard Hayes, decoded Nazi cipher codes during the last war. He did this by leading a team of cryptographic mathematicians to crack the Nazi Görtz cipher in 1943. Hermann Görtz was a Nazi spy that came to Ireland in the early stages of the war but was eventually arrested in 1941. He had provided substantial funds to the IRA in exchange for intelligence on the Irish coastal defences. The spy was captured along with several code books and documents that included the German plan Kathleen, which was the Nazi plan to invade and capture Northern Ireland by force, with considerable help and assistance from the IRA. Although Hayes came from Limerick, he worked in Dublin as National librarian and had access to countless documents, papers and material. He studied languages and was fluent in German. This specialist cryptographic work was carried out in a house in Montpelier Road, Dublin. Görtz was now considered to be the real prize of all the enemy agents captured, and would be personally interrogated by Hayes, who discovered various secret documents and plans while Görtz was being X-rayed for ailments in the prison hospital. These documents required further detailed study. Hayes managed to further break complex encoded ciphers of the Nazi SS and some of his team's work proved to be valuable to allied commanders when the Battle of the Bulge took place in Europe, in respect of acquiring enemy intelligence. The American Office of Strategic Services (OSS) in Dublin was able to benefit considerably from some of the cryptographic work done by Hayes, to make progress in reading Nazi encoded messages. The OSS was the predecessor of the CIA. Due to the Irish intercepts of encoded messages from the German embassy in Dublin, twelve enemy spies who parachuted or entered Ireland by other means were captured by the Irish Authorities. London was informed about this progress, and this helped seal the close bond between the countries during wartime, even though the IRA had other ideas.

Isle of Wight. There were various military installations and anti-aircraft installations on the island and listening posts with large aerials. It would also be involved with the PLUTO fuel pipeline to supply the D-Day Normandy ships. Shanklin had a large storage tank along the pipeline that passed via Sandown fort and then under the Channel. There was a female spy on the island, Dorothy O'Grady, who was caught, arrested and tried for espionage. The maps she had drawn of military installations and surrounding features were extremely accurate, based on detailed examination of the maps in 1995, and would have been like gold dust to the enemy if they had come into possession of them. The Germans were interested in the island as Hitler was keen on occupying it as a stepping stone to the mainland. It was tabled in Führer Directive No. 16 as an objective. They would obtain certain intelligence in anticipation of their invasion of England, Operation Sealion, which was aborted after the Battle of Britain. See *O'Grady.*

Italy. During the Second World War Italy was an ally of Nazi Germany and led by the fascist Benito Mussolini. Italy was allocated Enigma encoding machines, and Bletchley Park had some considerable success intercepting and breaking the cyphers, which resulted in a major victory at the Battle of Matapan when an attack on British convoys in the Mediterranean was thwarted. Mavis Lever at Bletchley helped crack some of the Italian cypher codes. The British admiral would later visit Bletchley Park and thank those responsible for the advanced intelligence that saved many British and Allied lives.

The Italian army's agency for intelligence, *Servizio Informazioni Militari* (SIM), did have a department that attacked the cryptographic systems of foreign governments. These intelligence intercepts included reading the communications of the US military attachés, including Cairo. The army's agency was based in Rome, managed by General Vittoria Gamba. There were three arms to the army cryptographic section: military & research; diplomatic; and commercial. The diplomatic section was in nine groups. On average, over 8,000 messages were intercepted each month. Around 75 per cent of these were studied in detail, and 3,500 would be translated after decoding. Intercept stations would be based upon four fixed units, and seven mobile, which also covered the occupied countries. Probably the greatest coup for the Italians was the copying of the US Military Intelligence code No. 11, used by military attachés, in 1940. US Colonel Bonner Fellers was the military attaché who joined at Cairo in 1940, and had access to British facilities and documents. His transmissions were unknowingly intercepted by the Italians. The Italians shared the code with the Germans, and messages were read for more than six months before the code was changed. The Germans benefitted considerably from the information up to at least 1942.

The navy also had a cryptographic section, divided into four sub-sections or branches. However, there are reports that some of the Italian systems and operational procedures led by Mussolini, such as against Greece, were poorly managed, and carelessness of radio protocols and methods would cause them heavy losses. They would share radio frequencies across infantry regiment stations, and failed to change call signs sufficiently frequently. Enemy direction finding would locate transmission points, whether fixed or mobile. Many messages were sent over the radio unencoded, and in plain Italian language. The Greeks, in contrast, had apparently acquired some enemy encoding radio systems, and used them to great effect.

Finally, the Italians penetrated many foreign embassies with spies, and used clandestine methods to copy documents, code books of foreign powers and associated information. The security and vetting of embassy staff and support staff was not always sufficiently thorough, leaving gaps at times in security and creating openings for spies.

Ivy Farm. The farm and adjoining land in Kent that was selected by the Foreign Office to position a specialist advanced listening station at Knockholt to support GC&CS at Bletchley Park. See *Knockholt.*

Japan. During the Second World War it was an ally of the Nazis and Italy, and therefore an enemy of the West and Britain. It used a version of Enigma for encoding messages. This was termed 'Purple' and both the USA and the British attacked it. However, 'Purple' was a diplomatic cipher. It was broken by the Signals Intelligence Service of the US Army. Wrens sent to Ceylon and other eastern countries worked on gathering intelligence against the Japanese. The Japanese attacked the American Navy base at Pearl Harbor, Hawaii, in December 1941, and brought America into the war, which was almost a relief for Churchill as Britain was creaking and groaning with limited resources and manpower against the Nazis. The breaking of Japanese codes in the build-up to the attack on Pearl Harbor was complex for the Americans, as the Japanese had prepared a long message in fourteen parts. It was only when the last part of the message was deciphered that it was clear an attack was inevitable, but it was too late by the time the information had been communicated and received by the admirals at Pearl Harbor. Later in the war, representatives of Japan such as General T. Yamashita visited Calais to see the progress on the Nazi defences. They were particularly interested in acquiring gold from occupied and other countries. The US Navy's codebreaking and intelligence OP-20-G division worked after Pearl Harbor to infiltrate the Japanese codes. They included Elizabeth Smith Friedman, Genevieve Grotjan, Ann Caracristi and Francis Steen. The Japanese were never able to break the US codes developed and used by the Navajo Indians, used by specialist teams of signals engineers who were considered to be 'code-talkers'. They had more success in breaking Soviet codes and ciphers. All the Japanese codes were eventually broken by the Allies, including code JN-25b, which had intelligence on the Battle of Midway. The Americans surprised the Japanese and won that battle, which had a major impact on the progress of the war in the Pacific.

Kensington, London. A training centre for WRNS personnel during the war was in Campden Hill Road, Kensington. According to one source the base was named *Pembroke I* for administrative purposes. This is of interest, as the later codebreaking outstations were termed either *Pembroke III* or, later on, *Pembroke V*. The HQ for Wrens was near Admiralty Arch in Trafalgar Square, and became HMS *President*, as if it were a ship. In training facilities and bases, dormitories for the Wrens were known as cabins. Tea trolleys would later be known as 'tea boats' with the dining area referred to as the mess deck. The Royal Navy would follow its traditions, and even shore-based bases would retain a strong link to naval discipline and terminology. See *Midway Island.*

PLACES

Kent. The south-east county was to prove important in collecting enemy intelligence with its specialist listening station at Ivy Farm, Knockholt, also known as 'the Pound'. Kent was additionally the base for the many American soldiers created artificially under the FUSAG deception to deceive the enemy during the D-day landings. Under the ETOUSA agreement between Britain and the USA a number of signals engineers came to Britain, and a proportion of these came to Kent in a support role, with others going to Bletchley Park and to Outstation Eastcote in Middlesex to operate a limited number of Bombe codebreaking machines. See *Ivy Farm* and *Knockholt*.

Kenya. An intelligence listening station was located as part of FECB in Kilindini during the war, prior to it being relocated to HMS *Anderson* in Ceylon in 1943. Wrens operated some of the equipment and were later transferred to Ceylon, which became a much larger base for their listening and decoding operations.

Kew, National Archives. This contains historic documents, photographs, diagrams and other material of national interest. Reference numbers of documents are preceded by letters such as HW. A complete reference might be, for example, HW14/164. Searches for documents and information can be made online or in person. It is an invaluable source of historical information. At the time of writing the National Archives hold the Bombe registers, which record the history of the Bombe codebreaking machines in two small hardback, lined books, with entries mostly in ink.

Knockholt. Ivy Farm, Kent. The site at Ivy Farm in Kent was taken over by the Government via the Foreign Office for use as an advanced listening station to intercept, among others, the advanced Nazi encoding teleprinter machines that were sending out non-Morse messages at high speed. This site was to be at Knockholt, situated near a small village. It was sometimes referred to as 'the Pound', and would be fully operational by early 1943. Radio intercepts would commence before this date. The special non-Morse messages generated by the enemy would be circulating across Europe by 1941 but grew in scale and geographical area over time. Landline non-Morse links would be difficult to intercept, so Bletchley decided that radio intercepts were the way forward and ordered selected Y-stations to concentrate on those.

Initially, officials spied on the farmer who was occupying the site and they had to wait for official papers to acquire it for their needs before moving in. They then brought in various experts and engineers including electrical engineers to build listening arrays to collect the data. The converted farmhouse came with 30 acres which would be greatly expanded over time to 160 acres with further substantial land acquisitions. The topography of Ivy Farm was of interest as it was at 240m above sea level on a form of plateau. This made it useful for the construction of a wide array of rhombic-shaped aerials for receiving radio transmissions and non-Morse transmissions. These aerials were huge in scale and could easily be seen from the air, which concerned the management, but some anti-aircraft guns were positioned nearby and eventually some barrage balloons. The aerials were around 300m across the major axis, and improved power supplies and cabling had to be brought into the site by electrical engineers as part of infrastructure changes and improvements.

Although commencing on a relatively small scale, Knockholt had approximately 600 key staff in 1944, and this number would increase further, with around eighty encoders, whose principal function was to intercept enemy messages and transmissions to pass them to Bletchley Park. Initially there were eight interception radio receiver sets, but this increased to twenty-five, in the converted farmhouse. They intercepted the first facsimile or fax message during the war.

The intention was to intercept specialised enemy traffic and intelligence termed 'Fish' over several different enemy communication links in Europe, each given a 'Fishy' name such as Gurnard, Bream and Jellyfish. It would take staff two to three weeks of specialised training to decipher tapes and the codes into letters of the alphabet. There were three shifts on the 24/7 operation of listening for enemy signals: 7am–2pm, 2pm–10pm and 10pm–7am. In addition to the farmhouse building, already filled with equipment, there were several Nissen huts around the site. The farmhouse staff were in the Foreign Office Research and Development Establishment (FORDE). Correspondence studied at the National Archives indicated that a third of the staff were on shift work, with the remaining two-thirds on daytime duties. There would be a night-time complement of up to sixty staff. There was a basic canteen for breaks. The Nissen huts would be freezing in winter and very hot in summer.

Teleprinter set-ups were established to connect to Bletchley Park, but some intelligence was couriered by motorcycle despatch riders. Radios were monitored constantly for enemy transmissions in the farmhouse. Female personnel, such as ATS, and RAF staff typed encoded messages onto tape for later analysis. The advanced messages being intercepted by their equipment was extremely fast, termed to be 'noise', and was based on a Vernon–Baudot code system. It was termed non-Morse and first discovered at a listening station in Denmark Hill above a police station, when Bletchley Park was alerted. The discovery eventually led to the design and building of the world's first semi-programmable computer, Colossus, to help in deciphering the enemy messages, intended for the German High Command.

Radio listening operators at Knockholt had to achieve Postmaster General (PMG) certificates by formal examination. They were expected to analyse twenty-five words per minute on the radio transmissions, find faults on equipment and understand Q-codes. Some would be issued with a first-class certificate of proficiency, which involved telegraphy and telephony.

The array of aerial masts was substantial, with some 48ft high and others 70ft, all stabilised by numerous guy cables and struts.[40] The Ministry of Works provided a detailed inventory of all the component parts. The site was a hive of constant activity, with typists, radio listeners, teleprinter operators, engineers and personnel to transfer messages on to tape for later analysis by HQ. By the end of December 1944 there would be 717 personnel working at Knockholt, excluding the security police and guards. This number was projected at the time to reach almost a thousand, so rapid alterations had to be made for improvements to the welfare facilities, lavatories, drainage, etc. There would be a limited amount of air raid damage at Knockholt by the enemy, including a raid on 18–19 December 1943, but not sufficient to stop the base from operating.[41]

The author has knowledge of a close relative of a colleague who worked on the base during wartime, but did not give anything away as to what her duties were. Secrecy was everything during wartime. Many in positions of trust on these and other listening bases would not even tell their families what they did in detail, even after the information was declassified in the 1970s. As D-Day approached, the intercepts at Knockholt became increasingly valuable and important. The specialist codebreaking Newmanry and Testery Sections at Bletchley Park would be working all hours to process the intelligence intercepted from Knockholt and equivalent advanced listening stations, and pass it on to the Chiefs of Staff. A summary would, of course, be provided for Churchill. In all, around 27,631 Tunny, German High Command messages were sent from Knockholt to Bletchley Park for codebreaking. Of these, 13,508 were deciphered successfully, around fifty per cent. Bearing in mind the complex conditions, missing letters in the transmissions, variable weather conditions and radio interference at times, this was considered to be a good success rate. The Ministry of Works thought that the complement of staff at Knockholt would reduce to around five hundred after the war against Germany ended in 1945.[42]

After the war many Y-stations were closed down, demolished or were planned for closure. Those in power had sent memoranda to try to establish which overseas listening stations should be maintained, and to seek views as to the possible threats that might still remain abroad or develop over time.

Königsberg. A German city where High Command 'Fish' encoded-teleprinter communication links were routed through, such as from Ukraine and other countries. Along with Berlin, this would be of great importance for encoded communication. It was bombed heavily by the Allies during the war. It was the most eastern German city at the time and is now part of Russia and named Kaliningrad.

Kursk. British intelligence was passed onto the Russians to help thwart a German surprise attack at Kursk in July 1943. This intelligence was obtained by the interception and decoding of certain Enigma messages at Bletchley Park. This might be seen as a turning point in favour of the Russians against the Nazis, but was not solely due to Bletchley Park. The Russians also had their own sources of intelligence that assisted them greatly. The source of the British-obtained intelligence was not passed on to the Russians, for fear of a security leak back to the enemy. Churchill had concerns in this respect, as did other senior officials.

Lauf, Germany. A key intercept and intelligence station during the war, gathering intelligence from the Poles, Russians and other western allies. It would be led by Wilhelm Flicke, who would go on after the war to write detailed accounts of the procedures and methods that the Nazis used in obtaining and processing intelligence. Most of these would be classified as documents until fairly recently. See also *Wilhelm Flicke*.

Letchworth, Herts. A town of importance, also known as the world's first Garden City (i.e. Letchworth Garden City), valued for its contribution in developing specialist factories, skilled people and other resources to design and build codebreaking equipment, such as the Bombe. The key factory responsible for this was the British Tabulating Machine Company (BTM), which originally specialised in punched-card technology and had links with the Hollerith company in the USA. It licensed their machines across Europe and the British Empire. Several buildings around Letchworth had staff and personnel, both men and women, building the Bombe machines and attachments for them.[43] BTM used a form of modular construction of the machines, using a considerable labour force. The company also took over part of the Spirella corset and ladies' foundation-wear factory due to the need to increase Bombe production. The factories were visited by Alan Turing and Gordon Welchman from Bletchley Park to assess and monitor progress. In 1951, BTM became interested in stored programme digital computers. In 1959, there was a merger between BTM and Powers-Samas Accounting Machines Ltd. The new company would be called International Computers & Tabulators Ltd or ICT. It employed 16,000 people. Over fifty years BTM had built a thriving business using Hollerith tabulating machines. It had over 1,750,000 sq ft of production space.

The BTM building is now gone, but the Spirella building, originally designed by architect Cecil Hignett, underwent a major refurbishment some years ago and is still a fine commercial building, opposite the small police station. It was reopened in the 1990s by HRH the Prince of Wales, now King Charles III. Spirella had a philanthropic ideology, and looked after its staff very well.[44] Today, Letchworth has the Garden City Collection, a museum with many interesting historical artefacts, pictures and books. It has a website and some photos of BTM and other features in Historical Letchworth can be found there. There does not appear to be any commemorative plaque or monument in Letchworth to indicate or inform the public how significant this location was in its support of codebreaking activities. It is hoped this will be rectified at some stage, as without those skilled workers and engineers the outcome of the last war could have been very different.

Lime Grove, Eastcote. An approach road that gave access to Outstation Eastcote during the Second World War and later to GCHQ post-war until the mid-1950s. This road was to the south of the site, giving access to Block A, where the accommodation and administration were established.[45] Codebreaking machines were to the north of the site in a number of connected finger blocks. An assembly block was constructed on the base adjacent to the Lime Grove entrance, part of

Pembroke V, and meetings and training events held there. Today, Lime Grove still exists, and is one of the entrances to the Pembroke Park housing estate, which replaced the base huts some years ago. Lime Grove was used by many personnel both during the last war and post-war, as it was the quickest route to the Eastcote High street, shops, cafes and the railway station. When the site became GCHQ in April 1946, the main access to it would have been via Lime Grove. Local residents around in the late 1940s and early 1950s would have seen a stream of principally civilian men and women making their way up Lime Grove to the security entrance at GCHQ. Even after it was no longer GCHQ, Lime Grove was still a key access route for personnel.

Lisbon, Portugal. One of the bases for Pujol Garcia, an agent for the Nazis and later a double agent for Britain and its allies in a deception plot. Garcia, or agent Garbo, had a false diplomatic passport printed in Lisbon. He would also travel to Madrid and make contacts with the *Abwehr* secret service. When in England acting as a double agent, Garbo would send secret reports in letters using invisible ink to his contact in Lisbon. He would play a significant role in convincing the Germans at D-Day that the main force, the fictitious FUSAG, would come across the Pas-de-Calais led by the American General Patton, and to hold back Panzer divisions in northern France.

While in Lisbon, and before being accepted by the British authorities as a double agent, Garcia would prepare reports for the Nazis by purchasing books and magazines on the British fleet, research in the local library, and make up false reports about shipping movements. Garcia also pretended to be in England, spying on troops and movements of shipping and the armed forces. Eventually, he was accepted by the British as a double agent. His travel arrangements to Britain were complex to avoid detection. Initially he was smuggled on a Spanish ship to Gibraltar, then to flown to Plymouth and met by MI5 officials.

Lithuania. One of the three Baltic states occupied by the Russians, Germans and then again the Russians during the war, but which eventually obtained independence in the 1990s. Lithuania worked closely with Germany up to 1933 to compromise Polish codes and ciphers. Note also that Lithuania's near neighbours, Estonia, and its Estonian Military Intelligence Service, had worked closely with Finland before the war to intercept Russian intelligence. Finland had also worked closely with the Japanese in this respect.

Little Brickhill, Bucks. A manor house became the posting base for the organisation of the American 6813th US Signals detachment, which supported Bletchley Park from 1943 with a complement of specialist signals intelligence army personnel.[46] This would be part of the ETOUSA co-operation agreement between Britain and the USA. The commanding officer based at Little Brickhill was Captain Bundy. This detachment was subordinated to SID Signal section, under the Headquarters European Theater of Operations (i.e. ETOUSA).

London. Early in the twentieth century this was the place of concentration of specialist minds on intelligence and intelligence gathering, which grew into Bletchley Park and GCHQ. Although GCHQ did exist for a time in north-west London, in Eastcote, Middlesex, both Bletchley Park and GCHQ were far outside the capital. However, the links that Bletchley Park had with London just prior to the war commencing and during wartime were very strong. Dollis Hill, near Willesden, had the Post Office Research Establishment that worked closely with Bletchley. The origins of GCHQ were in central London, and Watergate House off the Strand has a commemorative plaque acknowledging this.

Outstations Stanmore and Eastcote on the outskirts of north-west London also supported Bletchley Park with large numbers of codebreaking Bombe machines and Wren personnel. Denmark Hill Y-station, in south London, made an important discovery in non-Morse messages that resulted in a change of tactic and strategy for Bletchley. Knockholt wireless listening station at Ivy Farm in Kent, close to London, would be created as a direct result of the initial work and discoveries made at Denmark Hill. Barnet, on the outskirts of north London, was the Post Office Box location that collected intelligence from authorised radio amateurs listening in over the airwaves for enemy radio transmissions. Mill Hill was an important training base for WRNS recruits, or Wrens, as was Wimbledon in south London. The Cabinet War Rooms both at Westminster and the Paddock at Dollis Hill, were bases for Churchill to make strategic decisions and consult with his military advisers on intelligence. The Rooms (now Churchill Rooms) would also be the base where Churchill would hold secret telephone conversations with President Roosevelt, and later, Truman, using secure transatlantic communication links.

Other London locations included Berkeley Street, used for relocating GC&CS staff to the diplomatic section, and this expanded later to deal with Japanese intercepts and translations, amongst other countries' intelligence. This would house a substantial number of personnel, from administrative to translators and codebreaking, in flats and adjoining properties. Aldford House in Park Lane, where the commercial section was based, also formed part of GC&CS.

London locations would have a significant influence on both the outcome and strategy of the Second World War, using intelligence from a wide range of different sources. St James' Street would contain members of the XX or Twenty Committee, involved in deception tactics and intelligence feedback using double agents and spies. Much of the intelligence would be processed through Bletchley Park, but with telephone and teleprinter links to London, as well as an efficient document courier service on motorcycles.

Central London would incorporate many buildings and sites that were linked to clandestine operations, espionage and intelligence gathering. The Norwegian Branch of SOE planned the famous Telemark raid against the Nazis in a building near Baker Street station. A requisitioned boys' school at Hammersmith in west London was where General Eisenhower, Churchill and King George VI met in May 1944 to approve the final plan for D-Day.

PLACES

Modern London now incorporates the National Cyber Security Centre (NCSC), termed by staff as 'Nova South', in Victoria. This was established in 2016, and works under the umbrella of GCHQ to help defeat cyber-crime, terrorism and threats to the UK. See *Eisenhower*. See *Baker Street*. See *Cabinet War Rooms*. See *GCHQ*.

Loutsa, Greece. A site developed near a village approximately 160 miles northwest of Athens, where in 1941 the Germans set up a major listening station with twenty large reception aerials to cover listening for British and Allied radio traffic around the Mediterranean. The site was geographically perfectly situated for the needs of Captain Ferdinand Feichtner, who spotted it from aerial reconnaissance. The aerials would have direction-finding capabilities.

Malta. The Allied Mediterranean island was heavily bombed during the war, but was never captured by the Axis powers. It had the first Allied radio direction-finding system, and this superseded an obsolete system of acoustic 'mirrors' on the island. The island was awarded the George Cross for its resilience and resistance, maintaining its strategic position in wartime, which was crucial to the Allies. The submarines HMS *Safari*, *Saracen* and *Porpoise* returned to Malta in November 1942 having participated in supporting the build-up of Operation Torch in North Africa, and sinking enemy tankers. Bletchley Park would monitor the Enigma traffic intercepts relevant to Operation Torch, obtaining valuable intelligence for the Allies.

Malvern, Worcestershire. A radar research base known as the *Telecommunications Research Establishment* (TRE). Originally in Dorset, it relocated during the war due to fears of it being targeted by Luftwaffe attacks on the south coast, following a raid in France to capture a *Würzburg* German radar and its operator. Churchill insisted upon TRE being relocated inland when he was advised of the risk of attack at the coast. The War Cabinet prevaricated until they found a suitable location. It was to be either Marlborough College, or alternatively Malvern College for the relocation. A boys' school, Malvern College was eventually taken over, the site established and expanded exponentially over several years. The personnel included engineers, scientists, physicists and many support personnel. It grew into a huge base over time, and developed many important components and pieces of equipment, including complex components for the Robinson advanced codebreaking machine, and possibly even some component parts for the Colossus. Sir Bernard Lovell worked there during the war before he went into astronomy and moved to Jodrell Bank. The Ministry of Aircraft Production Research Establishment was already in Malvern, using it for signals training, so it made some sense moving there, even though the education of many boys at the school would be disrupted as they had to leave. The geographical location was also perfect as high hills were needed to experiment with radar and radio-based systems.

The locals wondered why there were so many men around the base and in the town, when they should perhaps be fighting the Germans and Italians in the armed services. This was a difficult dilemma, as the systems developed at TRE would go on to save many Allied lives and help shorten the war. The public would not have been aware of this due to TRE's secrecy. 'Window' or 'Chaff', was developed there by Joan Curran, using lengths of aluminium foil to confuse enemy radar when dropped by planes from height. Other radar-based systems were developed for the RAF, helping bombers find their way along transmitted electronic guide routes. The King and Queen went to TRE during the war in 1944 on a morale-boosting visit

The disruption to the boys' school and college was considerable, as they moved to Blenheim and later to Harrow school, sharing certain facilities and not initially being welcomed by the Harrovians, who generally considered it a bit of an imposition. Things improved over time. Measures were taken to ensure separation of the pupils and staff as far as possible. There was cooperation between the two schools, but traditions would be maintained wherever possible to maintain identity across both schools. After the war ended, when the Ministry had agreed to move TRE out within a year of the cessation of hostilities, they overstayed their welcome, and the matter was raised in the Commons to encourage TRE to move out to other premises and allow Malvern College to get back to normal.[47]

Numerous inventions, systems, and equipment came out of TRE in the war years. Many of the scientists and engineers went on to significant careers elsewhere. One of the most influential developments at TRE was centimetric radar, or centimetre waveband techniques. The development of this actually took place in the school house on the site. This would crush the U-boat threat much more significantly than Bletchley Park's interception and decoding of enemy messages. It was a game-changer, much needed, and welcomed by Churchill.

TRE was claimed to be the largest electronics factory in Europe during the war. Who would have thought that the work done on atomic systems at TRE in 1946 would lead to the development of the Large Hadron Collider? Few have heard of TRE, and it is one of the most underrated and least publicised sites and organisations, in the author's opinion.

In July 2000 the organisation was generally split into QinetiQ, a private company, and the Government Defence Science & Technology Laboratory (DSTL). Previously part of DERA, or the Defence Evaluation and Research Agency, QinetiQ has had great success with the invention and development of technical solutions for the military, aerospace, security and associated sectors. The author had a small connection with QinetiQ in his career, and many years ago frequently visited a QinetiQ site in Farnborough, where support staff worked. QinetiQ was floated on the London stock exchange in 2006, but DSTL remains under Government ownership. See also *Harrow School*.

Marston Montgomery, Derbyshire. A listening Y-station with wooden huts and operated between 1941 to 1947. It had 100 staff that listened to twenty-five radio signals, searching to locate and identify the enemy.

Mediterranean. A vicious battleground in the Second World War, with many convoys transporting men, armaments, fuel, materials and food across it. The

PLACES

Germans in North Africa relied upon the Mediterranean for a robust supply route and both sides lost many ships due to attacks from the air and submarines. Islands such as Malta were heavily exposed to attack and suffered greatly, but managed to survive and resisted occupation by the Nazis.

Gibraltar was an important British and Allied base near Spain, monitoring the movements of shipping. There were several deception plans used to fool the enemy into believing attacks would come from somewhere else, such as a plan to deceive the Nazis that Greece and its islands were of great interest to the Allies, whereas Sicily was really the objective. The use of intercepted encoded messages played its part in the plan. This saved many Allied lives due to relocation of enemy forces that most likely weakened the defence of Sicily.

The Mediterranean was the key to the Allied assault on Sicily and then to the Italian mainland, to penetrate the Axis powers. Both the Allies and the Axis powers realised that whosoever controlled the Mediterranean had a major strategic advantage in arranging supplies for their armed forces and in planning major assaults on occupied territory. In May 1941, the Western Mediterranean force of Admiral Sommerville, assisted in the closing in on the German battleship *Bismarck*, resulting in the elimination of one of the most important Axis ships by the British Admiralty.[48]

Mill Hill, London. A key training base for new Wrens was established here during wartime. Training lasted two or three weeks in basic naval discipline, including some Morse code work, a lot of cleaning, scrubbing of steps and floors and polishing. After the training, Wrens were tested for their knowledge and passed out on parade, known as Divisions, to be sent to various locations, usually onshore naval bases. Some would be selected for their aptitude and ability, to be sent to *Pembroke V*, Special Duties X sites, which included Bletchley Park and its five codebreaking outstations. There were other training sites at Wimbledon and in Scotland. Many Wrens have written accounts of their experiences through training and when posted to carry out codebreaking or support activities. However, they were unable to talk of this until the secret bases and systems were declassified in the 1970s. Some went to their graves without speaking of what they did, and most of their parents never knew what they got up to as Wrens in wartime, particularly if engaged on Special X duties. Some reports indicated that Mill Hill was named *Pembroke III* for naval administrative purposes.

Nearby, Mill Hill Barracks was home to the Royal Electrical and Mechanical Engineers (REME) in 1943. The site was used for postal training services in the 1950s, then redeveloped and the new Inglis Barracks were the target of an IRA bombing attack in 1989, with the death of a lance corporal Royal Engineer and injuries to nine other military personnel.[49] Mill Hill is approximately four miles from Dollis Hill, which was an important centre for research and development of codebreaking machines by the Post Office Research Engineering Station. See *Pembroke V* and *Dollis Hill*.

Midway Island, Pacific Ocean. The Americans had lost heavily at Pearl Harbor, but codebreakers would help in turning the tide in the Pacific against the Japanese

Navy in June 1942 at Midway. The Japanese Operational Naval code JN25, was complex and involved syllabic writing or 'KANA' in their code. Latin letters were used in a substitution to make sending the code practically possible. A five-digit code number in a message was modified by adding a different five-digit number from a cipher table, and that had around 100,000 permutations and combinations. The sender would transmit those messages with a numerical Key, which would then indicate the location and position of the cipher numbers from a table. An American naval intelligence unit, Hypo, (Project Hypo), was established based at Pearl Harbor with Captain Joseph Rochefort in charge and acquiring a cryptoanalyst, Elvin Urquhart, to assist in the codebreaking team. They worked night and day on the Japanese codes, using some trial and error to guess the word for 'ship', and other military words of interest. Another significant codebreaker was Commander Thomas H.Dyer, who was brought into the codebreaking team to work alongside Rochefort.

A mistake by the Japanese meant they delayed changing their codes on 1 May 1942, which gave the codebreakers an opportunity. A false message was broadcast by the Americans about Midway Island to state that they were running low on fresh water, which was not actually the case, but a deception, looking for a response. The Japanese transmitted then a coded message reporting this and inserted the letters 'AF' which the Americans realised was their code for 'Midway Island'. The Project Hypo team managed to read around one third of the JN25 code by April 1942 and with perseverance broke into more enemy messages over the next few weeks. They had eventually established the intentions of the Japanese, indicating that Midway was planned for attack, and even the date and time of the attack. The trap would be set to attack the Japanese when they were close to Midway Island by the American carriers, but the input of spotter planes was crucial, to identify the exact location of the Japanese fleet. Whilst Midway island was attacked heavily by Japanese planes, they managed to resist the force, and maintained occupation of the island, long enough for the American fleet to attack Yamamoto's carriers and battleships, which caught them by complete surprise. The value of codebreaking in the build up to the event was a key factor in favour of the Americans. See *United States of America*.

Murray Hill, New Jersey. Bell Telephone Laboratories was a centre for innovation before, during, and after the Second World War. There would be several sites over the years and many of them in, and around New Jersey. The original Bell Telephone Company was formed in 1877. In the early years, it designed and invented equipment and systems for the recording and record industry as well as movie equipment. It established extensive tests with stereophonic sound and full orchestras. Its roots were formed from AT&T and Western Electric in the early years, and telephone technology was the driving force for the company. The resources would develop further into acoustics, magnetics, radar and cryptography, In wartime, Bell Laboratories initially designed and then Western Electric built the voice-encoding system for transatlantic use, known as SIGSALY. This was used by Churchill and two American Presidents to communicate across the Atlantic and discuss strategy regarding progress in the war. Bell Laboratories built an initial prototype of the system. It was a highly complex system with twelve units made in total, and London received the second machine built, which was eventually installed within the basement of an annex to Selfridges, the famous Oxford Street department store.[50] The company would recover the equipment at Selfridges in London at the end of October 1945, after the war had ended. It would remain top secret for decades afterwards. The Nazis were unable to break into SIGSALY and it remained one of the true secret voice encoding/decoding systems in wartime. It involved using rotating recorded shellac discs, and record players of a special type, which had to be in complete synchrony on both sides of the Atlantic to work. Given the time differences across the 'Pond', it is truly incredible that the system operated exactly as designed. Other Allied scrambler telephones and systems were not as effective or secure.

Alan Turing visited Bell Laboratories while in the USA during the war, and made some suggestions to the designers. It is unclear whether those proposals and suggestions were taken on board. Work by Bell Laboratories in 1937 on speech vocoders, i.e. speech synthesis, may have given them a head start in developing SIGSALY. It used an advanced system known as pulse code modulation, or PCM. With a broad base of innovation as far back as the 1920s, a one-time pad cipher was developed at Bell, tested and confirmed as an unbreakable code.

Bell Laboratories also contributed to sonic deception techniques for the American 'ghost army' during the war, developing a non-Doppler acoustic audio that would be non-directional when transmitted at the enemy through large horn-loaded audio loudspeakers. This was technically important to make the noises and sounds projected through speakers sound realistic and not phased, which would otherwise have varied the sound in an unnatural way. Deception of the enemy was therefore more likely to succeed with the technical changes introduced by Bell Laboratories. Douglas Fairbanks Jr would take an interest in this work, and be actively involved in training strategies for the specialists, many of whom would be recruited from the film industry and supporting trades and professions.

In the early post-war period Bell came up with important developments such as the invention of transistors and charged coupled devices (CCDs). The 1947 invention of modern transistors by three Bell electronics engineers was probably the most significant invention of all though, and won them a Nobel Prize. In 1949 Claude Shannon at Bell had a paper published titled 'Communication Theory of Secrecy Systems'. This was, arguably, the basis of modern cryptography techniques.

When the Cabinet War Rooms in central London were being prepared for public use as a museum, Nokia Bell Laboratories would provide advice to the Imperial War Museum on the telephone set that Churchill used during wartime. Today, with various acquisitions and modernisation there are two principal arms to Bell Labs: Bell Labs Core Research and Bell Labs Solutions Research. The company developed the first lasers among many other significant technical achievements. See *Turing*; See *Selfridges*; See *Cabinet War Rooms*; See *Churchill*.

WW2 CODEBREAKING PEOPLE AND PLACES

National Physical Laboratory – Teddington. See *Teddington*.

New York. The base for Western Electric, which built twelve SIGSALY voice-encryption machines for the US, allocating the second machine to London, for the use of Churchill. This was for secure transatlantic telephone calls between Churchill and President Roosevelt, and later with President Truman. General Eisenhower also used the system. Bell Telephone Labs had developed the prototype SIGSALY. There were close contractual and company links between Bell Telephone Laboratories and Western Electric, which had bases in New York and Chicago. Prior to using SIGSALY, the A-3 voice scrambler developed by Western Electric was used, but was relatively insecure. The German Post Office had been able to infiltrate A3-based Allied transatlantic messages. See *Selfridges*.

New Zealand. Wrens in listening stations in New Zealand pioneered the technique of 'radio-fingerprinting', which helped identify the users and the sets of enemy Morse code operators. This became crucial in the fight against Japanese submarines communicating with their bases, and other submarines nearby. It was one thing identifying the type of transmitter, but another to focus on the transmitter itself, proving extremely useful for the military commanders of the Allies. Communication with the Royal New Zealand Navy, once the intelligence had been intercepted and decoded, would enable co-ordinated naval attacks in the correct locations against the enemy submarines. A bonus was the capture of a large quantity of Japanese code books, seen as the equivalent of gold dust, and a real prize for the cryptographers working to break into Japanese encryption systems and 'Purple'. New Zealand would establish a Combined Intelligence Bureau and Central War Room in Wellington. It would share and exchange intelligence information with FECB in Singapore.

Noordwijk, Netherlands. A town where the Nazis installed a listening station and decoded transatlantic phone calls between Churchill and President Roosevelt, initially in 1940 and 1941. The intelligence gained by the Nazis was of limited use at the time, as the Allies knew their system was not completely secure, so the conversations would be cautious. Eventually, a new voice-encryption system, SIGSALY, was developed by Bell Laboratories in the USA, and installed in several locations, including in London, operated by a team of US Signals engineers. There would be communication terminals in Downing Street, the Cabinet War Rooms, and at the American Embassy in London. Tests of the use of listening devices and associated research using aircraft occurred around Noordwijk and surrounding areas from 1936, some systems using UHF. Microwave technology was also considered for communication. Today, Noordwijk is the Headquarters of the European Space and Technology Research Centre (ESTEC). This forms part of the European Space Agency (ESA). See *Selfridges*.

Normandy. The French province and battle zone for the D-Day landings by the Allies in June 1944. Normandy was the starting point for the invasion and the eventual defeat of the Nazis. It was to form part of Operation Fortitude South to deceive the Nazis as to the significance of an invasion in Normandy, being sold as a diversionary tactic, where the main, principal assault would eventually come over the Pas-de-Calais in northern France. This tactic appeared to be successful, even beyond British and Allied expectations, but many brave troops were lost on D-Day and afterwards in the drive across France and Europe to Germany. However, the deception bought useful time for the Allies, and held back certain German Panzer divisions, awaiting an attack at Calais that would never come. The history of the Allied assault on D-Day is well documented elsewhere. Occupying the town of Caen, and in moving across to occupy Cherbourg, the major port further south, took considerable time. The main difficulty for the Allies, apart from getting off the Normandy beaches and being resupplied via numerous ships via special floating docks and pontoons, were the Nazi defences in the difficult hedged, bocage country, which was slow to penetrate.

Listening stations would be established on D-Day and afterwards, near the beaches and inland, to identify German troop and tank movements where possible. Not easy when one is constantly under fire from the enemy. Tactical intelligence would become almost as important as intercepting strategic intelligence in making real progress. The advantage for the enemy using Enigma machines was that they were portable pieces of equipment, contained in a wooden case. They could be easily set up and a team established to encode a message and send it via Morse code over the radio. However, it was not very practical for there to be only one person operating it and sending the Morse code as it would have slowed things down considerably. A two or three-man team was required to use Enigma effectively. Mistakes and errors could be made in sending the message or recording the received Morse code from another Enigma station. The advanced decoding machines back at Bletchley Park also helped decode the intercepted Tunny 'Fish' communication-linked enemy messages.

The work of those involved in the deception of the enemy prior to D-Day saved time and countless lives. It would be a combination of double agents, codebreaking at Bletchley Park and outstations that would give the Allied commanders sufficient and valuable enemy intelligence essential in moving forward with the D-Day plan, Overlord, to make it happen on 6 June 1944. In Normandy, the German signals engineers intercepted Allied signals intelligence, but were not equipped to do anything constructive with it. Even discovering American code books for use with Hagelin coding machines on abandoned landing craft near Omaha beach, the Germans failed to capitalise on this information, as they had insufficient mobile armoured resources to repel the Americans in the area. Hagelin machines were used by the Americans for enciphered communication, but the deception plan Fortitude South, plus the scale of the invasion, overwhelmed the enemy at a crucial time.

North Atlantic. The battleground between Allied convoys of shipping and Nazi U-boats, which relied heavily on Enigma intelligence transmissions to pinpoint the locations of their targets. Naval Enigmas tended to be more secure four-wheel Enigma machines, that is with four rotors instead of three. This increased the permutations for the settings considerably and improved security. The additional wheel could be set to any one of twenty-six positions based on a code book supplied to the captains and commanders. The fourth wheel was not interchangeable with the other rotors and had to be set manually. The U-boat commanders referred to the early years of the war as 'the Happy Time', when the loss of merchant and naval Allied shipping was substantial, and was gradually sinking cargoes of coal, fuel, vehicles, armaments, food and materials. Britain was being cut off from its supplies and suffering greatly as a result. The USA also suffered losses on the North Atlantic.

Bletchley Park had a name for the Nazi Enigma intelligence in this area, 'Shark', based upon the Nazi Triton Atlantic net. At one time during the war there would be a nine-month period when Bletchley codebreakers could not break the Enigma code settings, and losses in the Atlantic were huge. The turning point came through improved systems at Bletchley Park, and perseverance in attacking Enigma. Also, the centimetric radar developed by TRE in Malvern, the radar research base, made it much easier to detect Nazi U-boats and sink them. Arguably, the new radar had a bigger impact on U-boat losses than even the Bletchley Park intelligence. In an eight-month period in 1942, over 4 million tons of ships were sunk to the bottom of the Atlantic by U-boats. That was at an average rate of half a million tons per month. If this rate had continued Britain would have been starved to death and fuel supplies would have dried up almost completely, apart from coal in British mines.[51]

The German battleship *Bismarck* was pursued by the Royal Navy across the waters close to Greenland and Iceland, along the Denmark Straits, then south into the Atlantic, and was eventually sunk by three British warships on 27 May 1941, some 400 miles west of the French port of Brest. It had been sighted by a Coastal Command aircraft at 10.30am on 26 May and it was able to direct Navy ships to intercept it. Intelligence to locate and corner the battleship was crucial in the final decisive attack on the ship. The loss of *Bismarck* was a significant blow to the German Navy, although their U-boats remained active in the area and the nearby Mediterranean for some considerable time, creating havoc among Allied shipping and convoys.[52] The Dutch-designed snorkel applied to U-boats in 1943 enabled them to stay underwater for very long periods. Bletchley Park's priority was to decode naval Enigma transmissions, but this became difficult with the Nazis adding a fourth rotor wheel to a special version of Enigma.

North Sea. Part of the Second World War battleground for naval action, U-boat activities, and listening for Morse code intercepts from Y-stations particularly around the east coast of both England and Scotland. The gradual decline of U-boats in the North Sea area began around July 1943 to May 1944, and came with a retreat to Europe.[53] A list of various Y-stations is provided in an appendix to this volume.

Northwood Hills. Part of the north-west London suburb of Hillingdon, secret operations were carried out in Northwood Hills to support GCHQ Eastcote here, and after GCHQ went to Cheltenham there were still several years of support from this base. The activities ceased in 1978, and the unit was named the Services

PLACES

Communications Development Unit (SCDU).[54] Rented offices were at the junction of Chamberlain Way and Tolcarne Drive. There is now residential housing on the site where the secret rented offices were located. Those offices were only a mile or two north from GCHQ Eastcote.

Norway. Occupied by the Nazis in 1940, a substantial part of the German armed forces were located in the Scandinavian country for the duration of the war. This was partly due to the geographical and strategic position of the country, as well as resources such as timber and minerals. Operation Fortitude North would help to deceive the enemy in believing the Allies would be mounting a major assault across the North Sea to attack the forces in Norway. This plan appeared to work as intended and ensured many Panzer divisions were kept locked up, awaiting an assault that never came. The Allied advance following D-Day consequently had fewer troops to battle against, and fewer casualties than might have been the case if those Panzer divisions had been transferred to Normandy and France.

Daring SOE raids would occur in Norway, the most famous arguably being the Telemark raid on the heavy water plant.[55] These raids would be planned by the Norwegian division of SOE in London and take several sorties to achieve their goal of destruction of the factory and bombing of the ferry carrying valuable heavy water supplies across a lake adjacent to the factory. Accurate and timely intelligence would be essential before such raids could be given any chance of success. Wireless operators would work long hours on the mainland and on shipping to gather all the relevant information from the enemy and advise of the distribution of enemy troops. The Germans would use direction-finding mobile units to detect enemy soldiers, foreign agents and those dropped by parachute into the country by the Allies.

OSA Outstation Adstock. A country house estate near Bletchley Park used as a codebreaking outstation during the war. O.S.A. opened in March 1941. It was run by a complement of Wrens, who were billeted on site and operated a small number of Bombes to break enemy message settings of encoded Nazi messages. After a few years it closed down as an outstation and machines were transferred to other sites, such as Outstation Stanmore and Outstation Eastcote. It had five machines, but a number of additional Bombes passed through the doors before they went elsewhere. Some stables were used to house the machines, and the floor would have been damp and wet, which was a potential risk of electrocution for the female Bombe operators. There is evidence to suggest rubber mats were provided in some locations for people to stand on. The country house outstations were run on a slightly less formal basis compared with larger outstations at Stanmore and Eastcote, but naval routines and associated terminology were adopted at all five.

OSE Outstation Eastcote, Middlesex. The largest of five codebreaking outstations housing Bombes in Great Britain during the war. It was established in late 1943, known as *Pembroke V*, Outstation Eastcote, being the very last of the five outstations, and following Outstation Stanmore.[56] The outstations were largely operated by Wrens, who set up the machines, ran 'Menus' of instructions issued to them from Bletchley Park, and fed back the settings of the machine output for further processing at HQ. More than 800 Wrens operated the Bombes over three eight-hour shifts, day and night, and 365 days a year.[57] At the end of the war there were 103 Bombe machines on site. Many had to be modified, repaired, improved and updated, and major repairs were either carried out by Post Office engineers or RAF engineers. Alternatively, they were sent back to BTM at Letchworth.

Eastcote also accepted the training of a number of US Signals personnel, being the 6812th Signals, and they were allocated ten Bombe machines, with names such as Houston, Atlanta, Omaha, New York and other American cities. The introduction of American personnel to help Britain with the war effort was based on the ETOUSA agreement between USA and Britain. The Americans were very successful at processing Enigma Menus and determining settings for Enigma to be analysed further by Bletchley Park. They were trained by Wrens initially but had to live in tents in Ruislip Woods as management would not permit them to be billeted on site with the large number of Wrens. Outstation Eastcote was originally allocated as a military hospital for use on D-Day, but that was not to be and huts were built and modified with fingers to the long blocks, housing eight to ten Bombe codebreaking machines in each 'finger' or wing.

The Wrens on site effectively became data processors and very few would have even heard of Enigma, or the significance of what they were achieving working on the Bombes to find the Enigma settings. They would never see the final enemy messages, as their chief role was to assist Bletchley Park along with the other codebreaking outstations to establish the settings for a particular Enigma machine or machines. Promotion opportunities would be limited.

The Wrens initially required Menus of instructions, issued by Bletchley Park before the Bombes could be set up. These appeared strange to an outsider and had various graphical lines joining letters together forming links, based on clues that had been established by the mathematicians. The work would be tedious, boring, hot and stuffy, with very limited small high-level windows and ventilation. Noise levels in the Bombe rooms would be almost unbearable at times until one got used to it. Bombe wheel rotors would be positioned and aligned on the Bombes by the Wrens and wires plugged into sockets in the rear. Then one would have to wait for the machine to eliminate the many hundreds of thousands and millions of message settings by the wheels rotating on the front. All the machines were built by a factory in Letchworth and transported to Bletchley Park and the five outstations. Around seventy-two Wrens would sleep in berths (thirty-six two-tiered bunk beds) in a room that would be named after a famous battleship or naval ship. This would be in Block 'A', being the administrative, galley, stores, and sleeping quarters on the south part of the base. Large brick blast walls would be around the huts. RAF engineers would carry out maintenance on the Bombes. The Official Secrets Act would be signed upon arriving at a codebreaking base, and there were severe penalties for breaching it.

PLACES

The outstation at Eastcote was split into two parts by an existing public footpath going back to the sixteenth century. On the north part of the site were the codebreaking machines, and on the south side were barracks, sleeping accommodation, canteen, stores, equipment, first aid and miscellaneous offices. There was also, later on, a community building for dances and talks and training events, called the assembly block. Some social events occurred in non-shift time, including hockey teams with RAF personnel. This was a mixed team, which was quite unusual for the time.[58]

Special ancillary equipment would be brought into some outstations such as Eastcote, to make the Bombe machines faster and more efficient. The Cobra attachment had a bund wall surrounding it to contain any oil spillages. It was particularly noisy, dusty, and probably annoying and frustrating for the operators, such as the Wrens.

The site ceased operating as an outstation after the war, and was transformed into GCHQ on 1 April 1946, with a bank account set up in Eastcote by a Barclays Bank at the crossroads, now a coffee shop.[59] It gradually relocated GCHQ to Cheltenham between 1952 and 1954, where it remains now in the famous 'doughnut' modern building. In 1966–68 various local maps and descriptions indicate that some phase of refurbishment took place on the buildings. There would be multiple uses of the site, including: Joint Speech Research Department (JSRU); an American servicemen's children's school; a psychiatric health clinic; a zoological veterinary practice; a mortuary; rationing administration; census office; London Communications Electronics Security Agency (renamed Communications Electronics Security Department); PSA Government property management; GPO parcels logistics testing facility; and American Embassy marines security personnel.

Two of the last Colossus computers came to Eastcote after the remainder were destroyed at Bletchley Park on Churchill's instructions.[60] These were named Red and Blue, and it is not fully known what use was made of them while they were there. Some reports indicate that the Post Office parcels logistics department experimented with using Colossus for parcel movements programming, but that is unconfirmed. Eventually the two Colossus were moved to the new GCHQ in Cheltenham, where they stayed until the 1960s and were then dismantled. Around sixteen Bombes were operational at Eastcote after the war, salvaged just in time from Churchill's instructions to destroy them, and it is thought that some were used to decipher encoded radio messages from Europe, to listen out for possible splinter Nazi groups who may have wished to have a resurgence of National Socialism and follow Hitler's ideals. Eventually, the Bombes were dismantled or destroyed over time.

The Eastcote site was sold off for housing in 2007, and an estate was constructed soon after, with demolition of the old buildings taking place in 2007–08. Susan Toms of the Ruislip Eastcote and Northwood History Society has produced several papers and articles on Outstation Eastcote, and some are available in the society's archives online.

A commemorative plaque was placed at one of the entrances to the housing estate in 2014, and a small ceremony was held with representatives of the RAF and the Mayor of Hillingdon present. The plaque identifies the history of the site as a codebreaking outstation and as *Pembroke V*, and later as GCHQ post-war. The plaque states 110 Bombes were on site, but in fact after the war ended 103 Bombes were present based upon the official records held at the National Archives. *Pembroke V* was the administrative term for the group of stations that dealt with Special Duties X codebreaking support activities.[61] The plaque is partially concealed behind a railing, and few locals know it is even there. The author has given many talks and lectures on Outstation Eastcote for some years, to history societies, museums, universities, WIs and other organisations.

The key factors that separate Outstation Eastcote from other outstations during the war are that firstly it was the largest codebreaking outstation, with over 800 Wrens on shift duty, operating the Bombe machines. Secondly, it became GCHQ after the war, taking the name that was occasionally used at Bletchley Park previously. Churchill would have been on his honeymoon at Highgrove House in 1908, only a few yards away across a public footpath from the fields that were later to be the site of Outstation Eastcote.[62]

OSG Outstation Gayhurst. A country house estate near Bletchley Park used as a codebreaking outstation during the war. Gayhurst opened in September 1942, and was the third country house-based codebreaking support outstation, after Wavendon and Adstock. By the end of 1941 it would have five machines. It was run by a complement of Wrens, who were billeted on site and operated Bombes. Together with Outstation Wavendon, it would have several of the nineteen codebreaking Bombes in total, and an additional number went to other sites.

OSS Outstation Stanmore. The fourth codebreaking outstation to house Bombes and one of the largest sites supporting Bletchley Park, not far from the railway station in Stanmore and at a crossroads. It was approved to be situated at Canon's Corner in July 1942, and was fitted out with machine shops among other equipment.[63] The base was run by Wrens, who set up and operated the equipment. It was not far from Bentley Priory, the Fighter Command base to the west of Stanmore. On 26 October 1942 a letter with their 'Lordships' Approval' confirmed the administrative and associated personnel and staff for Outstation Stanmore as another codebreaking base, having dismissed Stowe School as an option. As some of the earlier codebreaking outstations closed or wound down, many machines were sent and transferred to Outstation Stanmore. With Bombes requiring modification, maintenance, updating, improvement and repairs, there were many machines being sent back and forth to the factory in Letchworth, and some were sent on to Outstation Eastcote as the war progressed and when OSE was later established.

Approximately 629 Wrens and 57 RAF mechanics would keep Stanmore operational during wartime, operating and maintaining the Bombes. The Official Secrets Act would have had to be signed by those working there. Equipment was delivered to the site in an unmarked lorry, and unloaded with an inbuilt crane on the rear. A cover story had to be created by management to deceive the public as to

PLACES

what the purpose of the Stanmore site was, bearing in mind there were many female personnel there. The official line was that the base was for confidential clerical work and administration duties, run by the Wrens. The cover story was produced on 21 October 1942 confirming the confidential work. Travis at Bletchley Park agreed, and so the background was set. The structure of the base had Wrens to operate the machines, others as cooks and kitchen staff, administrators, officers, as well as some RAF staff, maintenance personnel and armed guards from the Royal Marines

In the early years there has been found references to Stanmore as being called *Pembroke III*. However, this was changed so they fell in line with all the other outstations in becoming part of *Pembroke V*. There may have been accounting duties at Stanmore while it was designated *Pembroke III*, as other Pembrokes in Chatham, Kent, had accounting roles at onshore Navy stations.

Some publications state there were forty-nine operational Bombes at Stanmore, however, the author's investigation of the Bombe registers indicates that at the end of the war there were seventy-nine. As many as eighty-one machines passed through the doors there. Allowing for the total of 211 Bombes, 38 per cent of these were at Stanmore at some point. Some were sent on elsewhere such as Eastcote. Bombes had numbers as well as names and sometimes the names were changed, as can be tracked in the official register. One report indicated that in 1943 there were eight long rooms with ten Bombes in each room. A petty officer Wren would usually be in charge of up to ten machines, with assistants.

A V1 German flying bomb hit the outer walls on 18 March 1944, but fortunately none of the huts or equipment were damaged. This bombing would not have been targeted at the base.

After the war ended the site closed and the machines were dismantled and destroyed, although some parts may have been used as components for other equipment, and some parts might have been sent to specific universities for constructing early computers. Some Wrens wrote accounts of dismantling Bombes and playing skittles with the rotor wheels. Photos exist of parade, or Divisions, being held outside the huts at Stanmore.

A modern housing development is now situated on the site. As far as is known, there is no commemorative plaque such as is displayed at Eastcote.

OSW, Outstation Wavendon. A country house estate near Bletchley Park used as an outstation during the war. It opened in March 1941 and the first Bombe was installed there, named 'Victory'. It was run by a complement of Wrens, who were billeted on site and operated a number of Bombes. The huts with the machines had some automatic typewriters to print the machine 'stops'. It was closed down in January 1944 after Stanmore and Eastcote came on board, and around fourteen machines transferred, but it had up to nineteen when it was operational. The machines were installed in brick-built huts on the estate, similar to those at Gayhurst.

Outstations in England. Five codebreaking outstations existed during the last war, to support Bletchley Park. These were largely under the administration of the

Foreign Office. They would be at Adstock, Gayhurst, Wavendon, Stanmore and Eastcote. The last would become the largest outstation run by Wrens, and was not commissioned until September 1943. The sites were all part of *Pembroke V*, the Special X Duties section allocated from the Royal Navy to help support Bletchley Park. The largest outstation at Eastcote would become GCHQ after the war.[64] See *Outstations Adstock, Gayhurst, Wavendon, Stanmore, Eastcote.*

Paddock. See Dollis Hill.

Palmer Street, London. The headquarters in 1969 for the London Communications Security Agency (LCSA). This was at 8 Palmer Street, SW1. It was first established in 1953 and handled confidential paperwork by a number of discrete personnel teams. It was situated near St James's Park tube station. It would become a SIGINT co-ordination centre for Britain in 1953, known as Station UKC1000. Radio transmissions, telexes and telecommunications were routed through this site, including from British embassies around the world. BT staff were vetted for security in order to operate the equipment.

Paris. The French Resistance was active in and around the occupied French capital assisting Allied pilots who had been shot down and helping escaping prisoners of war. Radio messages sent by London via the BBC would be listened to in occupied countries and have coded phrases, giving information about something about to occur, or requesting assistance. Messages sent back to England would be risky, as the penalty was death by the Gestapo or SS. Y-stations in Britain would listen for these messages, as would Volunteer Interceptors if authorised to do so. It was critical that the Berlin–Paris German High Command communications link was intercepted through specialist listening stations, such as Knockholt in Kent. It was code-named 'Jellyfish', and would even influence the outcome on D-Day in June 1944 in helping to establish the strategic planning of the Nazis in France, the order of battle, and orders from Berlin to Field Marshal von Rundstedt.

South of Paris was the St Assise radio transmitter. This was previously the central communications link for the French Colonial Office. It had eleven pylons and five masts, providing an enormous aerial array. The transmitter would be extremely powerful and have a vast range. The Nazis would use this for transmission of instructions to U-boats in the Atlantic. Admiral Dönitz would be in regular contact with his U-boats via his officers, and both transmissions and responses were encoded via Enigma. The M4 Enigma was used with four rotor wheels for improved security over the three-wheel versions. The orders to U-boats were usually tested on another Enigma machine prior to it being transmitted. This was a type of quality check to ensure no problems would occur in the decoding of the orders and message. There was a link between L'orient in France and then the more powerful transmissions from St Assise. Lorient was also used for communications.

Pas-de-Calais. An area of land within the Hauts-de-France region and close to Calais in northern France. This is situated near the Straits of Dover, the narrowest

PLACES

part of the Channel for a crossing. It was significant as this was the area and the route from Kent that the Nazis and Hitler expected the Allies to use for their mass landings in France during the invasion., The Germans heavily fortified the Pas-de-Calais and northern France in preparation. However, a cunning deception plan fooled the Germans into expecting a larger, main force to come over from Kent and East Anglia, the First US Army Group (FUSAG), and this pretended that the Normandy landings were a smaller, diversionary force. The feedback of German communications from the deception was intercepted by listening stations and agents, to be decoded via codebreaking machines at Bletchley Park and the outstations. See *Operation Bodyguard*. See *Garcia* and *Garbo*.

Pearl Harbor, Oahu, Hawaii. The site of the surprise attack by the Japanese Navy on 7 December 1941, using planes from aircraft carriers to torpedo and bomb American warships at dock. The attack brought America into the war. Coded Japanese messages in several separate parts were being intercepted by the American intelligence services prior to the attack, however the last part was deciphered too late. A warning radar on part of the island by the coast detected some unusual activity on the screens on the morning of the attack, but when phoned through to the command post this was ignored. The Americans had the Naval Combat Intelligence Unit on the island at its Navy base, termed Station 'Hypo' or COM 14. Japanese Code JN 25 was eventually cracked by a combination of the Americans, those in the Philippines and the British through FECB.

The attack was considered a major victory by Japan to neutralise the US Navy in the Pacific during, allowing it to occupy many islands and occupy much territory unimpeded. However, the US recovered and pursued the Japanese, finally dropping two atomic bombs on Hiroshima and Nagasaki, ending the war and obtaining the Japanese surrender in 1945.

Pearl Harbor contains a memorial to all that lost their lives during the attack and is positioned at right angles over the sunken battleship *Arizona*, which is a war grave, only a few feet below the surface. Many of the tourist visitors to Pearl Harbor are Japanese.

Pembroke V. This was really an umbrella administrative name for certain specialist Royal Navy onshore bases where WRNS personnel worked to collectively bring together Special Duties X activities for codebreaking and support. More accurately, it would be formed across a number of individually separate land bases, and prefixed HMS, i.e. HMS *Pembroke V*. It was the administrative name given to outstations such as Eastcote and Stanmore, and the three country houses that hosted a substantial quantity of Bombe codebreaking machines.[65] *Pembroke V* would have been listed alongside certain outstations as a naval requirement for identification linked to intelligence administration. Note that at one time, Stanmore was once designated as *Pembroke III*, until it fell in line with the others as *Pembroke V*, and that was probably because of the accounting activities that occurred there before it became a codebreaking (machine) outstation.

Even Bletchley Park could be referred to as part of HMS *Pembroke V*, where Wrens would be allocated on Special Duties X.[66] Papers indicated that WRNS personnel were to officially cease referring to Bletchley Park as Station X from November 1942, and to call it HMS *Pembroke V*.[67] This was confusing, as other sites also were similarly named. If posted to a base designated HMS *Pembroke V*, the Wren would need to also know the location of the posting allocated to her, and this information would be typed alongside on her paperwork. Wrens would be specially selected at the end of their training course based upon their aptitude and performance for Special X duties at *Pembroke V* sites. The general public would have no idea of the significance of this designation, nor of the meaning of Special Duties X. Note that there were other Pembrokes, such as *Pembroke III*, which were mainly accounting bases. Chatham was one such *Pembroke III* for WRNS personnel. One report indicates that Mill Hill, a training establishment in north London for Wrens, was also termed *Pembroke III*.

Poland. The invasion in 1939, initially by the Nazis and shortly after by the Russians, triggered Britain and the UK declaring war on Germany. The significance of Poland in codebreaking is the three Polish mathematicians who, in around 1932, developed analysis of early German Enigma machines and by 1934 had largely solved the Enigma secrets. They also designed and constructed a basic machine, known as the Bomba, to tackle the permutations of Enigma settings. Marian Rejewski, Jerzy Rozyski, and Henryk Zygalski were the three mathematicians and cryptographer pioneers. Replica Enigma machines were constructed and worked alongside the new Bombas. The Enigma wiring and relationship to the reflector in the machine were established, based to a degree upon work done arising from access to a machine manual passed to the French by a disgruntled German called Schmidt. This information, when eventually passed to England, helped Bletchley Park considerably in penetrating Enigma. With the Nazis changing some of the Enigma design and procedures, the benefits of this early knowledge from the Poles was perhaps less useful over time as new techniques had to be established. However, the three mathematicians gave Bletchley's codebreakers a significant head start in enemy intelligence processing. Relevant organisations were the Polish Cypher School, and the Polish Cypher Bureau, which was started in the First World War. It is important to record that Alan Turing was not the first person to crack the Enigma message settings code, as that was achieved by the Poles.

The three Poles had previously developed a machine called the cyclometer, which had drums to simulate the Enigma rotors. The cyclometer would be helpful in checking rotor-generated displacements of the alphabet, as part of the encoding process. It was but one stage towards the building of their new machine. An important international meeting was held between Britain, France and Polish intelligence near Warsaw in July 1939. Analysis of Enigma by the Poles was passed to their allies, and these reports and data supporting them would prove to be invaluable. But all was not perfect, as ciphers from five rotors for Enigmas still needed to be cracked, and this large task was to be shared across the cryptographic sections of the countries attending the meeting. See *Zygalski*. See *Warsaw*.

PLACES

Portugal. Adjacent to the west of Spain, the country was used extensively by German agents to gather intelligence on shipping movements of the Allies and other data. Pujol Garcia or Garbo, known as Arabel to his German handlers, was a double agent who was based in Lisbon for a time before coming to England to work for MI5. He prepared misleading reports in Portugal of British shipping movements for the Nazis, but these were full of fictitious information supported by some articles in magazines on bookstands. Portugal was officially a neutral country during the war, but initially had leanings towards the Axis powers until later, when the British occupied the Azores. Both sides would use agents and contacts to gather intelligence in this region. See *Garbo*, See *Garcia/Pujol*.

Post Office Research Engineering Station. See *Dollis Hill*.

RAF Eastcote. One of several names for the post-war base at Eastcote in Middlesex after GCHQ was re-established at Cheltenham. It may also have been termed RAF Lime Grove, which was the main entrance to the base. A large contingent of American servicemen were present at Eastcote post-war, along with some RAF and civilians in a support capacity. *See GCHQ Eastcote and OSE Eastcote.*

RAF Uxbridge. Now the home of the Battle of Britain Bunker Museum, it provides an excellent taste of the critical time during the Battle of Britain. This was the No. 11 Group operations and group operations room at Uxbridge, in a fortified basement some 20m below ground where the 'plotting room' (i.e., control room) was situated. This was the centre for control of the RAF for the south-east England area during wartime, when command had been split into four discrete groups across England and Wales. Due to its location and the proximity to the south coast and the Channel, No. 11 Group had, arguably, the heaviest enemy action during the Battle of Britain. This group had been established in Uxbridge, west London, in 1936, and it had been a significant base for the command of air defence operations since 1925. It is now situated within the London Borough of Hillingdon. The operations room at Uxbridge had fortunately been built just before the start of the war by contractors Sir Thomas McAlpine, being a large basement structure, with steep steps.

WAAFs would be in the operations room taking instructions. Many famous people visited the operations room and bunker, including Sir Hugh Dowding, Churchill, King George VI, Queen Elizabeth and others. This was a base where the Official Secrets Act had to be signed if one worked there. It was essential to keep the base secret from the enemy, even though it had no runways and above ground were just a few wooden huts. This was a major administrative base for the RAF, and a substantial control board on the wall with illuminated lights indicated key information to command staff, as to which planes were up in which areas of the seven sectors of the group, the time to contact enemy, available reserves, etc. Special marked clocks gave further information. Information came to the operations room by telephone via a combination of Observer Corps sightings and chain radar detection across the country. Instructions were sent out to airfields within their sectors to get planes airborne and an indication of direction and time to contact. The system introduced by Air Chief Marshal Hugh Dowding (later Sir Hugh Dowding) improved the contact rate of locating enemy bombers and aircraft substantially. The intelligence required to make his system work heavily relied on radar detection and from the Observer Corps. There were those who doubted Dowding's plans, but he managed to save Britain from invasion and destruction of the RAF, much to the consternation of Hitler, who changed his plans.

The modern museum on site was built relatively recently, in 2018, contains various exhibits, and holds lectures on the history of air defence and related topics. The steps down are extremely steep, but the impression of the operations room once down in the underground bunker is spine-tingling. The map of south-east England dominates the room along with the wall indicator board. The scale of the operations control indicator board is substantial, and considering this was a huge, manual, illuminated indicator board, it could easily have been computerised had that technology been available at the time. But they managed perfectly well without computers with what they had at the time. It served its purpose to communicate the live 'real-time' situation to RAF commanders, day after day, under immense pressure, at a crucial time in our history. It was reliable, logical, easily understood, and it worked. Churchill must have been relieved that we had such a system to compensate for Britain's limited air cover, compared to the enemy. The Battle of Britain lasted until October 1940. RAF Uxbridge would also help coordinate air movements for the D-Day operations in June 1944.

Some ex-WAAFs who worked at RAF Uxbridge during those times have recorded brief accounts of their experiences in the operations room. It was a windowless, relatively dark room, overlooked by a glazed elevated gallery, where VIPs including Churchill could observe the progress on the indicator board and the actions of the WAAFs' movements on the raised map table below, showing the status during an attack.

Room 40, Admiralty. The origins of the British cryptographic intelligence division dating back to the First World War, and the origin of what we now term GCHQ, based currently in Cheltenham. Designated Room 40 OB or old building, it was part of NID25. The Division was formed in October 1914. In the early years, it would acquire several German Navy code books, which gave it a head start. Almost by accident certain German Navy encoded transmissions had been intercepted and passed to Rear Admiral Henry Oliver, who had no proper decrypt system to deal with them at the time. These messages were sent to Sir Alfred Ewing, who was interested and saw the decrypts as a challenge. This was the beginning of the development of cryptographic techniques and systems, with expansion of the organisation to cope with the volume of enemy intelligence, processing and analysing them. The combination of Room 40 and the War Office MI1(b) personnel resulted in the beginnings of GC&CS for intelligence and codebreaking.

The most famous activity here was the decoding of the Zimmerman telegram, the contents of which eventually brought America into the First World War, based on a threat from an adjacent country, Mexico, becoming an ally of Germany and considering an attack on the US. This telegram was a sensitive document and the Admiralty had to develop certain deception stories and techniques so as not to disclose exactly how the British came into possession of the contents, which were discovered by tapping US networks. As Britain was effectively spying on the Americans, their allies, they had to be extremely careful to avoid a diplomatic scandal and international rift. The director of Room 40, until mid-1917, was Alfred Ewing, and the personnel moved into other rooms and offices over time, so that it was established over several different offices as it expanded and the complement of staff increased. Room 40 would house some 800 wireless operators, plus ninety cryptographers and others in a support role. It would develop its technical and professional personnel, skills, and knowledge over many years, until significant changes occurred in the Second World War in cryptography, equipment, and systems of gathering and processing intelligence.

Ruislip Woods, Ruislip, Middlesex. The encampment site for the 6812th US Signals Engineers who would operate a number of codebreaking Bombe machines at Outstation Eastcote. Under the ETOUSA agreement between the USA and Great Britain there would be an exchange of military skilled personnel, some of whom went to Kent, some to Bletchley Park and some to Outstation Eastcote. As the outstation was largely comprised of Wrens, and effectively a 'Wrennery', it was thought that it would be inappropriate for the American visitors to be based at Eastcote as regards their sleeping accommodation. There was also limited room available at Eastcote, due to some 800 Wrens working there on the machines, plus several support staff. Some reports indicated that after a time, there would be some limited permanent accommodation billets in nearby Harrow for the men. The 6812th US Signals had a mix of officers and enlisted men to operate the Bombes in a specially allocated part of the huts in Block 'B' at Eastcote on the north part of that outstation.

Russia. An ally of Germany under various pacts and agreements until June 1941, when it was suddenly invaded by Germany. The Molotov–Ribbentrop pact was a non-aggression treaty between Germany and Russia. It was signed on 23 August 1939. Stalin had no confidence in his security advisers, and would not accept that the Nazis were planning a major offensive against Russia, Operation Barbarossa. He was unprepared as regards his armies and air force when it occurred and suffered heavy losses and the loss of large areas of territory. The Soviet Union then became allies of Great Britain and the West. The Russians were fed specific enemy intelligence by the British Government and its allies via Bletchley Park, although they would not be told of the sources, i.e. the codebreakers or about the codebreaking machines. A delicate balance was needed to avoid the Germans finding out about Bletchley Park. Russia counter-attacked the Nazis and regained territory eventually. Advance intelligence issued to the Russians before the Battle of Kursk by the British helped, to a degree, to turn the tide against the Nazis, and demonstrated how the codebreaking systems and people at Bletchley Park could make a real difference in a practical way. Some of the information and intelligence provided was a report from General von Weichs to Foreign Armies East, outlining the advance battle plans.

Britain chose to not declare war on Russia when it invaded Poland only a couple of weeks after Hitler invaded Poland. This was probably wise, although arguably hypocritical of the British, as Hitler's incursion into Poland had triggered the Second World War. Russia had difficult relations with the Germans before the start of the war, and agreements were changed and broken. The Baltic States were occupied by the Russians, then the Nazis, and after the war by the Russians again. There was a clear lack of trust between Hitler and Stalin, and the Russians were seen by Hitler as lower-class humans who would not be able to resist the Nazi war machine and invasion. The Russian winter helped to give an advantage to the Russians in their defence and counter-attacks. The duration of the Barbarossa campaign extended into winter and the German army and air force were unprepared for the conditions.

Soviet codebreakers were used in the Spanish Civil war as well as the Sino–Japanese war. It would be 1936 when special Russian operational groups would listen in to Franco's intelligence in the Spanish Civil War. In 1938, Russian cryptologists would go to China to attack the Japanese ciphers used in the war there, and exposed ten systems to aid the Chinese, an ally of Russia at the time. By 1939 cryptologists would assist General Zhukov in the Battle of Khalkyn Gol, by reading ciphers and codes.

Identifying the Russian contributions to codebreaking in the Second World War is difficult due to the secrecy of the state. However, a cryptographic department was established as part of the Russian NKVD in 1941. Further intelligence work established that Japan was not intending to attack Russia in support of the Germans during the war, allowing Russia to deploy its forces against Germany. This was due to the Russians deciphering the complex Japanese 'Purple' cipher. German Enigma machines were captured by the Russians in 1941, and their cryptologists would examine them in detail. There is a theory that Russian experts in codebreaking were able to read Romanian intelligence decrypts in Ukraine, giving them a strategic advantage in the battle plans for the area during that stage of the war. Direction-finding techniques by the Russians were perfected against the Germans, and identified groupings, military strength and positions of the enemy. Several German Panzer divisions were identified through radio interception of intelligence and direction finding, and this became crucial for the success in the Battle of Kursk.

While the Russians did acquire various enemy Enigma machines, there is no real evidence that they were able to decipher them cryptanalytically, even though they may have deciphered certain messages, i.e. they may not have been up to the same level of competence and cryptographical knowledge or experience as those engaged in the work at Bletchley Park, who understood the problems that needed to be solved and how to solve them, particularly using machines, or a combination of hand methods and machines. There also is no evidence available of Russian processing and decoding machines such as the codebreaking Bombe or Colossus, or of any Russian versions of them. However, it would be inappropriate to state that the Russians were illiterate in cryptography techniques during the last war. The establishment of cryptographic sections by them indicated they took the intelligence gathering process seriously.

Reports indicate that Russia did have its own cryptographic machine during wartime, which was termed M101-Izumrud, or Emerald. Code books were burnt and destroyed before Nazis could confiscate them at Russian embassies in Berlin and elsewhere in the early stages of the war. Hitler offered grand prizes for those in his armies seizing Russian code books or intelligence officers, but without much success. The methods used by the Russians in messaging their troops limited the opportunities for interception and analysis by the enemy. At the end of the war Soviet losses, after liberation from camps and recovering missing soldiers, amounted to 9,168,100. Total losses including civilians amounted to a staggering 27,917,000. This was far more than any other nation.

The sharing of intelligence between the Allies and the Russians helped a great deal in shortening the war and defeating Hitler. After the war it is likely that Russian personnel acquired a certain amount of discarded Nazi encoding equipment such as SZ40 Lorenz machines for their own use. Post-war, the Russians had a lot to learn and were somewhat exposed from a cryptographic point of view, but all that changed when they radically changed their own encoding systems and techniques, blocking out the USA and its allies, and leaving them blind for a time as regards the interception of intelligence. It may be of interest that back in 1914 the Russians gave the British a captured German code book. Room 40 in the Admiralty were able to make good use of this information to break enemy codes.

The spy John Cairncross had managed to infiltrate Bletchley Park for the Russians, feeding them intelligence on ciphers and other information. The relationship with Russia and the West over the years has been spasmodic and often lacking trust between the two sides. However, there have been times in the past when crucial intelligence has been shared, and countries have tolerated each other, working together for limited periods at least. The current situation with Russia at time of writing is potentially very dangerous for Europe, the West, for Russia, and indeed the world. It may be a very long time before trust is re-established and the sharing of intelligence is possible. The Cold War has become a lot colder in the twenty-first century.

Sandridge, Herts. A Second World War listening station or Y-station near St Albans. It may have been the first wireless secret listening station in 1939. Located at the top of Woodcock Hill, the station received transmissions from Italy, Germany, Tokyo and elsewhere. The messages were then forwarded to Bletchley Park. Teleprinters were also used extensively at Sandridge. The code name for the base was 5DG and personnel may have been seconded from the Foreign Office/MI6 or the Radio Security Service, as it was known. Bletchley Park was apparently coded CMY. It would be 1973 before the base was acquired by the Home Office for police and security research. Staffing would be 100 personnel, and around 25 per cent of these women. Listeners would be recruited from the Merchant Navy, Royal Navy, Cable & Wireless and the Post Office. Shifts at Sandridge would be either eight hours or twelve-hour extended shifts. Instructions after the war ended included destroying all books, documents and details of personnel addresses. Some reports indicated that Sandridge may have received some non-Morse messages later on in the war. Two aerials would be established here for radio reception intercepts. There was liaison with Knockholt Y-station in Kent on non-Morse messages, and a combined effort made to intercept messages where possible.

Sandy Hook, New Jersey. A beach used for major tests and evaluation of military deception techniques, organised by Douglas Fairbanks Jr, Naval Reserve Officer and famous American Hollywood actor and producer. The operation and test took place on 27 October 1942, with observers inspecting the training and deception techniques used in a dummy attack on a beach. It would be confirmed as successful and result in wartime action for the 'Ghost' army in Sicily, France, Holland and Germany. This would become the US 23rd Headquarters Special Troops. Intelligence would feed back the impact of such deception action to the commanders at HQ. See *Douglas Fairbanks Jr*.

Scarborough. Croft Spa was a listening Y-station on the coast in the north of England. It would specialise in direction finding of enemy U-boats and surface vessels. It had around twenty staff and operated from 1940 to 1975. It was established as a Royal Navy wireless telegraphy station in 1912. Scarborough was also a key listening station in helping to locate the battleship *Bismarck* in 1941. Scarborough would specialise in German Navy transmissions as well as air high-frequency traffic.[68] Scarborough had up to sixty-five receivers for listening to radio traffic.[69] The activities post-war were to provide intelligence and listening at the time of the Cold War. It provided some intelligence during that period relevant to the Cuban missile crisis relevant to Russian shipping movements, supplies for Cuba and associated radio transmissions. One report indicates it is the world's oldest continually operating signals intelligence site.[70]

Scotland. It played an important role in the deception of the enemy under Operation Fortitude North, helping to tie down Nazi occupying forces in Norway so they did not interfere with the D-Day invasion in June 1944. False radio messages would be sent from Scotland as part of the strategy and intercepted in the Scandinavian countries. It would also have various training bases for Wrens and military personnel across the country. Major General Sir Stuart Menzies, a Scot, would be the director of the Secret Intelligence Service from 1939 to 1951. Another Scot, General Sir Kenneth Strong, became chief of intelligence for General Eisenhower, under part of SHAEF. After the war, he would work at the Foreign Office and head up the Joint Intelligence Bureau (JIB), before becoming Director General of Intelligence for the Ministry of Defence.

PLACES

In 1940 three German spies were captured in Scotland who had been briefed to take special equipment down to London in preparation for Operation Sealion, the German invasion of the UK. In 1941 they were executed for spying and the invasion did not happen, thanks to the RAF repelling the Luftwaffe. Throughout the war, Britain promptly tracked down, captured and neutralised German spies operating in the UK. British double agent Garbo made an error by communicating to his German Nazi handler that 'a Glaswegian would do anything for a litre of wine'. Glaswegians did not generally drink wine, more likely beer and spirits, and litres were unknown as a measurement where imperial measurements were the norm. The Germans did not take the bait.

In Greenock and adjacent Gourock, an intercept and signals wireless radio station run by Wrens was known unofficially as Signal City. There were around 200 Wrens plus many maintenance staff operating there in 1942. See *Signal City*.

Selfridges, Oxford Street, London. A famous department store that concealed a special secret during wartime. It had in a basement annex a very large and complex electronic voice encoding communication machine called SIGSALY, developed by the Americans at Bell Laboratories. It was built in New York at Western Electric, and in all they built ten machines, the first going to the Pentagon in Washington, and the second to London. It was used to encode telephone conversations between the American President and Churchill. Prior to the introduction of SIGSALY, the Germans in Holland would intercept international phone calls between Roosevelt and Churchill, and descramble them with sophisticated equipment. One phone call lasted just five minutes but discussed the forthcoming Allied invasion in principle.[71] Fortunately, the location and detail were not discussed.

The SIGSALY machine terminal cost $1 million in 1943, a substantial amount but worth it to improve secrecy and confidentiality in wartime. A quantity of signals engineers and officers from the 805th Signals Services Company operated the large machine in the basement of Selfridges, and used recorded discs on a record player to add a form of digital noise to be added to the voice message over the telephone line. The Prime Minister could use the system from the underground War Cabinet Rooms in Westminster. There were also terminals in the American Embassy and Downing Street, i.e. phone terminals. The equipment was so large it could never fit within 10 Downing Street. The power use and heat output of the equipment was significant. It weighed in excess of 50 tons and had to be electronically synchronised with identical equipment thousands of miles away over the Atlantic. It was nicknamed 'the Green Hornet' due to the buzzing sound the equipment made when operational. Recorded discs that added noise to the encrypted voice conversation would be destroyed afterwards, preventing the conversation being reproduced by the enemy or enemy agents. Churchill supposedly did not care much to use the equipment, and preferred a less secure red scrambler telephone. However, in time he did use it, and spoke with Roosevelt and later Truman on war strategy, terms for the forthcoming German surrender and related issues. The general public using the department store and Selfridges staff would not have been aware the encoding machine was in the basement, and may only have seen the occasional American uniformed soldier entering or leaving through a side door. Special security measures were additionally put into place to prevent the SIGSALY communication line being hacked or interfered with by enemy agents between the connected sites.[72]

Alan Turing visited the manufacturers of the machine during the war in America and gave his thoughts on the design. The machine worked effectively, and although highly complex, it provided a secure voice-encryption system that the Nazis were never able to penetrate and decode. Some of the design features of SIGSALY were very advanced for their time, and included the first voice transmission using Pulse Code Modulation (PCM).[73] The security was also assisted by use of a one-time pad cipher, which made it very difficult to crack by the enemy. SIGSALY commenced operationally in April 1943 and was still in use in 1946. However, the London SIGSALY machine was dismantled and taken away by the Americans after the war had ended.

Sicily. Located in the Mediterranean and part of Italy, it had strategic importance during the war. It was heavily fortified by the enemy, but deception plans implied the Allies would be making an assault in Sardinia, Corsica, and Greece, resulting in movement of troops and Panzer divisions. The Nazis were caught off guard when the combined forces of American, British and Canadian troops made the Sicily assault in a massive amphibious air and sea landing under Operation Husky on 10 July 1943. The combined deception tactics employed would help in terms of time and reducing casualties, at least until they came to the Italian mainland, when fighting the enemy would be problematical, such as at Monte Cassino. There would be almost 25,000 Allied casualties while taking Sicily. Use of the American specialist 'Ghost' (23rd Special Troops) army in Sicily would help with diversionary tactics and confuse the Nazis. *Operation Mincemeat* helped relocate Nazi divisions to Sardinia and Corsica, buying time for the Allies and saving countless lives. This operation involved a body of a man disguised as a British officer carrying strategic plans for invasions by the Allies in the Mediterranean being washed up on the shores of Spain. German agents were suspicious at first, but Berlin was convinced this officer and the documents he was carrying were genuine, and the plan worked. Intelligence feedback in the Mediterranean was crucial for the Allies. North Africa, Malta, the Straits of Gibraltar, Sicily, Italy, Greece and surrounding areas would be under constant scrutiny by both the Allies and the Axis powers. The invasion of Sicily would be the first stage in the long, drawn-out battle to neutralise Italy and the Nazis.

Signal City, Greenock, Scotland. From 1942, the designation in and around Greenock for naval signals communication operations, comprising a wide range and spread of different buildings and headquarters. A signals commander would be in charge of personnel. Two hundred British and Canadian Wrens would operate a wide range of signals-based equipment from semaphore to teleprinters, and cipher machines. Many other Wrens would be in a support role for the base accommodation in the 'Wrennery'. As an official Wren Depot, a large proportion were taken on so they could not be transferred or redeployed to other bases, and had to remain carrying out their duties there. They would be termed as 'Immobile' Wrens. There would also be substantial quantities of male supporting personnel on the base. Training of Wrens and personnel would also form a major part of the operations. The personnel included operators of teleprinters, cipher officers and Morse code telegraphists. Additionally, it would be a fall-back signals communication centre for the Admiralty in case of Nazi occupation elsewhere in Britain. There would be a strict 'pecking order' of military bases across Britain to take over signals communications in the event the Nazis occupied parts of the United Kingdom, and Greenock was down the Admiralty list due to its geographical position in the north.

The Wrens' accommodation included an old asylum building, and was spread over a large area, with an additional number of Wrens who were needed for the management and running of the accommodation buildings across the site. Wren communicators would be involved in the following jobs: Wireless telegraphy, radio direction finding, coder, teleprinter operator and signal distribution officer. Greenock had a torpedo factory, and was also the home of the Free French Navy. It also hosted one of the largest naval transport divisions in the UK and incorporated a major supporting infrastructure. See also *Scotland*.

South Africa. This country would provide various armed forces to support the Allies and would have various listening stations across the country. These included Johannesburg, Durban, Port Elizabeth, Simonstown, Komatipoort and Bloemfontein.

Spain. Notable for its involvement with the Nazis, who supported General Franco in the 1936–39 Spanish Civil War, which was a valuable testing ground for the new German armed forces prior to the start of the Second World War. It was in Madrid in June 1944 that Pujol Garcia's (Garbo's) message to the Nazis was encoded into an Enigma machine by the authorities, for transmission to Berlin in the early hours of D-Day, with Garbo being a double agent acting for the British. This important message was part of Operation Fortitude South to help deceive the Nazis and divert their attention away from Normandy. The German High Command responded not only back to the double agent, but Bletchley Park managed to decode the intercepted High Command instructions, giving the Allies comfort that the deception plan seemed to be working against the enemy. The decoding of the agent's message in Madrid indicated a security weakness, and one that was taken advantage of by the codebreakers at Bletchley Park and the listening Y-stations supporting them at the time.

Spain had declared itself neutral at the start of the war, but Franco met with Hitler to discuss offering support for the Axis powers. That meeting did not result in anything constructive, but Franco did provide some support during the war. However, the Franco–Hitler alliance was on shaky ground and there would be disagreements about geographical territories that both parties wanted under their belts. Franco allowed Germany to provide and establish within Spain various Nazi radio listening stations to monitor the Atlantic and Mediterranean for enemy shipping.

The Enigma message exchanges in Spain were geographically much nearer than Germany, and more advantageous for Britain to try and intercept in England. Dilly Knox, at Bletchley Park, had a breakthrough in decoding Enigma messages from Spain in 1937, and gave the Bletchley codebreaking team confidence in moving forward. The Russians were also intercepting messages during the Spanish Civil War.

Two hidden secret Enigma machines were discovered in Spain and handed over to GCHQ in 2012. It is understood these modified machines were used to communicate with the German Condor Legion and the Spanish forces under Franco during the Spanish Civil war. The machines were located in a secret room in the Spanish Ministry of Defence. In return for the pair of Enigmas, a single German four-rotor Enigma, rotor box and various related documents were given to Spain to establish a codebreaking museum there. It is thought the Enigmas given to GCHQ were without plugboards, and therefore less secure than the ones the Germans would generally use.

Spaso House, Moscow. The US Ambassador's residence in Moscow, in 1952, which was bugged by the Russians using a listening device within the carved wooden US Great Seal emblem hung on the wall. This was during the early part of the Cold War period with Russia. The gift of a replica carved, wooden, US Great Seal to the ambassador after the war by the Russians would be taken as an act of friendship to recognise the co-operation and bond between the Americans and Russians during the war. It would be several years before the Americans realised that conversations by the American Ambassador had been intercepted by the Russians. Several excerpts of conversations in the embassy were accidentally intercepted by British military listening personnel but dismissed as there were insufficient clues and a lack of evidence of a bug at the time. The replica of the Great Seal had been a gift to the American Ambassador in Russia by the Vladimir Lenin Pioneer Organisation. It was then hung on the wall above the Ambassador's desk; a perfect spot for listening into private conversations. The listening device would remain undetectable except when operational and in use. This clever design feature made it very difficult to detect. An electronic 'sweep' in 1952 by security officials finally identified the security breach in the Great Seal. The seal had been made in two separate pieces so the bug could be installed and then the joint was disguised with plaster of Paris. The device would be a small condenser microphone within a resonant cavity within the seal. It had been in place on the wall of the Ambassador's residence for several years undetected as a listening device. The Great Seal replica with the listening device was held up at a United Nations Security Council meeting when the Russian delegation were present to show the lengths that the Russians would go to as regards espionage and bugging of Western officials for intelligence.

A much earlier espionage plot had been discovered in the attic of the residence in 1937, but a telephone operator was caught accessing the space and dealt with.

PLACES

The Americans would be just as devious as the Russians, with them digging lengthy secret tunnels under the streets in Berlin to connect to Russian military telephone lines, with help from the British. That tunnel was eventually exposed by George Blake, a British senior MI6 officer, who was spying for Russia and passing secrets to them. The tunnel became a propaganda coup for the Russians following its discovery and exposure. People would travel from around the world to see the secret tunnel for themselves, and there would be guided tours. This was to humiliate the Americans and the West. Surprisingly, even though Britain had been involved in part of the tunnel and phone tapping, the Russians concentrated on humiliating the United States. See *George Blake*.

Spirella, Letchworth, Herts. A women's corset and foundation wear manufacturer, which made parachutes during the war and then was used by BTM to expand its 'Cantab' Bombe codebreaking machine factory using women operatives.[74] The Garden City Collection at Letchworth has a photograph, 'Wizards with Wires', showing factory women assembling component parts in the Spirella factory for BTM. These cables, sockets and components would be transferred to the main factory for final assembly of the Bombe machines. There would be both daytime and night shifts for production, including over 300 workers by September 1942, and a further expansion as the war progressed.

Spirella was originally an American company but was later acquired by the British, as can be seen by the signage on the front of the main building. Due to labour shortages, some women workers were accepted as outworkers to wire the machine rotor drums, and some of these would have been residents in the villages surrounding Letchworth. By September 1942, there would be 215 workers at Spirella, mainly women on the day shift, and a further 105 on the night shift.[75] See *BTM* See *Letchworth*.

St James' Street, London. The base for the Twenty Committee formed by the British security services to obtain feedback from intelligence using the skills of Bletchley Park and the codebreaking outstations, together with agents and double agents. A 'to let' signboard was displayed outside the building to make the public think it was an unassuming London address. Numerous plans and plots were formulated here, including the handling of double agent Garbo, that had an impact on the build-up to D-Day. Also, the *Operation Mincemeat* deception plan to drop a corpse in Spain to convince the enemy that Allied landings would come in Greece and not Sicily was dreamed up here. The art of deception was developed to a high degree. See *Masterson*.

St Malo-Paramé, Normandy. One of four Nazi listening stations to listen for and to collect radio transmissions across the Channel. This signals intelligence network of stations was established by the *Abwehr*. See *Y-stations*.

St Paul's Boys School, Hammersmith, London. This school is famous for the location of the strategic meeting and the final planning of the D-Day assault plan, with General Eisenhower, Churchill and His Majesty the King, King George VI, present on 15 May 1944. The plan offered was approved by all.

During wartime, the school was requisitioned by the Government for the 21st Army Group. The school was also used by Poles as a spy base, and they burnt and destroyed many documents in 1945 after the war had ended. These documents were requested to be handed over to the British, but they were destroyed in large volumes, to the concern of the British authorities. The instructions to burn documents was given by the Polish intelligence chief, Colonel Stanislaw Gano, who had created intelligence networks in occupied Europe as well as America and North Africa. He acted due to fear the information would fall into the hands of the Russians after the war. This fear was also shared by Churchill to a degree, in that he instructed the complete destruction and dismantling of all the codebreaking machines used during wartime in case the Russians found out about their technology. Prior to the Poles using the school, their headquarters were at the Rubens Hotel in London. That hotel was also the base for the headquarters of the Polish Free State Army in exile.

The school building was demolished in 1968. A plaque commemorating the D-Day meeting is displayed affixed to the external boundary wall on the main road.[76] See *Eisenhower*. See *London*.

Stanmore, Middlesex. A north-west London borough with famous sites including Bentley Priory, the Fighter Command base during the war. A V2 rocket bomb apparently came close to Bentley Priory in the early hours of 27 January 1945 but thankfully missed the site. Aircraft movements were managed below ground at Bentley Priory as a precaution. Stanmore also housed the Balloon Command centre for barrage balloons. These balloons would be strategically positioned in the capital and elsewhere to deter low-flying enemy aircraft. A Polish radio intelligence centre was also based in Stanmore managed by Heftman, a Pole who had worked for a Polish radio factory, AVA. They made replica Enigmas there.

Stanmore also established the fourth (in sequence) satellite codebreaking outstation, not far from the main Stanmore station and at a crossroads adjacent to Elstree Road. This was an important outstation to support Bletchley Park. It would receive many Bombe machines from not only the Letchworth factory, but also from smaller country house outstations, some of which closed down before the end of the war. John Tiltman of Bletchley Park would be gathering intelligence in conjunction with the Polish SIGINT at Stanmore in February 1944.

Like many parts of London and its suburbs, Stanmore suffered enemy bombing. A detailed map of the Harrow and Stanmore area is available for inspection from the London Borough of Harrow, and shows close bombing near the outstation, and also near the Bentley Priory Fighter Command station nearby. See *OSS Outstation Stanmore*.

Stowe School, Bucks. Bletchley Park considered finding a larger site to accommodate the Bombe codebreaking machines, as space was running out at the three country houses nearby. Stowe School was considered as a location for new Bombes being manufactured, but instead, Stanmore was used as the next codebreaking outstation. The reasons for abandoning Stowe are unclear, but it may have been that either the pupils and staff would have had to be relocated miles away in an equally large site, or that the headmaster would have been concerned that the use of the site for semi-military purposes might have made it a target for the Luftwaffe. If Stowe had been chosen and implemented for Bombe machines, it is highly unlikely that either Stanmore or Eastcote Outstations would have been established. The Stowe School site falls under the National Trust, with extensive grounds and landscaping. See *Outstations in England*.

Swakeleys House. A Grade II listed house and grounds within the London Borough of Hillingdon. It was used by the military during the war, with a searchlight battery located there, and taken over by the Foreign Office until 1955. Some reports indicated that it was used for a period for rest and relaxation by codebreaking support personnel from outstations and associated departments. Tennis courts, club rooms and rooms for socialising were made available for staff who needed a break from the codebreaking support activities. It was not geographically far from Outstations Eastcote or Stanmore. See *OSE* and *OSS*.

Sweden. Although it was classed as a neutral country during wartime, from June 1940 it allowed Germany to pass troops, goods and supplies across its territory. Norway and Denmark were neighbours and yet they were now in the hands of the oppressor. Sweden wanted a peaceful existence with Germany. It was only later on in the war that it took a stronger position against Nazi Germany, allowing safe passage for escaping Allied airmen and those involved in covert operations. Ball bearings were crucial for the German war machine and for a long time Sweden supplied these materials and components to the Nazis. The RAF and USA were bombing production factories in Germany and elsewhere to slow down the pace of the Nazis in the production of armaments, military vehicles, trains and equipment. Many firms and organisations had direct links to German companies in Sweden, or alternatively, had 'cloaked' companies, which had strong economic and financial connections with Germany. Nazi troops and equipment were allowed to be transported through Sweden en route to Finland, to help fight the Russians. It was not until May 1943, when the war was turning in favour of the Allies, that Sweden reopened trade negotiations with them. Some advanced encoding machine links were land-based cables instead of radio transmissions, and it is suspected the Swedes intercepted some of these. Even 'neutral' countries had the need for intelligence to be kept informed of developing situations during wartime. A Swedish cryptographer, Arne Beurling, was head of the Russian Section and managed to decode a T52 *Geheimschreiber* (secret writer) German teleprinter encoded message by hand. No one understood how he managed to achieve this brilliant achievement. The T52 was far more complex than Enigma. This way, he was able to inform his government what the Germans were planning in the adjacent occupied countries, such as Norway and Finland. See *Norway*, See *Finland*.

Switzerland. Although declaring itself a neutral country during the war, Germany would be interested in the financial sector of Switzerland and secretly listen in to the communications of banks and government officials. Many different countries and organisations would use its banking and investment system. Germany was curious as to what goods and funds were being transferred across nations, and when. Enigma machines were acquired by the Swiss, commencing in 1938, and a special model was made for them (Swiss Enigma K). The Nazis would attempt to obtain code books, listen in to the transmissions, or use other means to intercept the intelligence. Some 265 machines were used by the Swiss across various departments, including the army and air force. Their models of Enigma were unique in having an additional external lamp panel on an extended cable. The box housing the machine was wider than others, in order to accommodate the external lamp panel. The Poles, Germans, Americans and British were able to read the Swiss Enigma intelligence with relative ease. In 1947 after the war, the Swiss developed a hybrid machine of Enigma called Nema, with many more rotors. They were used until 1970s and around 640 machines were distributed in Switzerland for principally army and also government use. In December 2014 the auctioneers Christie's sold a 1948 Swiss Nema machine for $20,000. The description can be read online. See *Germany*.

Teddington, England. The location for the National Physical Laboratory (NPL), which was established in 1900 and developed various innovative technological solutions and inventions. A Government-funded research laboratory, it concentrated on physics and scientific research by a team of scientists. Alan Turing would join the staff of NPL in 1945 as a temporary senior scientific officer. NPL would later introduce and develop advances such as 'data packet switching', which is used as the basis for the internet and modern computers today. Donald Davies developed this packet switching technology, joining NPL in 1947, and was briefly an assistant to Turing for a time. Turing would produce a paper on his ACE computer and work on its development until he left in 1948. This was shortly before he published his paper on intelligent machinery in 1950. 'Computing Machinery and Intelligence' would set out the 'Turing test' for intelligence. Today, the NPL has expanded its research programme into biosciences, environmental science, acoustics, quantum technologies, ionising radiation, medical physics, time and frequency and others. See *Turing*. See *London*.

Tehran, Iran. Location of the conference in November 1943 for the Allies to discuss strategy between for the continuing war. President Roosevelt, Churchill and Stalin attended and a draft plan was prepared initially. Arising from this came Operation Bodyguard, a plan for the deception of the enemy in terms of military strategy. Approval of decisions and planning would take place in December 1943. The background was the need to disguise the build-up of troops, equipment and resources in England prior to the invasion of occupied France and what was to become D-Day in 1944. At the conference the leaders issued 'A Declaration of the three powers regarding Iran'. Much was discussed, including arrangements to allow Russia to acquire the Baltic States (via a referendum in each state and with guaranteed non-interference from the West), relocation of the German–Polish border, and other political discussions. This was all about trade-offs and providing incentives, with the major Western political powers giving away land in exchange for wartime cooperation from Russia, and encouraging a declaration of war against Japan by the Russians. Assistance to Iran for their help against the Nazi oppressors was additionally discussed and agreed. The conference was also significant for setting out the principles of a new United Nations, post-war, to be established and dominated by a combination of the three powers plus China. The second front was encouraged by Stalin, who was under great pressure, but D-Day would not arrive for another six or seven months. Churchill would be able to communicate across the Atlantic by secure telephone using the American SIGSALY system installed in the basement of Selfridges department store in London. The Germans would not be able to penetrate this communication link. See *Selfridges*.

The Pound, Knockholt, Kent. The name used for the site at Ivy Farm in Kent, which was to be identified as Knockholt, the advanced listening Y-station during the war. See *Ivy Farm* and *Knockholt*.

TNMOC, The National Museum of Computing, Bletchley Park. A separate trust, independent charity and museum within the grounds of Bletchley Park (i.e. the Bletchley Park Estate) and housing a range of codebreaking and encoding/decoding equipment, some being replicas but many operational. It is home to the world's largest collection of working historic computers. A replica of the Turing–Welchman Bombe is at the museum, also the replica Colossus, which was based on the world's first semi-programmable computer that assisted in deciphering the encoded teleprinter messages from the German High Command during the Second World War. The replica Colossus was built under the direction of Tony Sale and volunteers, and took over nine years to build. It is a working model, as is the replica Bombe. All the original Bombe and Colossus machines were destroyed after the war. TNMOC is housed in 'Block H'. It was granted charitable status on 6 June 2005, noted as sixty-one years after D-Day. See *Bletchley Park*. See *Sale*.

Tower of London. A prisoner-of-war camp was established at the Tower during wartime, and clandestine methods were used to 'bug' inmates to listen in to their conversations and eavesdrop in order to collect intelligence. The Post Office Research Engineering Station in Dollis Hill became involved, particularly in installing listening microphones and equipment, also utilising Trent Park at Cockfosters, a stately home in north-east London, for testing and installing systems in conjunction with RCA, an American company, for the Combined Services Detail Interrogation Centre (CSDIC), which worked closely with MI5 and other agencies.[77] This type of Government support for various secret agencies continued throughout wartime. Nazi officer Rudolf Hess was imprisoned at the Tower after he parachuted into Scotland. A number of captured German officers and men were interrogated here, at the Tower prisoner-of-war collection centre, before being sent off to other camps in Britain. That centre would eventually move to north London due to lack of space and high volume of detainees. See *Dollis Hill*.

Ukraine. European country geographically close to Russia that at the time of writing is being fought over by Russia, which attacked it in February 2022. During the Second World War Ukrainians would be part of eastern Poland or Soviet Ukraine, with the occupation of Poland by the Germans bringing the two together for a brief time. The Soviets had seized Ukraine for themselves in September 1939 as the occupation of Poland took place. There would be resistance, particularly in the west of Ukraine, to the Russian occupation. German codebreakers would be sent Russian signals by partisans, and be able to decrypt them. A partisan leader had assembled a few thousand men in 1941 to assist the Germans in fighting against the Russians, but all did not go well, and the partisans were then forced to make a truce agreement with the Russians. By the end of 1941 almost all of Ukraine was under Nazi domination and control.

In some ways, there is an analogy between this region and that of the Baltic States, although the latter countries' situation was further complicated by the non-aggression pacts[78] between Germany and Russia in exchange for Russia occupying Estonia, Latvia and Lithuania without the Soviets having to worry about external opposition. Any country that is invaded and occupied by different adjoining enemies in a relatively short period of time faces instability, uncertainty and fear. There would also be mass murder of Ukrainian Jews by the Nazis running into the millions, and mass deportations for slave labour. Different partisan groups fought against the Nazis but also against other partisans, who were pro-Russian. With the Russian counter-offensive against the Nazis, by the end of 1944 Ukraine was back again under Russian control. The politics of the area during wartime is very complex, and has trickled further into the twenty-first century with terrifying consequences for Ukraine, Europe and the world.[79]

A total of four German High Command communication, teleprinter, non-Morse links would be spread across Ukraine, and largely connected to Königsberg in northern Europe from north, east, south and western Ukraine. These links would be termed 'Squid', 'Octopus', 'Stickleback', and 'Smelt', respectively by British codebreakers. Intelligence intercepted from these communication links would be invaluable to the West. See *Königsberg*.

United States of America. Allies of Great Britain once the attack on Pearl Harbor in December 1941 brought it into the Second World War against Japan and the other Axis powers. Intelligence interest started before the war and the Zimmerman telegram, which involved Mexico and Germany as potential allies. That telegram, decoded by Britain's intelligence services, brought the USA into the First World War. As regards the Second World War, there was close contact between Churchill and President Roosevelt, and exchange of intelligence using Bletchley Park, its outstations and listening wireless stations. America would have problems working quickly enough to decode the Japanese fourteen-part encoded message to their embassy in America, prior to Pearl Harbor being attacked. A combination of errors and mistakes, aided by a degree of complacency, would give the Japanese an initial advantage of complete surprise with the attack, and create a situation that the American military base in Hawaii, on the island of Oahu, was unprepared for.

The contribution of the USA to the war effort was immense, not just in men and armaments but in the establishing of the Lend-Lease policy, which lent equipment worth millions of American dollars to Britain, Russia and its allies.[80] The USA suffered greatly along with Britain in the loss of shipping in convoys across the Atlantic due to constant U-boat attacks. Bletchley Park was able to intercept a number of Enigma messages giving U-boat locations, but these were spasmodic and there would be large gaps in acquiring the decoded messages and the settings of the machines, helped by the occasional capture of U-boat code books.

Senior American military staff knew Bletchley had machines to assist codebreaking, but eventually they decided to create their own four-rotor-based Bombe machines, and these were transported to Washington to attack German naval Enigma messages. Alan Turing visited America during wartime and discussed codebreaking, intelligence and machines with selected personnel. Offering a British Bombe to them did not go down well, and they declined the offer, probably because they were designing and building their own improved version in the Midwest. The voice-encoding, highly complex SIGSALY machine was designed and built by Bell Laboratories and used successfully at the Pentagon initially. Later, a second machine was installed in an air-conditioned basement room of Selfridges department store in London and operated by a complement of American signals engineers and officers. Churchill would use that encoding system to successfully communicate via telephone across the Atlantic with President Roosevelt, and later with President Truman. A quantity of other SIGSALY machines would be used, some installed on warships in the Pacific for use against the Japanese. Military radio equipment for communications supplied by America to Britain and elsewhere was robust and well-built. It was used extensively in Britain during the war, and helped to intercept numerous messages by Voluntary Interceptors (VIs) and at formal listening Y-stations across the country.

The USA would have not only the standard German Enigma machines to deal with for interception of enemy massages, but also the Japanese 'Purple' encoding machines, being versions of the Enigma. They would have some assistance from Bletchley Park on this, and many Wrens were transferred to places such as Ceylon and further east to assist with 'Purple' intercepts of transmissions, particularly after VE day. The war with Japan culminated in the use of the Hiroshima and Nagasaki nuclear atomic bombs. The secrecy that guarded and protected the development of the bombs including tests in the desert would be crucial to their successful use in 1945. Furthermore, both sides of the war were looking to develop weapons of mass destruction, commencing with the Nazi's advanced V1 and V2 rockets programme, plus the introduction and testing of advanced high-speed jets. The destruction of Deuterium, or 'heavy water', supplies in Norway by the Norwegian branch of SOE in a daring commando operation bought the Allies time to delay Germany's production of nuclear armaments. The intelligence shared with allies on such matters had to be distributed sensitively and strictly controlled to prevent leaks to the enemy.

The ETOUSA agreement between the USA and Britain was an exchange and support programme of military personnel and this enabled divisions of US Signals engineers to travel to Britain and assist with intelligence intercepts, and even operate a quantity of British Bombe codebreaking machines at Outstation Eastcote in Middlesex. The operational records of the 6812th US Signals indicated considerable success in breaking many Enigma keys while at Eastcote, where operators were trained by Wrens. Other American officers and enlisted men would be sent to Bletchley Park in Buckinghamshire, and to Kent in a support role. They would gain additional knowledge on intelligence systems and processing while in Britain.

Innovative methods of security were introduced by the Americans, such as use of First Nation dialects in the Pacific to thwart the Japanese, with messages encoded by specialist signals personnel. The establishment of a considerable number of American listening radio stations across the country proved successful, and some had a considerable geographical range, using shortwave transmissions. The use of many women from WAVES to build Bombe codebreaking four-rotor machines helped to replace the resource of limited manpower available at the time. Improvements would be made to the codebreaking machines to make them even more efficient than the Bombes in England.

The Navy Intelligence organisation OP-20-G would be actively seeking out enemy intelligence for many years, aided by the American four-rotor Bombe machines and other systems. The NSA would develop post-war to work closely with GCHQ in Britain, and help to counter the potential threat from Russia and the East. Several British cryptographic experts would act as consultants to the NSA after the war ended, and these included Gordon Welchman, who worked in a principal position at Bletchley Park during the war. Although Welchman did have significant problems with his book, *The Hut Six Story*, when published on both sides of the Atlantic, it must be stated that the Americans obtained a great deal of useful techniques, ideas and knowledge from papers and documents produced by British mathematicians, cryptographic experts and academics. Many of them would have worked at Bletchley Park or been associated in some way with that specialist site. The issue for the NSA and security and intelligence organisations post-war was to stay one step ahead of the Soviets and to a degree, the Chinese, in security systems and gathering intelligence to identify serious threats. President Kennedy would have the Cuban Missile Crisis to deal with in the 1960s, a scenario that came very close to nuclear war. The advancement in technology would give America an advantage in developing computers and computer systems, leaving Britain far behind in that period, partly due to the restrictions imposed by the Official Secrets Act and the secrecy of Colossus, the first semi-programmable computer, developed in north London during the war. There are currently a number of important museums in the USA preserving cryptographic machines, systems and the history of the topic, including the National Cryptologic Museum, on the site of the NSA at Fort Meade, Maryland.

In 1985, two American Navy officers were revealed to have stolen sensitive cryptographic secrets using a Minox C spy camera and supplied them to the Soviet Union since the 1960s. Jerry Whitworth and John Walker were both caught and imprisoned for life for their espionage deeds. The Minox model 'C' is a sub-miniature camera but was not advertised for espionage or spying in marketing literature, until a brochure was issued by the firm of Leitz in 1979.[81] However, this was at a time when Bond films and spy films were becoming popular, and was done tongue in cheek. See *Selfridges*. See *Dayton, Ohio*.

Uxbridge. A large town in west London within the London Borough of Hillingdon. It contained during wartime the base for coordinating England's air defence system, and is now the Battle of Britain Bunker and Museum,[82] with an underground wartime control room, where guided tours are provided for the public. Intelligence from the Observer Corps and spotters would be passed to Uxbridge and they had to coordinate the fighter defences against the Luftwaffe, who attacked day and night. It is interesting that Uxbridge, Stanmore, Eastcote and Dollis Hill are sites that, while they may have carried out different activities, are relatively close together to the west and north-west of the capital. Uxbridge and the other areas are now far more populated today as compared to wartime, and there has been much construction of housing, offices and commercial buildings, as well as extensions to the underground railway system that have affected the area. See *RAF Uxbridge*.

Vint Hill Farms, Virginia, USA. A specialist listening station that was able to intercept radio transmissions from Berlin and elsewhere using substantial aerials and masts. It was purchased by the US Army in June 1942 and Monitoring Station No. 1 was then established here. It was staffed by the Women's Army Corps, who were trained in Morse code. People were recruited with skills in maths and foreign languages. On 10 November 1943 the station intercepted a crucial message by the Japanese ambassador that would become useful in future planning for D-Day by the Allies. See *USA*.

Virginia, USA. Arlington Hall in Virginia, incorporated the US Army's Signal Intelligence Service. In 1943, it had investigated, on a relatively small scale, Russian cipher messages linked to the Foreign Ministry in Moscow and sent across the world. There would be five organisations involved: diplomats, trade representatives, GRU and two divisions of the MGB. Eventually there would be sharing of information with the British and a joint UK–US team would work on the analysis of Soviet traffic. Canberra, Australia, was one location where the Russians would be active in intelligence gathering and distribution, using the diplomatic service as a cover, based upon findings in 1948. The joint investigation and analysis of Soviet intelligence messages would have initially a cover name of 'Bride', later on 'Drug', and finally 'Venona'. GCHQ Eastcote in England would work on project Venona, i.e. analysing and decrypting the Soviet messages along with the US, but only a fraction of these messages would actually be read and deciphered initially. It was a long-term project that would continue on until the 1980s before the project was closed down. GCHQ moved to Cheltenham in the 1950s, when it was transferred from Eastcote. Arlington Hall would be the base for the US Army's signals intelligence service from 1942 to 1989. It took over the Arlington Hall Junior College educational campus for its new role in signals and intelligence analysis and an investigation of cryptographic techniques and activities of enemy states. In 1989, the Signals Intelligence Service was relocated to Fort Belvoir, Virginia. See *USA*.

Warsaw, Poland. Significant for meetings and research that was established regarding cracking Enigma and German cipher codes. It regained its status as capital of Poland after the First World War. Meetings would be held just outside the city by intelligence services of different countries before the Second World War. Earlier, in 1928, a package arrived at a Warsaw station parcel office. It was en route from Germany to the German embassy/foreign office, but was opened by the Polish staff, who found an Enigma machine within. This was a diplomatic item, and technically protected from customs interference. Polish military intelligence were contacted to arrive at the parcel office, where they found the much-prized machine, to their delight. The delay in passing the package to the Germans caused the embassy personnel some displeasure, and they were advised it had not arrived, but the Poles were able to study the workings of the machine at least for a limited time. It was carefully repackaged and passed to the embassy as though the Poles had no knowledge of what was inside. This was years before the Second World War began, and yet, intrigue and clandestine operations would be common to find out what adjoining countries and neighbours were planning.

The AVA Radio company in Warsaw would be commissioned to make fifteen replica Enigmas in 1933, for the codebreakers to experiment with cracking the message settings. The design of Enigma did become more sophisticated and developed over time, increasing the permutations of settings as more rotors were added, and a *steckerboard*, or plugboard, with cables at the front linking letters together. Warsaw suffered greatly in the war and is remembered for the tragic anti-Jewish operations, which were to spread across Poland and Europe. It is likely that Enigma was used to help communicate instructions and orders to Nazi officers for the transfer of Jewish and ethnic people to Nazi concentration camps, as around 150,000 or more Enigma machines were built and used by the Axis powers. See *Poland.* See *Zygalski*.

Washington DC. The home of the President of the USA. Two American presidents spanned the Second World War period, Franklin Roosevelt and Harry Truman. Some codebreaking Bombes built in the USA were transferred to Washington to tackle Nazi naval codes. They were all high-speed, four-wheel-based machines to counter the four-wheel Enigma threat. The Americans developed their own machines even though Alan Turing, who visited the USA during the war, offered them a British Bombe. They refused as perhaps they had already designed their four-wheel Bombe or were too proud to accept a 'Limey' piece of electronic engineering. As it turned out the USA Bombe was faster than the British design and more efficient. They were built by special teams that included many women in the US Naval Reserve (Women's Reserve), which was created in 1942. The organisation was better known as WAVES, which stood for Women Accepted for Voluntary Emergency Service. It was set up to release resources to allow women to serve in the Navy in shore-based roles to release men to fight abroad. This work involved women both building and operating Bombes. There are photographs of WAVES operating cryptanalytic Bombes from 1943 to the end of the war. In some ways these women would be doing similar work to Wrens, although on different models of Bombes. However, in England, the Wrens did not build the Bombe machines, only operated them. In comparison, the WAVES were principally there to support the Army and Navy. It would be interesting if a WAVES codebreaker could compare notes with a Wren counterpart, but it is not known if that ever occurred after the war, when documents on Enigma were declassified.

The first US Naval Bombe codebreaking machines were shipped from the NCR factory in Ohio to Nebraska Avenue in Washington in September 1943. These were a heavily modified British Bombe design, with a four-rotor Enigma machine basis. There would be many electrical switches to reduce the mechanical parts, and the machine would work more efficiently. The coding of the machines would be N-530s. It is recorded that 121 of these would be manufactured initially. Improved versions would be coded N-1530s. They would be sent to the Naval Communications Complex in Nebraska Avenue. It is understood that by the end of 1943, seventy-seven US codebreaking machines had been constructed, and by then were in operation on Naval intelligence Enigma decrypts. The combined effort of Britain and the United States in decoding many enemy encrypted Enigma messages would help turn the tide of the war in the Allies' favour.

Washington was also an important centre for training and operational codebreaking staff, such as the female codebreakers recruited to work on Japanese intelligence after Pearl Harbor. These would be both cryptographers and cryptanalysts, termed 'Codegirls'. They would be recruited in the thousands, and a training and operational centre would be established at Arlington Hall Junior College for Women. Both the US Navy and Army made use of women in large quantities to support their codebreaking and intelligence operations. Considerable success was achieved in collecting and decrypting information, which resulted in the sinking of Japanese shipping in the Pacific.

Similar to the gender split at Bletchley Park, by the end of the war almost three quarters of the US Army's codebreakers and analysts were women. In 1944 prior to D-Day, many of them would send misleading messages out by radio to support the FUSAG deception, and Operation Fortitude South, forming part of Operation Bodyguard. The National Security Agency (NSA) developed from many of the techniques, systems and procedures that were developed by the female codebreakers and improved over time. See *USA*. See *Bletchley Park*.

Watergate House. Located off the Strand in London, not far from the Savoy Hotel, the site is considered to be the first home of GCHQ. A plaque marking the centenary of the GCHQ was unveiled by HM Queen Elizabeth II at Watergate House in 2019. The plaque acknowledges that GC&CS, the origins of GCHQ, was formed from an amalgamation of the British Admiralty's Room 40 and the War Office's MI1(b), i.e. British Army intelligence. The date of the establishment of the new GC&CS organisation was 1 November 1919 and it had fifty personnel. It relocated to Queen's Gate in Kensington in 1921. This number would grow substantially over time as it relocated to larger premises. Watergate House is Grade II listed and is used for offices today, with a commercial company occupying it. The reception area to the offices features a pseudo-electronic reproduction of Bombe rotor wheels rotating to simulate an Alan Turing 'Bombe' codebreaking machine, to recognise the building's use and heritage. At time of the author's visit in 2019, not long after the plaque was unveiled, on the front window sill stood a boxed Monopoly board game, 'The Alan Turing edition'. See also *Bletchley Park* and *GCHQ Eastcote*.

Whaddon Hall. A listed country house and estate, which was the Secret Intelligence Service (SIS) headquarters during wartime. They would be sending Ultra intelligence to military officers to make decisions and use the intelligence to best advantage. There would be a transfer of certain roles from Bletchley Park in early 1940, but principally in communication distribution. Codebreaking and the development of cryptographic systems would remain at Bletchley Park.

Whitehall, London. Part of central London within the Borough of Westminster, used by the Government and its agencies. The beginnings and early seeds of GCHQ, and British intelligence, was developed from Room 40 on the first floor of the Old Admiralty building in Whitehall, before relocating eventually to Watergate House in the Strand some years later. It then grew considerably, in terms of personnel and resources, over time. The amalgamation of the Admiralty's Room 40 together with Army intelligence, MI1(b), after the First World War formed the new GC&CS. By 1919 the division had transferred and relocated to Watergate House. This was around twenty years before GC&CS was situated at Bletchley Park in Buckinghamshire, away from London. See *Watergate House*. See *Bletchley Park*.

Wimbledon. One of several training bases for Wrens and similar personnel. Mill Hill was the principal base in London for training Wrens. The famous tennis club grounds in Wimbledon were converted into a military camp and also a working farm for food and rations, although the tennis courts were left untouched.

Woburn Abbey. During the war, this country house and estate housed many Wrens working at Bletchley Park on codebreaking and support duties. It was a 'wrennery' for the duration of the war. It also housed Government departments in a support role. Wrens would have to commute into Bletchley Park on a daily basis to do their shift work and return to Woburn at night or after their shift ended. Woburn also housed the Political Warfare Executive, which had a link to Bush House in London. It is now a tourist attraction in modern times. Although not a codebreaking site, Woburn supported many of the 1,676 Wrens who worked on Special X duties codebreaking across six separate sites, including at Bletchley Park. See *Bletchley Park*.

Worldwide Y-stations. A series of different locations across Britain, Europe, USA, Africa and Asia for listening to radio-transmitted intelligence. The name 'Y-station' was abbreviated from wireless station. A radio was often termed a 'wireless' at the time. Numerous Y-stations were spread across the UK.[83] They were on sites owned by different organisations including the Foreign Office, RAF, Army, Navy and GPO. Some were organised by the Marconi Wireless telegraphy company, often at bleak coastal stations. The stations further north in Scotland were particularly useful for intercepting radio communications from Norway and the Baltics. Norway was occupied territory during the war, and heavily fortified with German divisions. The listening stations would be manned by different personnel from the armed services, and civilians too in the specialised bases. Members of the ATS, RAF, WRNS, WAAF and others would sit, concentrate and listen to enemy transmissions on headphones during long shifts covering both day and night. They would have to be competent in taking down Morse code and some could even identify a specific enemy 'key', transmitter or operator. The information would be sent back to coordinating bases such as Bletchley Park, either via courier motorcyclists or via teleprinter transmissions on telephone lines installed by the Post Office engineering division. Names of some of the British Y-stations include: Beaumanor, Cheadle, Chicksands, Sandridge, Whitchurch, Flowerdown, Denmark Hill, Hawklaw, Knockholt, Montrose, Ford End, Wincombe, Cupar, Valance, Highbridge and Whitchurch.[84] Beaumanor is referred to in a British film *Enigma*, for which British composer John Barry composed the music.[85]

Using shortwave radio, places like Rhode Island in the USA could receive transmissions from Cairo in Egypt, some 8,767 km away, or Berlin, 6,139 km away. However, this would require extremely large aerial arrays at the listening station, complete with thousands of feet of wire and cabling. Clearly, large aerials and masts of listening stations could attract the attention of the Luftwaffe in Britain, so were risky. Anti-aircraft guns would be positioned not too far away for some limited protection. Knockholt, at Ivy Farm in Kent, was a listening station that was rather specialist as it intercepted enemy non-Morse messages from encoded Nazi teleprinter attachments. This data transmission via teleprinter was so fast it had to be converted to punched tape, and later analysed by Bletchley Park with a combination of machines and hand-codebreaking methods. Some listening stations would be in the east, such as on the island of Ceylon, and help the Allies in their fight against the Japanese.[86] Several Wrens were transferred to Ceylon, now Sri Lanka, for intelligence support duties. Those abroad in tropical countries complained of the excessively high humidity, and having earphones clamped to their head with sweat running down, listening on the airwaves to faint radio transmissions for hours at a time. Y-station listening would occur abroad at overseas embassies, including Canberra in Australia and Bangalore. Around nineteen stations were in the USA alone, and picked up intelligence from North Africa and Europe, thousands of miles away. The Germans had no idea of the extensive listening stations across America as their agents had been located and all were arrested.

Most Y-station operator staff did not tell their children what they were doing in wartime, or even if they mentioned the base they were stationed at they gave very little away, being wary of the secret nature of their duties and consequences even after the war had ended, until the activities were declassified. While the Nazis knew the Allies would be listening into radio transmissions, they had no idea that advanced Y-stations such as Knockholt would be intercepting non-Morse messages, converting them to punched tape and processing them with a view to decoding them at a headquarters in the British countryside. They would have been astonished at the organisation of the British codebreakers, the systems and methods used.

However, none of it would be possible without the listening stations, which were always the first stage of the codebreaking process. Operators and listeners would need to have skills in sending and receiving Morse code, and be able to identify the non-Morse radio transmissions. Many could detect the 'key' of an enemy operator with experience. Landline enemy communications did not form part of operations as the interception of these was considered too difficult or risky. Sweden did, however, intercept various landline cables. Fortunately, the enemy heavily relied upon radio Morse code or non-Morse teleprinter transmissions for military communication. Radio equipment for listening at Y-stations would be standardised as far as possible, but the Lend-Lease US arrangement with Britain and its allies would go some way to providing certain electronic equipment to aid the continuing war effort against the enemy.[87] A proportion of Voluntary Interceptors or VIs who were radio amateurs, would eventually go into the services and become Y-station listeners, and take less time to be trained in use of Morse code and equipment than others due to their enthusiasm, knowledge and communications experience. If one includes all the RAF bases, Admiralty listening bases, plus Army listening bases there would be several hundred listening stations in total during wartime. Some sources have indicated worldwide there were more than six hundred listening stations. See *Bletchley Park*. See *Knockholt*. See *PORES*.

World powers of co-operation (UK–USA Agreement). A combination of specific countries and places around the world that agreed to share intelligence during the Second World War. These countries included USA, Canada, Australia, Britain and New Zealand. This was continued post-war under the USA–UK accord, whereby it was agreed to share intelligence and co-operate between countries for the benefit of the nations. While the initial agreement came from a 1941 Atlantic Charter, it was developed further with the 1943 BRUSA agreement. This was enacted in

March 1946 after the war had ended and signed by the USA and Britain. The other countries were added soon after. The club of countries that were relevant to this expanded agreement were nicknamed 'the Five Eyes'.[88] Thus, GCHQ in England, protecting Great Britain's interests, will be permitted to share intelligence with the intelligence divisions of other member countries, such as the NSA, and vice versa. The signing of the original agreement in 1946 paved way for the 'Special Relationship' between the USA and Britain, and this phrase has often been referred to by Presidents and Prime Ministers over the years. Each of the member countries to the agreement had English as their principal language, although Canada would also have French in parts of the eastern states. The formation of NATO in 1949 across many different European countries and America in the West further upset the balance of power with Russia in favour of the NATO members. The expansion of NATO in the twenty-first century, which may potentially include new countries applying to join, such as Finland and Sweden, further troubles and angers Russia, which sees NATO as a potential threat, with some member states' territory coming closer to its borders.[89] Alliances can be impacted by political situations in countries as they change over time. However, NATO has survived and has become extremely relevant to modern times. See *Australia,* See *USA.* See *Canada.*

Commentary on Places

Although Bletchley Park might be considered the most well-known place within codebreaking, intelligence gathering and processing during wartime, many other locations in the UK and around the world either supported it directly, or influenced it one way or another. The unique mix of Bletchley being a hub of activity for both military personnel and civilians made it a somewhat strange place in wartime, tucked away in the Buckinghamshire countryside, away from prying eyes. The main mansion building and lake dominated the Park, but the addition of numerous huts for intelligence analysis and processing, administration and others, would somewhat detract from the aesthetics of the place. It was formed as GC&CS to be a type of school or university for investigating intelligence intercepted from abroad, and evolved into GCHQ in modern times through a type of metamorphosis of personnel, systems and leadership. GC&CS would become the specialist university to which academics with exceptionally bright minds were seconded. Many others who may not have been to university, but became adept at applying systems, logic and trial and error to help crack and process Ultra intelligence, would find they had an important role to play at the Park. Thousands of people worked at this strange site and collected data from codebreaking outstations. Those outstations were following the special instructions from Bletchley's codebreakers termed 'Menus', weird arrangements on paper of combinations of lines, letters and numbers.

The outstations were effectively data processors, rather than employing codebreakers. Sadly, most at the outstations had never heard of Enigma, had never seen one, didn't know how Enigma worked or what it could achieve.

Advanced listening stations

The development of Ivy Farm and Knockholt, used to intercept non-Morse enemy messages, would become more important as the war went on to help defeat the advanced German teleprinter encoding machines. The modern analogy might be for a nation to be dealing with the Covid virus and its profound and devastating impact on society. Just when you believe that you are now on top of the situation a series of variants of that virus materialises and you must now adopt a different strategy and approach to deal with it, find resources and act quickly. People's lives are at stake.

Get it wrong, and the results can be disastrous. In wartime, getting the non-Morse messages wrong, or failing to deal with them, could have seriously affected the outcome on D-Day and caused the prolongation of the war, an invasion of Britain by the Nazis and the loss of millions more lives. The V2 rockets could have been increased in number, and possibly led to the development of more serious weapons of mass destruction by Hitler. We know that 'heavy water' was being processed at a hydro plant in Norway by the Nazis to progress a nuclear weapon and was stopped by brave members of the Norwegian SOE.

Non-Morse messages

Few members of the general public would have been aware that there were two parallel problems for Britain and its allies during the war: the Enigma machine and its development over time on one hand, on the other, the non-Morse high-speed messages from the Nazis' advanced encoding machines. It would not have been quite so bad if Turing's decoding Bombe machine could have been used to tackle the advanced machines, but it simply could not. It was never designed to do that, so Turing and Welchman could be afforded no blame. The later Colossus was based upon a different system, and could process different problems if you had the knowledge and expertise. The Bombe, by comparison, was much more limited, designed and built for one specific purpose. New systems would have to be trialled and tested, developed, then materials found and built. This included locating, ordering and testing many hundreds and thousands of valves. Problems would have to be resolved, resources including men, women, materials, electrical power found, and progress reports prepared for the Prime Minister. Many of the places listed in this glossary would be part of the bigger picture in intelligence and processing it. Families may well have had relatives that worked at these bases or locations, which were often top secret.

PORES

It is little known that the PORES research station also played a significant part in assisting government agencies throughout the war in installing eavesdropping equipment, or 'bugs', in buildings to help gather intelligence from suspects and prisoners of war. However, the greatest contribution there was surely the development and construction of advanced codebreaking machines and components for them. There, brilliant engineering minds such as Tommy Flowers, Gill Hayward, Dr E.A. Speight would work together supporting Bletchley Park to develop engineered solutions to the challenging Nazi wartime threat. Post-war, several of those engineers would go on to develop peacetime inventions and developments such as electronic security seals and random number generators for lottery gaming purposes. Britain was truly fortunate to have such a diverse collection of people to help with the war effort.

Malvern and TRE

TRE in Malvern was an interesting site. The largest electronics factory in Europe at the time of the Second World War, with numerous physicists, scientists and engineers designing systems for radar and telecommunications. TRE was instrumental in inventions and achievements across a broad range of technology, assisting with components for advanced codebreaking machines and designing systems to identify U-boats. Many of the materials we take for granted today were simply not available then, and researchers had to use whatever they could get hold of. Add the complication of restricted resources of certain materials due to Hitler's occupation of Europe and the Japanese influence in the Far East, and the challenge for the Allies became greater still. The displacement of Malvern College to accommodate TRE would have been upsetting and disruptive for both pupils and staff. However, it was a necessary inconvenience to allow TRE to expand further into a significant research and development organisation, helping to shorten the war with electronics. So many of the people who worked at TRE and many other supporting bases received little or no recognition after the war. A fortunate few went on to make a name for themselves in careers such as atomic science, astronomy, telecommunications, and engineering.

What's in a name?

It can be somewhat confusing for members of the general public to track the history of GCHQ, the Government Communications Headquarters, particularly in the early years when it was the Government Code and Cipher School (GC&CS). The plaque at Watergate House off the Strand in central London goes some way to explain this. However, it does not indicate on the plaque that GCHQ was officially formed at Eastcote on 1 April 1946, which had previously been the codebreaking outstation Outstation Eastcote, or OSE. Probably there is not sufficient space to show this.

GCHQ relocated to Cheltenham between 1952 and 1954 as additional space was required for expansion. Of course, today GCHQ is still there, and most people are aware of its purpose to protect the nation. Also, to additionally support the intelligence networks of Europe and the USA as our allies. The increasing threat from terrorists, hackers of computer systems who wish to bring down the British economy, the Government or the NHS is increasing and must be monitored continuously. The encoding and decoding machines may have become a bit more sophisticated, using advanced computers and the internet, but the principles of listening in to enemies and potential enemies have not changed.

Teleprinters, cables and noises

People are invariably linked to places. Considering the infrastructure of the complex codebreaking organisations and support, the Government needed the different sites and locations to make the system operate reasonably efficiently. A balance had to be struck to have divisions close together geographically, while spreading them apart to avoid the Luftwaffe destroying all our codebreaking capacity in one brief bombing raid. This is the reason that Bletchley Park had several country houses for support as codebreaking outstations, and two others substantially larger, at Stanmore and Eastcote, some distance away in Middlesex. Stowe School was considered as an outstation, but was dismissed at an early stage for reasons unknown. The methods of communication between sites and bases had to be thought through carefully, developed over time and became established. A combination of using the telephone, motorcycle despatch riders, often Wrens, and teleprinters were used. Teleprinters were much faster than couriers, but they could break down and needed maintenance. Codebreaker Gordon Welchman commented that in the early years the teleprinters struggled to cope with the large quantity of messages that were intercepted.

The despatch rider and courier service offered by Wrens was generally very reliable and worked in all weathers through day and night. The pressure would have been on the Post Office engineers to lay the cables needed for telephones and teleprinters across miles of countryside. Then, there was always the risk of an enemy agent tapping into a landline and listening. However, much of the time all they would have heard is a peculiar noise, which would have to be de-noised at Bletchley Park, and then decoded via different methods. The identification of most of the enemy agents in the UK by the authorities made it safer from the potential risk of the enemy understanding it was breaking their ciphers and codes. If Hitler had realised this was the case, bombing raids would have targeted key sites eventually, but as Britain then had a significant number of outstations, not all would have been lost. It was about spreading the risk; Churchill understood the need to do this, and quickly.

Naval shore-based outstations

The sites and places of a support nature to HQ, Bletchley Park, were many and varied. From farms taken over at Ivy Farm/Knockholt to country houses with stable blocks for machines, and hutted outstations built on open fields. Several hundred Wrens, even in the low thousands, operated many of the codebreaking machines. A handful were at Bletchley but most would be at outstations. All these women required somewhere to eat, sleep, wash and rest, as well as operate the codebreaking equipment. These were run as Naval onshore 'ships', with terminology to indicate you were on a ship and not land. Quarterdeck, galleys, cabins, berths, divisions, tea boats … the list is fascinating, but was there to maintain tradition and assist somewhat with naval discipline. Armed guards and high brick walls around the huts and buildings would have to be the main security, and a constant checking of security passes of all personnel. Social etiquette and military regulations would prevent a number of American signals codebreakers 'berthing' on site with the Wrens, after a hard shift on the codebreaking Bombes. They would have to put up with tents in Ruislip Woods some distance from the base, and travel into Eastcote. They appear to have acted like true gentlemen, according to accounts from Wrens on that base.

Letchworth

And what of Letchworth, the town in Hertfordshire that apparently has no plaque of commemoration or recognition as to how it assisted Britain to defeat the Nazi enemy? With engineers and personnel at BTM and at Spirella, plus other locations around Letchworth, it designed, manufactured, assembled, and tested codebreaking machines, which started as a concept idea by mathematician Alan Turing. He would visit BTM from Bletchley Park with Gordon Welchman to monitor the progress and output of machines. Turing would discuss with chief engineer Harold Keen how to make the machines more efficient. The factory had taken up almost a third of its floor space just to manufacture Bombes. They would even build a 'Super Bombe' which was enormous and so heavy and large they could not lift it off the ground to get it to Bletchley Park. It would later be split back to the four component Bombes.[1]

BTM and Philpotts

BTM was a unique and highly specialist organisation. It had a large presence in Letchworth with its substantial factory, and it acquired other buildings and locations around the town over time. All these helped to assemble parts of the Bombe machine, in a modular approach. To design, obtain the correct materials, plan, organise, train and manager the workforce, liaise with Bletchley Park as to the distribution of the completed machines, and also the codebreaking outstations that took in the majority of the machines, would have been challenging enough with modern computers. To have achieved it without computers in wartime is quite astonishing, with restriction on power supplies, air raids, materials and labour shortages. No wonder the Chairman of BTM, R. Philpotts, held a celebratory dinner after the war, and issued certificates of merit to key staff and personnel. Bearing in mind this work was still classified and top secret, and even the innocent-looking dinner menus for the meal with the Bombe 'Cantab' code reference printed on could have been confiscated by a raid of the authorities under the umbrella of the Official Secrets Act.

Although BTM was fortunate not to have been identified by the Luftwaffe as a prime target due to its manufacture of codebreaking machines, the modular approach, with parts made in other buildings and locations around Letchworth, gave it a degree of comfort. However, a major bombing raid flattening BTM would have seriously put back the efforts of Bletchley Park and the codebreaking outstations if the production of machines and modifications had been stopped by the enemy. Bletchley would then have had to go back to purely manual codebreaking methods, much slower output, and would not have been able to cope with the vast volume of encoded intelligence messages coming in on a daily basis. Additionally, the more complex and secure four-wheel Enigmas take more time to attack, so the whole process would have slowed down, and fewer messages would have been broken. Thankfully, luck was on side of the Allies.

Post-war, some of the buildings and sites survived for a time, but many did not. Some sites would be demolished and redeveloped for much-needed housing. Some of the buildings and sites should have been designated as listed, for architectural or historical significance, but were not, so the bulldozers got there first. Others would be converted into factories, or offices, and there would be little evidence of what went before. Once buildings have been demolished, there is often no indication there as to what was previously on the site, its former use, or impact during wartime and beyond.

The Spirella building in Letchworth had a change of use to commercial offices from the original factory, and was grade II listed. It was reopened after a major refurbishment by HRH the Prince of Wales in the 1990s. Bletchley Park was nearly demolished and sold, but thankfully was saved in the nick of time. Outstation Stanmore and Outstation Eastcote were not so fortunate. The sites were demolished, and housing developments were built in their place. If they were lucky, they got a small plaque, commemorating what had happened there, but that was the exception not the rule. As far as I can ascertain, the site at Stanmore has no plaque or note on the redeveloped housing site. Not even the girls' secondary school, down the road from the old site, knew it even existed until I gave a talk to the pupils about the base and its significance. This is all about the need to preserve local history in our society.

A famous London department store with a secret in the basement

If you have visited the Churchill War Rooms in Westminster, you can understand the claustrophobic conditions of having to work there under difficult circumstances. There is a maze of rooms and corridors, with sleeping quarters on a sub-floor basement, accessed by a ladder, for personnel who had to stay there during the night, perhaps on shift work. One can still see the narrow room used by Churchill to make transatlantic phone calls to President Roosevelt. A lonely place, as there would be no other staff present during the calls. Yet Churchill would not have been aware of the complex American equipment and signals engineer operators situated in the basement of Selfridges, the department store in Oxford Street, making the conversation with the American president secure. There were windowless rooms for the Prime Minister to meet in, and discuss difficult issues, but issues that required urgent decisions. Decisions affecting human life and survival, knowing that your ships were being sunk in great numbers by the U-boats, and that Bletchley Park needed to crack those Enigma codes to give Britain any chance of coming through and defending freedom from Hitler. Churchill had to have a character that balanced his sense of humour with his serious side, and know when to make his displeasure apparent with others. He had to maintain his credibility as a statesman and leader, confiding in the monarch and listening to advice. He had to take the responsibility for his decisions and actions, and explain to Parliament his reasoning and direction, to help crush Hitler. He had to use the intelligence gained from breaking Enigma in a constructive but sensitive way, being cautious as to who, even in his team, should even know Enigma existed, or that the codes and ciphers were being broken by some very clever people and a large support team in top secret bases in England.

Deception as an art and a science

Listening stations in occupied France and the Netherlands provided the Nazis with radio transmission intelligence during the war, listening across the Channel. Of the many stations established, they relied on four key ones for the bulk of British radio traffic. Later, as the war progressed, the British, with the assistance of the Americans, fed false misleading radio traffic across the airwaves. This was part of a major deception operation, Fortitude South, to fool the Germans into thinking there was another major US Army based in southern England waiting to come across the Pas-de-Calais. The radio traffic would include conversations on supplies and equipment, training dates and locations, weather reports, disputes and arguments, even wedding announcements of military personnel. This would have been largely uncoded, open speech radio transmissions and lasted for several weeks prior to D-Day in June 1944. This amazing act of military deception appeared to work, and along with other factors held back Panzer divisions in the north of France awaiting an assault that would never come.

Those intelligence organisations that were rather complacent with their codes and ciphers, such as France both before and in the early stages of the Second World War, suffered greatly as a result, and gave the Nazis a head start for their Blitzkrieg. The British Expeditionary Force at and around Dunkirk was also exposed cryptographically. Lessons should be learnt from having weak ciphers that can be easily penetrated by the enemy. This is just as important in peacetime as in war. Peace always precedes war action, so it is a huge advantage for any state to have up-to-date and accurate intelligence, either before they are attacking an adjacent country or are about to be attacked. They require the resources to maintain secure codes and ciphers, and that is a combination of the cryptographic experts, mathematicians, etc., plus the funding and organisation, together with appropriate leadership. This is where Bletchley Park eventually progressed to have the systems in place, the people, the secure space and buildings, and the effective leadership. Without Churchill it is arguable that the codebreaking and intelligence-gathering system would have lacked resources, and not been as effective.

My research on listening stations that operated during the Second World War surprised me a great deal; the geographical spread of them across the world, those across the British Empire and the USA. Some American Y-stations were collecting German High Command intelligence from thousands of miles away, and they also managed to help control the serious U-boat threat, working alongside other agencies. They were listening to and locating German spies, who were providing information on troop movements so that U-boats could home in on shipping and send them to the bottom of the Atlantic. Without the listening stations, the work of Bletchley Park and the outstations would have been almost insignificant by comparison. They would be the first initial stage in the chain of events to help collect and process the data that the Allies badly needed. The volume of intelligence was increasing daily during the war and it had to be recorded on log sheets, the frequencies identified and checked, direction-finding equipment aligned and tested, and repairs and maintenance carried out. The consistency of the operators was crucial.

COMMENTARY ON PLACES

The random nature of weather conditions and atmospheric pressure would affect the signal reception at times, and incomplete encoded messages would occur frequently. Yet, the overall system generally worked. It was better organised than that of the enemy, and communication between departments appeared to be more efficient, at least to a degree. The involvement of the Americans and Canadians gave Britain a broader listening base to work with than previously. However, the reader is advised to read the book *The Third Reich is Listening* to get an overall, balanced impression.[2] The Allies made mistakes and missed opportunities at times. With so much information needing to be collected, processed and decoded, this is unsurprising.

Special X duties

Most of the codebreaking bases were listed under *Pembroke V*, the administrative name for the Special X duties bases. Mill Hill Wren training base and Outstation Stanmore would be designated as *Pembroke III* for a time, until they fell in line as *Pembroke V*. Some of this can be evidenced in the officers' records of the WRNS, listing different locations and bases. The Wrens were formally instructed to discontinue using the term Station X for Bletchley Park, and it to be redesignated as *Pembroke V* from 15 November 1942. All of this must have been most unsettling and confusing for the Wrens.

Billets for codebreaking and support staff would be in a variety of places, some ornate country houses and rooms, some very basic wooden or brick huts or homes, and rented rooms often with no boiler to heat the water for washing or cooking. Outside toilets were common and freezing in winter. Coal for heating had to be carried in with buckets and scuttles. Those military staff able to bed down in a country house large room with quality carpets or parquet flooring were fortunate. However, women trying to 'spend a penny' at night were wary of going down the long, dark corridors to the bathroom, especially if there were rumours of ghosts in an old, historic building. Woburn Abbey was used as one location for Wrens who worked at Bletchley Park; a beautiful estate to pass through on the way to work in the morning.

Many personnel would be reposted to different locations, and it would not be unusual to train initially at Mill Hill, north London, to be posted to Outstation Eastcote, then posted to Bletchley Park to train others. Then again staff could be reposted to Outstation Stanmore, north London, and just as they settled in reposted again to a base in Scotland, many miles north. They would make friends, compare notes on the different places and learn new skills. But it would be very tiring, all that travelling, and they welcomed a bit of home leave now and again after the very long shifts working on codebreaking machines and activities.

TNMOC, volunteers and veterans

The National Museum of Computing in Buckinghamshire (TNMOC) is unique in that many of its exhibits and items are operational. The proximity to the Bletchley Park Museum is excellent, as one can visit both on the same day. Some items that had previously been in the larger, main Bletchley Museum have been transferred across to TNMOC, such as the working Bombe machine. TNMOC is a source of learning and education, as well as a basis for research on codebreaking machines and items associated with them. It claims to have the world's oldest digital computer. The late Tony Sale, who worked for years on the Colossus replica, would have been proud of the museum and its objective to share learning and education in this specialist field with others. The volunteers who support it put in many hours of their own time to make it the museum it is today.

Spreading confusion

The places of interest where deception techniques were used or developed to confuse and mislead the enemy were spread across the continents to varying degrees: Sandy Hook, in New Jersey, USA, for training and evaluation on a beach with troops being confused as to the direction of an attack; a place on the west coast of Scotland where techniques and training were developed; Virginia, USA, where a camp assembled specialists from a wide variety of trade backgrounds and supplemented them with other soldiers. Then there was the use of dummy vehicles in North Africa and in Europe to imply to the enemy that their resources should be spread more thinly than otherwise would have been the case. While arguably the greatest deception in the war was that of Operation Fortitude South that affected the potential success or failure of D-Day, others on a smaller scale would pay dividends for the Allies too.[3] To establish if those deception actions worked, one had to rely on radio reports, interception of enemy intelligence, confiscation of maps and documents, and contact with the French Resistance. The Y-stations would be kept busy listening to enemy traffic daily, and it would be a major task to filter the encoded messages to ensure the information was passed quickly to relevant commanders.

Signal City

Signal City, at and around the Scottish town of Greenock, was a hive of activity during the war, collecting and processing naval signals. A multiple of different buildings and smaller sites made up the complex, one of the largest communications bases in Britain. Looking at the maps of the area, one house was for Norwegian forces, which makes sense as Norway is just across the North Sea, and there would be several clandestine commando-type operations in the occupied country during the war, although the famous Telemark raids were planned in London. The base was also designated to be a reserve location for transfer of the Admiralty HQ should Hitler invade England.

Bell Labs

Bell Laboratories would make a significant contribution to the war effort in America. From the development of the SIGSALY system to developing a non-Doppler, non-directional sound audio for deception purposes, they would provide technical innovation and modifications that aided the Allies considerably. Their SIGSALY system would be studied by Alan Turing, who visited their factory and secure building laboratory.[4] It would provide a high degree of confidentiality and security between the Prime Minister and Presidents Roosevelt and Truman when talking across the Atlantic. It would also be used at the Battle of Midway in the Pacific. After the war ended, the Americans would come and collect their SIGSALY machine in the basement of Selfridges' annex. An alternative secure voice-encoded scrambled system would have to take its place for post-war discussions with President Truman.

London, intelligence and codebreaking sites

Living in London, I have been intrigued at the relatively close proximity of various historical sites that were either used for codebreaking during the war or had a support role. The Greater London Rail map shows Eastcote, Stanmore, Dollis Hill, Knockholt and many areas in central London listed of historical importance in this field. Knockholt is within the county of Kent, but is not far away from the capital, to the south-east. Letchworth, where Bombes were designed and built is just north of London in the county of Hertfordshire. The Spirella[5] building in Letchworth still exists, after a major and significant refurbishment some years ago. The Post Office Research Engineering Station, PORES, was at Dollis Hill, which is not far from either Eastcote or Stanmore, both of those being codebreaking outstations. Hendon, north London, was the location of the safe house where double agent Garbo was kept by the British Intelligence Service MI5, and who influenced the outcome of the Second World War around D-Day with his false and misleading messages to the Germans. Mill Hill, where Wren training took place, is in north London, again close to places such as Stanmore and Dollis Hill. Barnet, the collection point of data for the wireless Voluntary Interceptors, is in north London, slightly to the east. Watergate House, with historical importance in intelligence and codebreaking as a precursor to development of GCHQ, and with a commemorating plaque on the front wall, lies off the Strand, not far from Trafalgar Square. Churchill's Rooms or Cabinet War Rooms are in Westminster. St James's Street is in central London nearby, and was used for the Twenty Committee to prepare deception plans against the enemy and to monitor double agents and spies. It is only when one travels north from London, past Letchworth, into Buckinghamshire that one encounters Bletchley Park, and some of the outstations nearby that were country houses. Not all the sites remain intact, many have been redeveloped for housing, but some, like Bletchley Park, are museums open to the public. A few more commemorative plaques in and around London would not go amiss and help to keep alive the history of intelligence gathering and codebreaking. There would, of course be numerous listening stations spread across Britain, a proportion of them being RAF stations or Army controlled, with several others coming under the Foreign Office, such as Knockholt, in Kent.[6]

Overseas and UK listening stations

There were hundreds of listening stations or Y-stations during the war, many in Britain but a good number of them overseas. We must not overlook those places and listening stations or Y-stations in the east, such as in Ceylon and on the Pacific islands such as Guam. Australia too had listening stations, and they were also in Kenya during the Second World War. Some were in the Caribbean, while the Falkland Islands also had one. There would be a concerted effort across the continents to help the Allied effort in defeating the Axis powers in Europe, and the Japanese in the Pacific and the east. Australia, New Zealand, India and many other countries would play their part in the overall battle against our enemies. Sharing of intelligence would not always work out well, or efficiently. Such a large operation across the world, with many hundreds of thousands even millions of people, across many different intelligence organisations would lead to mistakes, mishaps, poor communication, rivalries and technical problems. However, that was to be expected and the positives would outweigh the negatives overall. There would be some problems between intelligence services and data analysis of codes in Hawaii, and across the world in Brisbane, Australia. It seems that the Americans may not always have communicated information back to the eastern command efficiently. However, the British made mistakes too, and all this was under extreme wartime pressure, where people were also tired, suffering from fatigue, working very long hours without breaks or holidays. The mix of different social classes across the services would be a mixed blessing. Some from different classes worked well together, such as within the Bombe rooms setting up equipment together in teams, while others created barriers to the promotion of personnel, purely due to their accent, background or their social class. The class system during wartime would remain alive and well.

The stations in the United Kingdom would be listed and reviewed annually, with some modified, others expanded, others merged or close down.[7] Military personnel would be sent out to run the facilities overseas, including many Wrens and RAF personnel. The climate and conditions would be very different to those in Britain. But it was an opportunity to see more of the world, when travel abroad would otherwise have been limited for the average person. Bletchley Park would require the support of many of the outstations to build a picture of Japanese enemy intelligence, although other nations would equally want a slice of the intelligence pie for themselves. Some of the RAF personnel would form small listening teams to warn Allied shipping of potential Japanese air attacks, and would have to be mobilised at short notice as priorities could change quickly.

Moral and legal positions in wartime and post-war

There will always be challenges post-war by society and politicians as to the moral and legal issues surrounding difficult questions. For example, the Germans were using IBM calculating machines to document and calculate data including, reportedly, Holocaust statistics, and unpleasant matters. How much IBM knew of this, and whether it was in a position to do anything about it, would be a matter for others. If the enemy happens to have acquired some of your equipment, and are using it for their benefit, they are unlikely to give it back during wartime. Spare parts might be supplied via third-party countries, however. Siemens in Germany used forced labour, effectively slave labour, during the war, to build equipment in its factories for the Nazis.

A proportion these companies with questions to answer still exist today, and some have acknowledged their past formally, while others have not. War is never black or white, but with numerous, almost infinite shades of grey in between. Somewhere along the line, cryptographers and codebreakers would be intercepting horrendous reports of enemy atrocities, either that had already occurred or were being planned. It would be the job of others, higher up the command chain, to prioritise those intercepts and to take action either during or after the war had ended. Many of the enemy's activities had been concealed and documents and reports burnt, particularly as the Allied forces approached Berlin and Hitler's headquarters. It would be for the War Crimes Commission to determine in the Hague which officers had committed war crimes and which had not.

Technology and progress

In modern times intelligence gathering has been amplified by advances in technology, including satellites observing land and oceans on earth, and helping to identify changes from high up in space. The resolution of some of the new satellite cameras is quite incredible. This has benefits for observing things like climate change, but many are spying on other nations and provide an early warning for troop movements, tracking aircraft, rockets and missiles, military ship movements, and so on. Intelligence gathering has moved on from human spotters and observers with binoculars in balloons, to satellites, drones and other systems. Some drones are highly sophisticated. The observer can now be thousands of miles away from the observed action, and matching this intelligence with decoded encrypted messages. The generals and commanders in the Second World War would have given their eye-teeth to have some of the modern technology to aid them in battle in respect of intelligence-gathering systems.

Social media also plays a massive part in communication nowadays, even though that is generally unencrypted. The existence of the JSSU, or Joint Service Signal Unit, in Lincolnshire is of interest, as there is a coordinated common approach between the British and Americans on surveillance, and electronic cyber-warfare, involving the three main armed services with American input. Based at RAF Digby are the Headquarters of the Joint Cyber & Electromagnetic Activities Group (JCG). There are additional JSS units abroad such as in Cyprus. The Royal Corps of Signals within the British Army has a Volunteer Reserve unit, JSSU(V), and includes specialists such as electronic warfare signals intelligence operators. The Royal Corps of Signals provide specialist communication, cryptographic, linguistic support and advice to the British armed forces. The Americans have their Maritime Cryptologic Integration Center. Joint co-operation is essential to deal with modern-day threats and challenges in the twenty-first century.

Ukraine

I have mentioned Ukraine within this glossary and referred to some of the complex issues surrounding that country today, which have arisen (in part) from events during the Second World War and its volatile history. The use of partisans to share intelligence signals with the Germans, and later be at war with those same Germans, is curious. Different factions of partisans would be fighting one another across Ukraine, and things would change quickly. In history, alliances can and do change. Your friend one minute can become your enemy the next. There were four German High Command communication links across Ukraine back to Königsberg, and no doubt the listening and Y-stations in Britain and abroad would be very interested in those intercepts of non-Morse messages. Knockholt in Kent would have been kept very busy intercepting them and the other Fish links.

Huts at Bletchley

Within this volume of the glossary I have mentioned Huts 6, 7 and 8 and Blocks C and D within Bletchley Park. Why not the rest of them? The huts mentioned were specifically important locations within the Park where enormous progress was made in deciphering ciphers and codes used by the enemy. The others may be mentioned in a forthcoming volume to varying degrees. After all, Bletchley Park does have considerable mention within this book, and space is limited to include other relevant places and people. Additionally, the Park was constantly being worked upon, altered, new blocks built, with equipment, departments and people relocated and transferred elsewhere. One example is the Hollerith records section under Freeborn, based for a time at Bletchley and then relocated some miles away.

Wartime statistics and losses

Codebreaking and the gathering and processing of intelligence was but an adjunct to the act of war, important though it was.

To put this into perspective, it is prudent to show the reader the losses of military and civilian casualties by country, and by quantity, giving examples of some of those countries involved. Listed below are the combined military and civilian *losses*, i.e. deaths, expressed as a percentage of the population in 1939:

COMMENTARY ON PLACES

Country	% of Population that died in the Second World War (Losses)
Germany + Austria [Third Reich]	11.05% of population (8.66 million)
Japan	4.72% (3.365 million)
Italy	1.15% (0.51 million)
USA	0.32% (0.418 million)
UK	0.76% (0.363 million)
British Empire	0.34% (0.439 million)
Canada	0.39% (43,600)
Australia	0.58% (40,400)
France	1.26% (0.523 million)
Poland	18.77% (6.54 million)
Greece	7.02% (0.507 million)
Russia	14.8% (27.917 million)
China	2.9% (15 million)

These figures have been abstracted from *The Second World War Infographics*, that publication being an excellent analysis by the authors of statistical data on the war, also using excellent graphics, and worth studying in some detail. Russia by far exceeded all countries for the heaviest losses in terms of millions of men and women. This was largely due to it being attacked during Operation Barbarossa by the Nazis, culminating in a particularly bloody campaign that saw it fighting for survival over a prolonged period. Brave men and women across the world, and on both sides, fought and died in a war that would result in relative peace within the second half of the twentieth century. Expert historians have given opinions that indicate the Colossus codebreaking machine may have reduced the length of the war by around two years, saving many millions of lives.

Finally, experts at GCHQ, MI5, the NSA, and other intelligence organisations around the world have the benefit of studying in some detail the history of codebreaking, to learn lessons from those who came before and achieved great things, or improved the efficiency of collecting information. They accept that risks sometimes will have to be taken, and that you will only intercept a tiny proportion of everything out there. Then the data needs to be prioritised by humans and via computer-based algorithms. Not all humans are trustworthy, as can be seen from history with some passing secrets to the enemy, but fortunately most are. If mistakes and errors are made, as they will inevitably be, then learn from them quickly. Never forget that, ultimately, irrespective of which codebreaking machines, computers, cryptographic techniques and tools we have at our disposal, in the end it is humans who have to make the difficult judgements that affect all of us.

APPENDICES

Abbreviations

ACSWSA	Admiralty Civilian Shore Wireless Service
AFSA	Armed Forces Security Agency
A I	Artificial Intelligence
ASDIC	Anti-submarine detection investigation committee (Sonar)
ATS	Auxiliary Territorial Service
BP	Bletchley Park
BTM	British Tabulating Machine Company
CESD	Communications Electronic Security Group
CESG	Communications Electronic Security Department
COMINT	Communications Intelligence
CPC	Communist Party of China
CSDIC	Combined Services Detail Interrogation Centre
CSO	Composite Signals Organisation
D/F	Direction-finding
EDSAC	Electronic Delay Storage Automatic Calculator
ELINT	Electronic Intelligence
ERNIE	Electronic Random Number Indicator Equipment
ETOUSA	European Theater of Operations United States Army
FECB	Far East Combined Bureau
FRUEF	Fleet Radio Unit Eastern Fleet
FUSAG	First US Army Group
GC & CS	Government Code and Cipher School
GCHQ	Government Communications Headquarters
GPO	General Post Office
HUMINT	Human Intelligence
ISK	Intelligence Services Knox
JDU	Joint Discrimination Unit
JISD	Japanese Intelligence Signals Digest
JSRU	Joint Speech Research Unit
JSSU	Joint Service Signal Unit
JTLS	Joint Technical Language Service
LCSA	London Communication Security Agency
LEO	Lyons Electrical Office

ABBREVIATIONS

LSIC	London Signals Intelligence Centre
MCIC	Maritime Cryptologic Integration Center
MI 1(b)	War Office/British Army intelligence in Whitehall, London
NASD	Naval Air Signals Intelligence Digest
NATO	North Atlantic Treaty Organization
NCSC	National Cyber Security Centre
NSA	National Security Agency (USA)
OKW	Oberkommando der Wehrmacht (High Command of German armed forces)
OKW-Chi	OKW-Chiffrierabteilung. Decryption department of the German High Command
OSA	Outstation Adstock
OSE	Outstation Eastcote
OSG	Outstation Gayhurst
OSS	Outstation Stanmore
OSS	Office of Strategic Services (USA)
OSP	Outstation (Bletchley) Park
OSW	Outstation Wavendon
PLUTO	Pipeline Under the Ocean
PORES	Post Office Engineering Research Station
RNELH	Ruislip Northwood Eastcote Local History Society
RSRE	Royal Signals & Radar Establishment
SIGSALY	Signal voice encoding/decoding US-built machine
SIS	Signals Intelligence Unit
SCAG	Special Cryptologic Advisory Unit
SCDU	Services Communication Development Unit
SIGINT	Signals Intelligence
SLU	Special Liaison Unit
SOE	Special Operations Executive
RAF	Royal Air Force
RN	Royal Navy
SHAEF	Supreme Headquarters Allied Expeditionary Force
TA	Traffic Analysis
TICOM	Target Intelligence Committee
TNMOC	The National Museum of Computing
TRE	Telecommunications Research Establishment
WAAF	Women's Auxiliary Air Force
WATU	Western Approaches Tactical Unit
WAVES	Women Accepted for Volunteer Emergency Service
WEC	Wireless Experimental Centre
WRNS	Women's Royal Naval Service

British Y-Station Listing

[Note D/F: Direction-finding station, W/T: Wireless Telegraphy Station]

Abbotscliffe
Anstruther
Ashford
Baldock (D/F)
Barwinnock (D/F)
Barrow (D/F)
Beachy Head
Beaumanor Hall
Beeston Hill
Bishop's Waltham
Broadstairs
RAF Canterbury
Capel-le-Ferne
Chacewater
Cheadle (W/T)
Chelmsford (D/F)
Chicksands (D/F) (W/T)
Chilbottom
Clayock (D/F)
RAF Clophill
Coverack
Crail
Crawley
Croft Spa, Scarborough
Cromer
Cupar Foxton (D/F)
Cupar Magask (D/F)
Denmark Hill
Fayreness
Felixstowe
HMS *Flowerdown*
Flowerdown (D/F)
Forest Moor
Fort Bridgewoods
Gilnahirk
Gorleston
GPO TRS Scotland
Hanslope Park
Harpenden
Hartley (Blyth)
Hawkinge
Hawklaw
Helston
Highbridge (W/T)
Ingoldmells (W/T)
Kedleston Hall
Kilwinning (D/F)
Kingask
Kingsdown (W/T)
Knockholt
Land's End (D/F) (W/T)
Lewes
Lydd (D/F)
Lydford (W/T)
Markyate
Marston Montgomery
Meonstoke
Met Office Dunstable
Milstead
Milsted
RAF Monks Risborough
Montrose (W/T)
Mortehoe, North Devon
Newbold Revel (RAF training school)

BRITISH Y-STATION LISTING

North Walsham	Stockland
Norwich, South Walsham	Stockton-on-Tees
Oakhill (W/T)	Stranraer (W/T)
Oban	Strete
Pembroke (D/F)	Sutton Valance (W/T)
Perran (D/F)	Thurso (D/F)
Perton	Torquay
Peterhead	Upton Grey
Portland	Ventnor
Portrush	Waddington (W/T)
Sandridge	Weaverthorpe (D/F)
Saxmundham	Wincombe
Shenley Brook End	Winterton
Shetlands	Whitchurch
Skegness	Wick (W/T)
South Walsham	Withernsea
Southwold	Wrotham
St Davids	Wymondham
St Erth	

Note: This listing is a significant proportion of the listening stations and Y-stations (including several direction-finding stations) in Britain during the war. Some of these were on sites occupied by the RAF, some by the Army, some managed by the Foreign Office, the Post Office, and some miscellaneous bases. A large amount of the listing above is taken from the National Archives HW41/401 Lists and locations of Y-stations.

A temporary listening station was established at Bletchley Park in May 1944 using staff transferred from the Scarborough Y-station. This was due to the approach of D-Day in June and the need for speedy processing of radio and morse intercepts. It was set up in one of the huts on the site, known as Hut 18. We have not listed Bletchley as a formal Y-station in the listing above, however, due to the specialist nature of the station.

Prior to the second world war, Bletchley Park had a radio transmitter on the site until January 1940, when it was not used. The temporary use of Bletchley Park as a Y-station during wartime around D-Day was limited between May 1944 to July 1944. The risks of enemy air attack at Bletchley due to visible radio aerials at the time, were considered relatively low, but were a possibility.

Overseas Listening Stations (examples)

Ascension Island
Falkland Islands, South Atlantic
Faroes
Georgetown, British Guiana
Gerdar, Iceland
HMS *Anderson*, Colombo, Ceylon
Kingston, Jamaica
Lumley, Freetown, Sierra Leone
Naharia, Palestine
St Helena
Terceira, Azores
Tristan da Cunha

The listing above is taken from the National Archives reference HW41/401 of Y-stations. A selection of others include the following: Mauritius, Mombasa (Kenya), Malta, Melbourne and Gibraltar.

Note that lists and locations of Polish Y-stations from 1940 are recorded in National Archives WO 208/5092.

German naval Y-stations are recorded in National Archives ADM 223/6 1945.

Canadian Y-Stations or D/F
St Hubert, Quebec
Hartlen Point, Nova Scotia
Esquimalt, Vancouver Island, British Columbia – station managed via Ottawa
Toronto

Terms and Names

Abwehr The German Secret Service during the Second World War.

Banburismus A system devised by Alan Turing, mathematician and codebreaker at Bletchley Park, to improve efficiency of codebreaking when attacking enemy messages to establish Enigma settings.

Baudot International teleprinter code invented by Emile Baudot. A version of special binary digital code applied to punched paper tape using the alphabet, and some additional characters and commands.

Beach Jumpers American forces operating by sea, which were part of complex deception techniques to deceive the enemy in beach landings, to divert the enemies' attention away from the genuine attacking force.

Bodyguard The code name for the Allied deception operation in 1944 comprising Fortitude North and Fortitude South.

Bureau B A name given to conceal the identity of Bletchley Park.

Cadix The code name for the intelligence centre used by the Poles in southern France at Uzès, under the control of Vichy France before German occupation of the area.

Cambridge Five A group of five British individuals educated at Cambridge University in England, in positions of trust, such as within MI5, who passed secrets to the Soviet Union and acted as spies either during the Second World War, post-war or both.

Cantab The name given to the project for design and construction of codebreaking Bombe machines at BTM in Letchworth.

Cobra A separate and specialist piece of codebreaking equipment that would be attached to Bombe machines with a long thick cable to improve the performance.

Code Synonymous with the term cipher or cypher, a code is a set of rules applied, usually in secret, to enable communication with others who can access those rules. It can be based upon a system of letters of the alphabet, numbers, hieroglyphics or images applied in a particular sequence, or via a specific set of rules. The object is to maintain secrecy and to have control over who can access the message or data being encoded. One person encodes messages or data, and then another decodes them, using the relevant rules.

WW2 CODEBREAKING PEOPLE AND PLACES

Code book A book or document that contains the rules applicable to a particular cipher or code, to enable consistency of approach by those who wish to encode messages or data. Distribution of such code books must be controlled to maintain secrecy.

Colossus The world's first semi-programmable computer designed and built by the engineering part of the Post Office for Bletchley Park. It was designed utilising 1,500 valves, and used to attack the German Lorenz and advanced teleprinter-based encoding machines used by the German High Command. A Mk 2 version was produced near the start of D-Day in 1944, which was several times faster than the original.

Crib Clue.

Cryptanalysis A method of codebreaking using a mathematical or statistical approach.

Cryptography Writing of hidden messages also known as encrypting.

Cryptology A codebreaking method that uses a more linguistic approach.

De-Chi Part of the Colossus decode element of advanced teleprinted non-Morse messages, which was stripped away using the Colossus and Robinson codebreaking machines.

Divisions The naval term for parade used by the WRNS.

Enigma A rotary-based encoding machine designed by Arthur Scherbius and used by the Nazis and other enemy countries during the Second World War. Enigma literally means riddle or puzzle. Different versions were made.

Fish Communication links across Europe used by Hitler and his generals for German high command communication. Nineteen links were established. The routes were given names of fish by the Allies to identify them, such as 'Gurnard' or 'Bream'. Fish was a Bletchley Park code name for this traffic. Fish link messages were often 10,000 characters long, and needed special equipment and processes to analyse and decode.

Some examples given below:

Squid – To Army Group South
Octopus – To Army Group A and 7th Army
Tarpon – To Luftwaffe in Romania
Trout – To German authorities in Memel
Perch – To Army Group centre
Bream – To Rome
Herring – North Africa
Gurnard – Berlin to Zagreb
Jellyfish – Berlin to Paris

Note that Octopus was replaced by Stickleback

TERMS AND NAMES

Fortitude The operation for deception of the Nazis, split into two parts, Fortitude North and Fortitude South.

Fortitude North The code name for the operation by the Allies to deceive the enemy, with activities and radio transmissions in Scotland, to tie up Nazi forces in Norway in 1944. Part of Operation Bodyguard in deception activities.

Fortitude South The code name for the operation by the Allies to deceive the enemy as regards where the main Allied force in England would attack occupied France in 1944, and relevant to preparations for D-Day.

Freebornery A name given to the tabulating section under Freddie Freeborn from BTM, processing message data deciphered from codebreakers at Bletchley Park, for a database using Hollerith punched-card machines.

Geheimschreiber A Nazi 'secret writer' advanced encoding machine.

Ghost army An American specialist division that acted using deception techniques and operations to support main forces and commando units during the war.

Green Hornet The nickname for the SIGSALY voice-encoding and decoding system designed by the Americans during the war.

Heath Robinson See Robinson.

HMS *Pembroke* See Pembroke.

Hydra A cipher key used by U-boats for Enigma communication.

Jellyfish The Berlin to Paris High Command Nazi communication link, being one of several 'Fish' communication links used by the enemy in the Second World War.

Kriegsmarine German Navy.

Lorenz A German teleprinter-based attachment used by the Nazis during the last war to encode German high command messages.

Luftwaffe German Air Force.

Medusa A cipher key used by OKW to command U-boats in the Mediterranean with Enigma.

Menu A set of instructions using letters and graphical connected lines provided by Bletchley Park codebreakers to set up the Bombe codebreaking machines to tackle the message settings of Enigma.

Morse code Communication system of dots and dashes transmitted electrically via an electro-mechanical key, sent either via wires or transmitted via radio telegraphy. Often encrypted during wartime.

Non-Morse A type of system for communication of messages and data that was used extensively during the last war by the Nazis for high-speed, teleprinter-based communication. It was based on the Baudot code of dots and crosses to communicate the alphabet, plus certain punctuation marks. This was used to communicate messages from the German High Command using teleprinter attachments, and machines such as Lorenz and more advanced German secret writers.

Overlord The code name for the D-Day invasion in June 1944.

Paddock The secret underground facility at Dollis Hill, London, for alternative Cabinet War Rooms for the Prime Minister. (Used for only a limited period by Churchill.)

Pembroke The first part of the naval term for administration and associated bases, which were Special Duties X bases, and often established as codebreaking outstations. *Pembroke V* was the most used term for codebreaking stations from an administrative viewpoint, but *Pembroke III* was previously used at some locations, if only for accounting purposes. Official naval onshore bases were termed HMS *Pembroke*, and run as though they were Navy ships.

The Pound A name sometimes used at Knockholt listening station in Kent for the base that occupied Ivy Farm.

Purple A Japanese cipher machine termed 'Purple' by the allies. This was the Type B Cipher machine, the equivalent of Enigma, but designed in a different way with specific features.

Robinson A codebreaking machine used at Bletchley Park to decipher message settings of the advanced German encoding machines. Also sometimes referred to as Heath Robinson, although not designed by that inventor.

Rodding A system to assist decoding of enemy messages at Bletchley Park.

Room 40 British Naval intelligence HQ based in London, and evolved from the First World War.

Rotors Wheel rotors used in the Enigma series of machines, and similar rotary-based encryption machines. These were installed using a code book with instructions and the sequence could vary.

Secret writer An advanced type of Nazi encoding machine.

Settings (Enigma) The configuration of the Enigma machine prior to either sending or receiving an encoded message. The settings must match exactly on both the sending machine and receiving machine in order to be able to read and decode the message.

Shark Naval encoded German messages, often with U-boat positions, movements, and associated intelligence, transmitted over the airwaves using Morse code and enciphered via Enigma. It was the German Triton U-boat communication, given another name.

SIGABA An American encoding machine.

SIGSALY A voice-encoding system invented, designed, and built by the Americans.

TERMS AND NAMES

Special Duties X Another term for a top-secret base with intelligence processing and codebreaking. Many WRNS were allocated to such bases and specialist duties, although their administrative name for the onshore locations was *Pembroke V*, or HMS *Pembroke V*.

Tea boat Name used by the Wrens for the tea trolley on their naval bases, including codebreaking outstations.

Triton This was a cipher used by U-boat HQ to operational Atlantic U-boats. Bletchley Park called Triton 'Shark'.

Tunny An advanced British-designed and built machine to encode secret messages that used a teleprinter by the enemy, and which was prefixed SZ. Also, the range of enemy intelligence and 'Fish' traffic from advanced encoding machines, such as Lorenz, which had to be intercepted by the Allies during wartime. It would also be the British nickname for the Lorenz SZ40 advanced teleprinter attachment used by the Nazis for encoding messages for the German high command.

Sturgeon The code name for the German T52 secret writer encoding machines and group of machines.

Ultra The intelligence encoded by the enemy during the last war, and largely or substantially decoded by personnel at Bletchley Park with the support and assistance of others.

Venona A post-war project to expose and examine foreign intelligence intrusion into the secrets of Western powers, which had used a number of different methods of espionage, including use of foreign agents to infiltrate Western security services. Initial clues of espionage by the Russians were exposed as far away as Canberra, Australia.

Women Accepted for Volunteer Emergency Service (WAVES) American female volunteer personnel, also used to construct the American naval version of the British codebreaking Bombe machine.

Wren Name associated with British WRNS female naval personnel. Wrens operated most of the codebreaking machines at Bletchley Park and the outstations.

Wrennery Buildings near, or attached to, an operational base and usually being adjacent to an onshore naval base with accommodation for WRNS personnel or Wrens. Woburn Abbey was one such 'wrennery', during the war, although it was not a naval base but a country house estate. The Wrens had accommodation there so as to be able to quickly access Bletchley Park to carry out their duties.

Author's Note

When I studied various sources on codebreaking and military history for writing this book, I came across certain differences of opinion of events and of the importance of contributions by individuals, as well as some errors and mistakes. This is inevitable, as the subject matter is so vast, relying on millions of memoranda, documents, photographs, diaries, personal experiences and accounts, dates, times, places, charts, maps, diagrams, organisation charts, listings, etc. I have tried to provide a reasonably balanced view in the glossary. The incorporation of entries across the world confirms that the efforts in codebreaking and intelligence gathering and processing during the war were truly an international task. While Britain had gifted cryptographic experts, mathematicians, physicists and linguists, so did many other countries.

Points of Interest on Intelligence and Codebreaking

- Electronic interception was used as early as 1900 in the Boer Wars.
- In the late 1890s the Royal Navy had Marconi radio sets on some ships.
- The first Bombe, named *Victory*, was only out of action for a total of forty-two hours in the first fourteen months.
- Most codebreaking bombes had names of places, such as cities of the world. All Bombes had a number, but some had more than one name when it was modified, sent for major repair, and refurbished.
- Outstations Eastcote and Stanmore combined had around 85 per cent of the Bombe codebreaking machines built. However, a small proportion of these Bombe machines had also been sent from the country house outstations; Adstock, Wavendon, and Gayhurst, as the new sites were established.
- Some Wrens and operators of both Hollerith tabulating machines and Bombe codebreaking machines claim to have lost some of their hearing due to the excessive continuous noise levels produced when they were present on shift at the bases.
- By D-Day 1944, twenty-six different Fish communication links were being used by the Germans. Four of these links covered Ukraine, which were based around the points of the compass.
- A mobile Lorenz encoded teleprinter caravan with two army vehicles containing cryptographic equipment was used by the Germans in the Second World War, even though the machine was extremely large and heavy, and not really designed to be portable.
- Around a quarter to a third of BTM's factory was involved in Bombe production during wartime. Construction was spread over several buildings with final main assembly and testing in the main factory.
- Some radio receiver sets under the US Lend-Lease agreement with Britain were dumped down a deep well by American personnel after the war ended, as America didn't want them back, preferring the loan to be repaid in full by the British.
- Two Colossus codebreaking machines (out of ten machines built) ended up at GCHQ Eastcote after the war ended, termed Red and Blue. This was prior to

- them eventually being sent to a secret location and then to GCHQ Cheltenham. They were dismantled and destroyed in the 1960s.
- Post Office research engineer Tommy Flowers' car broke down on the way home after the day of installing and testing the Colossus codebreaking machine at Bletchley Park. The date would be 5 February 1944. His diary entry confirms this.
- The SIGSALY voice encryption machine designed and built by the Americans, and installed in the basement of Selfridges during the war, was promptly removed by them after the war. This left the British Government with a problem to ensure secure communications across the Atlantic post-war.
- Converted stables and outbuildings were sometimes used at some of the country house estates where codebreaking outstations were located. Bombe machines would be operated by Wrens in conditions where standing water on the floor would pose a potential safety risk to the operators next to electrically operated codebreaking equipment.
- None of the larger codebreaking outstations exist, both OSS and OSE having been redeveloped for housing. However, the public footpath dividing Blocks A and B at Eastcote still exists, and has history going back to the sixteenth century.
- A chef from the Savoy Hotel worked at Bletchley Park in the early years, preparing food for the codebreakers. However, he left after a while as he could not get on with the personnel and their requirements.
- The book *The Hut Six Story* by codebreaker and mathematician Gordon Welchman was reprinted some years later. Following threats against Welchman by the NSA and British for allegedly breaching security in the information that the original book contained, it was not permitted to be marketed or advertised. The reprinted editions in 1997 later substituted one of the chapters, but that was purely down to the new publisher and not a specific requirement of the security authorities. A summary is below:

Original First Publication *The Hut Six Story*, 1982 (hardback).

Penguin Paperback published 1984.

US Publisher McGraw Hill remaindered last 1,125 copies of US edition.

M&M Baldwin edition published 1997, omitting original 'Part Four' and substituting a new chapter on Welchman's last thoughts on his Second World War work, based on a paper submitted to the journal *Intelligence & National Security*.

Parts One and Two were also published in their entirety. Part Three also published in its entirety but with minor text correction amendments.

(Author's note: Prime Minister Margaret Thatcher of Britain and President Ronald Reagan of America jointly agreed in 1982 that the content of the original book was a potential security threat to the West, based upon reports from the NSA and the advisers to the British Government. The NSA interviewed Welchman about the book's contents in America.)

POINTS OF INTEREST ON INTELLIGENCE AND CODEBREAKING

My sincere thanks to Mark Baldwin of M&M Baldwin publishers, of Kidderminster, for this clarification to my original publisher and myself on 27 October 2020 by letter. There is also some information provided in Appendix III Publishing History, in the paperback edition of the reprinted book of The Hut Six Story.

Experiences of a Codebreaking Wren During Wartime

Eileen Lawrence, (née Hughes), a wartime veteran, shares some of her recollections while a Wren in uniform.

What year did you join the WRNS or Wrens and how old were you at the time?
It was 1943. I was seventeen and a half.

Where did you have your WRNS training and how long was it?
It was at Mill Hill, and I was there two weeks.

Can you recall what sort of things you did while being trained?
The choices were either kitchen duty or cleaning duty. They seemed to be deciding whether they wanted you or not and that you wanted to stay in the Wrens.

When were you told you were going to work on Special X duties at an outstation? Where was your first posting?
Yes, after our training we were told we would work on Special Duties. Outstation Eastcote was the first posting.

What was the accommodation like at an outstation and what were the sleeping conditions there?
There were long rows of huts and bays of four double bunks where we slept with our Wren colleagues.

Did you work on shifts and if so, what was the shift pattern that you had to work to?
Eight-hour shifts, 8–4pm, 4pm–12, and 12–8am. At the end of a long run of shifts we had four days off, which they called 'stand-off'.

Did they make you and others sign the Official Secrets Act when you arrived at the outstation?
Yes, we all had to sign the Official Secrets Act.

Did anyone tell you about the Enigma encoding machine? Did you and your other Wren colleagues understand what the purpose of the outstation was?
Not until arriving at Eastcote were we told anything about this. Once we arrived there, we were told the purpose of the outstations.

EXPERIENCES OF A CODEBREAKING WREN DURING WARTIME

Can you recall the food at the outstations, and the sort of things they gave you to eat?
I can't remember specifically the actual meals, but it was all pretty revolting! I stopped having sugar in my tea as the only sugar available was brown sugar then.

What did you do in your free time?
We went into London, by train. We also explored the local area as to what was there for entertainment and things. I did have a bicycle so I could get around.

At the outstation were there Post Office engineers and RAF engineers to help maintain the Bombe machines?
I recall only RAF personnel.

When working and setting up the Bombe codebreaking machines in the huts is there anything you specifically remember about them?
You tended to get little electric shocks from the wires.

Did you work alone on the machines or as a team?
We worked always in pairs.

You also worked for a time at Outstation Stanmore, I believe? Did you meet people there you had known from Eastcote or your training?
The outstations of Stanmore and Eastcote were very similar from memory, at least as far as the set-up and buildings. Some of my colleagues did move to Stanmore at the same time as I did.

I think you told me that after one long shift on the machines at Eastcote, you came outside the huts and heard a nightingale bird singing. Is that memory still clear from all those years ago?
Yes, it is.

I understand you were at a base in Scotland during the war on a posting. What was that base?
At the end of the war I was sent to Skegness, which was a Butlin's holiday camp, and there were four of us to a chalet. We were not permitted to walk on the beach. From there after nine weeks, we went onto Donibristle Fleet Air Arm, in Scotland, and I was employed as a writer.

What happened to you after that?
I ended up working at MI5, until I got married.

Anything else would you like to share with us on your wartime escapades?
I remember arriving at Euston station from Glasgow during an air raid!

Author's Note: We thank Eileen for sharing the above with us, of events and experiences so many years ago. This book is dedicated to Eileen by the author.

Selected Papers of Alan Turing

Item	Ref	Dates
The Physical principles of the Quantum Theory	Ref AMT/B/43	1930
On Computable Numbers with an application to the Entscheidung problem [Note this is often abbreviated to 'On Computable Numbers']	Ref AMT/B/12 N/Archives	Issued May 1936, published Jan 1937
Zeta function machine	Ref AMT/C/2	17 July 1939
The Rules of 'Go'	Ref AMT/C/22	1930–39
Wartime research papers of Alan Turing released by GCHQ. National Archives HW25/37, HW25/38	GCHQ	GCHQ 1945–46
The History of Hut Eight 1939–45	Ref AMT/B/27b	1945
Computing Machinery and Intelligence	Mind 59 AMT/B/19	Oct 1950
Proposed Electronic Calculator		1946
The Automatic Computing Engine (Turing Wilkinson)	Lectures	1946/47
Intelligent Machinery/Man as a Machine	AMT/C/11 AMT/B/28	1947/1969
Mechanical Intelligence (An internal document under the National Physical Laboratory and National Archives Reference: DSIR 10/385)	Lecture	Typescript in early 1946 published 20 Feb 1947
Pure Mathematics	papers	August 1952
Mathematical Logic		1937–1945
NR 964 CBCB55 9024A 19390000 Turing's Treatise on the Enigma	AMT/C/30	1939–1942

SELECTED PAPERS OF ALAN TURING

Item	Ref	Dates
Mathematical Theory of Enigma Machine (also known as 'Prof's book')	Nat. Arch HW 25/3	1939–1942
Report on Speech secrecy system DELILAH. A technical description by A.M. Turing & D. Bayley REME	Nat. Arch HW 25/36	
Programming a Digital Computer to Learn	AMT/B/51	1952
The Chemical Basis of Morphogenesis	AMT/C/26	Published August 1952
	AMT/C/9	1954–1977
Can digital computers think?	AMT/B/5	15 May 1951
Can automatic calculating machines be said to think?	AMT/B/6	1952
Alan Turing's original proposal for the development of an electronic computer	AMT/B/25	1972

Note: Some of the above are held at the Cambridge University King's College Archive Centre or the Turing Archive. A few of the above had other joint contributors also. *Computing Machinery and Intelligence* poses various questions that Turing suggests in terms of the thinking machine, i.e. thinking from the process of learning. *The Imitation Game* film title was probably taken from this paper as it appears as a heading early in the 1950 published paper.

Sources

The National Archives at Kew
Bletchley Park Heritage Trust
The National Museum of Computing, Block H, Bletchley Park, Milton Keynes, MK3 6EB
GCHQ – Government Communication Headquarters
The National Cryptologic Museum, Maryland, US
The Association of Wrens
The Royal Navy
The Radio Society of Great Britain (RSGB)
The Association of Estonians in Great Britain
Uxbridge Reference Library, LB Hillingdon
Pembroke Park Estate and Public Footpath, LB Hillingdon
Letchworth Tourist Information Office
Letchworth, Garden City Collection, www.gardencitycollection.com
Letchworth Garden City Heritage Foundation
The Imperial War Museum, London
The Churchill Rooms, London
Bentley Priory Museum, Stanmore
Historic England
Ruislip Northwood Eastcote Local History Society
Eastcote Residents' Association
The London Borough of Harrow
The London Borough of Hillingdon
Headstone Manor and Museum, LB Harrow
The Science Museum, London
BBC and BBC News, online sources
BBC, WW2 People's War (online)
WinstonChurchill.org
Bletchley Park, emails, Dr David Kenyon, Research Historian
Bletchley Park, emails, Guy Revell, Museum Archivist
Bletchley Park, Outstations – A Brief history
Bletchley Park – Podcasts
WRNS, *Wren History 1939–1945* online source
British Telecom (BT) archives
The Channel Islands Military Museum, St Ouen, Jersey, C.I.

Bibliography

Books, articles, and publications

Agar, John, *Turing and the Universal Machine* (London: Icon Books Ltd, 2001)
Agar, John, *The Government Machine – A Revolutionary History of the Computer* (Cambridge/London: MIT Press, 2003)
Aldrich Richard James, *GCHQ* (London: Harper Press, 2010)
All The King's Men – British Codebreaking Operations 1938–43. Thesis by Andrew J. Avery – East Tennessee University (2015)
Avarez, D., *Allied & Axis Signals & Intelligence in WW2* (London: Routledge, 1999)
Batey, Mavis, *Dilly – The Man Who Broke Enigmas* (London: Biteback Publishing, 2017)
Boon, Rachel, PhD student, University of Manchester, 2020. Thesis: *Research is the Door to Tomorrow – The Post Office Engineering Station Dollis Hill 1933–1958* (University of Manchester, Centre for History of Science, Technology and Medicine.
Buttar, Prit, *Between Giants – The Battle for the Baltics in World War II* (Oxford: Osprey Publishing, 2013)
Campbell-Kelly, Martin, *ICL – A Business and Technical History* (Oxford: Oxford University Press/Clarendon Press, 1990)
Cawthorne, Nigel, *Alan Turing – The Enigma Man* (London: Arcturus Publishing Ltd, 2016)
Coghlan, Peter & Dr Thomas Cheetham. *Knockout Punch* (*Ultra* Bletchley Park Magazine Issue 18, 2022)
Copeland, B. Jack plus others, *Colossus – The Secrets of Bletchley Park's Codebreaking Computers* (New York: Oxford University Press, 2010)
Corera, Gordon, *Intercept The Secret History of Computers and Spies* (London: Weidenfeld and Nicolson/Orion 2016)
Cox, Colleen A., *A Quiet and Secluded Spot-Ruislip, Northwood, and Eastcote* (London: Ruislip, Northwood and Eastcote Local History Society, 1991)
Dunlop, Tessa, *The Bletchley Girls* (London: Hodder & Stoughton Ltd, 2015)
Erskine Ralph & Smith, Michael, *The Bletchley Park Codebreakers* (London: Biteback Publishing, 2011)
Ferris, John, *Behind the Enigma The Authorised History of GCHQ Britain's Secret Cyber-Intelligence Agency* (London: Bloomsbury Publishing, 2020)

Gannon, Paul, *Colossus-Bletchley Park's Greatest Secret* (London: Atlantic Books, 2006)
Gladwin, Lee A., Article: *Alan Turing, Enigma, and the Breaking of German Ciphers in World War II* (Archives.gov, Fall 1997)
Greenberg, Joel, *Alastair Denniston* (Barnsley: Frontline Books, 2017)
Greenberg, Joel, *Gordon Welchman* (London: Frontline Books, 2016)
Hinsley & Stripp, *CodeBreakers – The Inside Story of Bletchley Park* (University of Oxford: Oxford University Press, 2001)
Jennings, Christian, *The Third Reich is Listening – Inside German Codebreaking 1939–45* (Oxford: Osprey Publishing, 2018)
Kasekamp, Andres, *A History of the Baltic States* (London: Red Globe Press, 2018)
Kenyon, David, *Bletchley Park and D-Day* (New Haven and London: Yale University Press: 2019)
Kerrigan, Michael, *ENIGMA How Breaking The Code Helped Win World War II* (London: Amber Books, 2018)
Kippenhahn, Rudolf, *Codebreaking – A History and Exploration* (New York: Abrams, 1999)
Koorm, Ronald, *Backing Bletchley – The Codebreaking Outstations from Eastcote to GCHQ* (Stroud: Amberley Publishing, 2020)
Lamb, Christian, *Beyond The Sea – a Wren at War* (London: Mardle Books, 2021)
Large, Christine (Director at Bletchley Park), *Some Human factors in codebreaking* [From a paper published in 2002 given at RTO HFM Symposium
Levine Joshua, *Operation Fortitude* (London: Harper Collins Publishers, 2012)
Lopez, Aubin, Bernard, Guillerat. *World War II INFOGRAPHICS* (London: Thames & Hudson, 2019)
Lucas, Russell, *German Secret Service* Glossary chapter (2016)
Macintyre, Ben, *Double Cross* (London: Bloomsbury Publishing, 2012)
Matthews, Peter, *SIGINT* (Stroud: The History Press, 2018)
McKay, Sinclair, *The Secret Life of Bletchley Park* (London: Aurum Press Ltd, 2011)
McKay, Sinclair, *The Secret Listeners* (London: Aurum Press Ltd, 2013)
McKay, Sinclair, *The Lost World of Bletchley Park* (London: Aurum Press Ltd, 2013)
McKay, Sinclair, *The Spies of Winter* (London: Aurum Press Ltd, 2016)
McKay, Sinclair, *100 People you never knew were at Bletchley Park* (London: Safe Haven Books Ltd 2021)
Messenger, Charles, *The D-Day Atlas* (London: Thames & Hudson, 2014)
Miller, Russell, *Code Name Tricycle* (London: Pimlico, 2005)
Montefiore, Hugh Sebag, *ENIGMA – The Battle for the Code* (London: Weidenfeld and Nicolson/Orion 2011)
Morris Moses & John Wade, *Spycamera – The Minox Story* (West Sussex: Hove Collectors Books, 1998)
Page, Gwendoline, *We Kept The Secret* (Norfolk: George R. Reeve Ltd, 2008)
Paterson, Michael, *Voices of the Codebreakers* (Barnsley: Greenhill Books, 2018)

BIBLIOGRAPHY

Pearson, Joss, *Bletchley Park's Secret Room* (Stroud: Amberley Publishing, 2015)

Philpott, Colin, *Secret Wartime Britain* (Yorkshire: Pen and Sword Books Ltd, 2018)

Ramsey, Winston G., *The War in the Channel Islands – Then and Now* (Poland: After the Battle Magazine Publications, 1981/2012.

RNELHS, *The Home Front Ruislip, Northwood and Eastcote in Wartime* (London: Ruislip, Northwood and Eastcote Local History Society, 2007)

Vogal, Steve, *Betrayal in Berlin* (London: John Murray 2018)

Roberts, Captain Jerry, *Lorenz* (Stroud: The History Press, 2018)

Singh, Simon, *The Code Book* (London: Fourth Estate Limited 2000)

Smith, Michael, *Station X The codebreakers of Bletchley Park* (London: Pan Books, 2004)

Smith, Michael, *The Debs of Bletchley Park* (London: Aurum Press Ltd, 2015)

Smith, Michael, *Bletchley Park – The Code-Breakers of Station X* (Oxford: Shire Publications, 2014)

Storey, Neil R., *WRNS The Women's Royal Naval Service* (Oxford: Shire Books/Osprey Publishing, 2017)

Summers, Julie, *Our Uninvited Guests* (London: Simon & Schuster, 2018)

Taylor, Neil, *Estonia – A Modern History* (London: Hurst & Company (Publishers), 2018)

Tidy, Josh, *Letchworth Garden City in old photographs* (Letchworth: Heritage Foundation Letchworth Garden City, 2016)

Tidy Josh, *Letchworth Garden City Through Time* (Stroud: Amberley Publishing Ltd, 2015)

Turing, Dermot, *XY & Z The Real Story of How Enigma was Broken* (Stroud: The History Press, 2018)

Turing, Dermot, *PROF – Alan Turing Decoded* (Stroud: The History Press, 2016)

Welchman, Gordon, *The Hut Six Story* (Kidderminster, M&M Baldwin, 2018)

Weller, A., *Secret Eastcote* (London: Friends of Eastcote House Gardens Community Archive Publication, date unknown)

Whitehead, David, *COBRA* Paper by David Whitehead CEng MIEE (1994)

Wilcox, Jennifer. *Behind the Enigm a- History of the Cryptanalytic Bombe* (NSA - Centre for Cryptologic History Reprinted 2015 United States of America)

Articles

After the Battle, Issue 37 (Historical society)

Atlas, company historical information ICL and ICT

Grace's Guide to British Industrial History, Graces Guide, 2012 (Graces Guide Registered Charity), Information on BTM Co.

Local paper article (2014) on unveiling of the plaque at Pembroke Park

The Rutherford Journal, The Turing Bombe (Online)

Sale, Anthony, *The American 6813th Technical History 1945* – reformatted by Tony Sale © 2003

Signal City, Geoffrey Dykes/RN Communications Branch Museum/Library
The Independent, Article on Dorothy O'Grady (Date unknown)
The National Archives. *Operational Selection Policy OSP28 – Government Communications Headquarters and Its Predecessors* (Revised January 2006)
Toms, Susan (RN&E LHS) *The History Behind the Road Names for Pembroke Park, Eastcote*
Toms, Susan (RN&E LHS) Papers and articles from The Ruislip, Northwood, Eastcote Local History Society – *Codebreakers at Eastcote*.
Toms, Susan (RN&E LHS) *Enigma and the Eastcote Connection – 2005* The Ruislip, Northwood, Eastcote Local History Society
Tony Sale, Menus

Other sources of information/websites

Bombe Types, www.Bombe.org.uk
www.Chris-Intel-Corner -Blogspot (Italian Cryptograph
www.codes and ciphers.org.uk (The British Bombe, 6812th Signal Security Detachment (Prov) APO 413 US Army, pdf scan via Tony Sale)
www.commsmuseum.co.uk
www.Cryptomuseum (Netherlands)
www.Firstworldwar.com
www.goldbeach.org.uk
Hertsmemories.org.uk (BTM webpage)
www.history.mil
www.HistoryNet

Online Podcast E80 by Bletchley Park, October 2019, on Outstation Eastcote
Online Podcast E145 Torch to Tunis-Bletchley Park

Online Podcast E128 by Bletchley Park, 'Whitehall 7947'
PastScape, Drayton Parslow
www.Prabook.com
www.theintercept.com
Radio Boulevard, Western Historic Radio Museum
Ruislip Online, online source, including extracts from DTI staff articles relevant to Eastcote, post-war
Russia Beyond, www.rbth.com
www.Stmuscholars.org
www.subbrit.org.uk
Subterranean Britannica
www.usni.org
War History online
The wartime memories project, www.wartime memoriesproject.com
Wikipedia.org/wiki/Typex
Wikipedia WATU

BIBLIOGRAPHY

Miscellaneous Sources

Bill Thompson USN (Ret)

Correspondence and discussions with an ex-Wren Eileen Lawrence (née Hughes), who worked at two outstations during the war.

Discussions with managers of various military-based museums on wartime historical events.

Discussions, letters, and communication with certain ex-Wrens (WRNS) who worked on codebreaking machines and equipment during the war and who contacted the author's publishers after reading his book *Backing Bletchley*, published in 2020.

Damien Horn. My particular thanks to Mr Damien Horn of Jersey, C.I., curator of the Channel Islands Military Museum at St Ouen, Jersey, to allow reproduction of certain photographs of wartime military equipment from a private collection.

Discussions or emails with individuals who worked on the outstation base at Eastcote or had family members who had links with the base or Y-stations. This included some ex Wrens.

Discussions with individuals who have had some knowledge of the Eastcote Outstation, mainly post-war, several of them locals.

Discussions with Betty Hollingberry, ex Wren, based at Eastcote during wartime as Betty Vowles.

Discussions with a Bletchley Park Voluntary Guide at Northwood Hills Library in 2018.

Discussions with a member of the National Museum of Computing at both Northwood Hills Library and at Ruislip Manor Libraries in 2018.

Discussion with a number of ex British Telecom engineers who trained at Bletchley Park after the war.

Discussions with Mr T. Voore, ex BBC test engineer, on radio equipment and electronic equipment used in wartime. Additionally, discussions with him on the George Blake prison escape outside Wormwood Scrubs.

Emails and correspondence with members of the Association of Wrens over the last few years.

Examination of local maps of the Eastcote and surrounding areas sourced at Uxbridge Reference library and elsewhere.

Exhibition at the Science Museum in 2019 on GCHQ and codebreaking.

Extracts from Microsoft Powerpoint Presentation (R. Koorm FRICS) on Codebreaking Outstations – Eastcote to GCHQ (copyright 2018).

Extracts from Microsoft Powerpoint Presentation (R. Koorm FRICS) on Support Services to Intelligence Operations during WW2 (copyright 2019).

Extracts from Microsoft Powerpoint Presentation (R. Koorm FRICS) on D-Day and Codebreaking during WW2 (copyright 2019).

Extracts from Microsoft Powerpoint Presentation (R. Koorm FRICS) on Fake News or Deceiving the Enemy During WW2 (copyright 2020).

Investigation and study of the two volumes of the Bombe registers on loan to the National Archives at Kew (HW25/19 and HW25/20).

Maps, photographs and information via the Collections Officer at the Garden City Collection, Letchworth.

Radio Society of Great Britain (RSGB) Emails exchanged with the Radio Society of Great Britain (2021/2022) (RSGB).

Smithsonian Channel television broadcaster various documentaries on the Second World War.

Various Television documentaries on codebreaking and intelligence and the Second World War.

Various TICOM reports: TICOM Secret Intelligence in Nazi Germany – Fish and the Jellyfish Convoy.

NB a proportion of the above presentations were prepared by the author for museums, history societies, and similar. Some were given in person and some online. The presentations are the copyright of the author. Photographs within the presentations are credited to the source or sources where appropriate.

Some of the National Archives reference documents (reference codes) researched are listed as follows, but are not a complete list, only a snapshot of some that have relevance to the subject. Note that the endnotes also contain references in places to specific National Archive documents:

HW 25/19, HW 25/20 (Vols 1 and 2 Bombe registers)

HW 14/9, HW 14/57, HW 14/48, HW 14/43, HW 14/56 (cover story for Stanmore and WRNS staff recruitment), HW 14/123

HW 14/48, HW 64/63, HW 64/65, HW 14/51, HW 14/60, HW 34/17, HW 34/21, HW 47/1, HW 64/25, HW 14/164

HW 64/63, HW 64/25, HW64/45, HW 64/68, HW 64/76, HW 14/164, HW 14/62

FO 366/2221 (Financial arrangements GC&CS Eastcote)

WO 208/5092 (Polish outstations), HW 4, HW 2/69, HW 25/22, HW 41/401, HW 50/72, HW 55/1, HW 64/28, HW 192/420, HO 391/12, HW 8/97

Other Acknowledgements

Photographs supplied via GCHQ are By the kindness of the Director of GCHQ © Crown copyright.

Access to the National Archives for research by the permission of The National Archives, Kew, Surrey, England.

Selected information relevant to Ex Wren, Eileen Lawrence, (Née Hughes), via Eileen's daughter, Jane Frusher.

Those individuals who provided papers and information on BTM, ICT, ICL and associated history of the BTM development, including post-war.

Several volunteers from Bletchley Park attending talks on codebreaking given by the author at various times, and discussions with them.

Museums of Interest in England

The Imperial War Museum, Lambeth, London (www.iwm.org.uk)

Bletchley Park, Bucks. (bletchleypark.org.uk)

TNMOC, The National Museum of Computing, Bletchley Park, Bucks (www.tnmoc.org)

Bentley Priory Museum, Stanmore, Middlesex (bentleypriorymuseum.org.uk)

Battle of Britain Bunker Museum, Uxbridge, Middlesex (battleofbritainbunker.co.uk)

Royal Signals Museum, Blandford Camp, Dorset (www.royalsignalsmuseum.co.uk)

The National Army Museum (www.nam.ac.uk)

Endnotes

Introduction

1. The Association of Wrens is the main organisation for ex Wrens who served in the Royal Navy.
2. TNMOC, The National Museum of Computing.
3. National Security Agency (USA).
4. Non-Morse is a teleprinter-based system using Baudot encoded symbols used on advanced encoding machines.
5. *Backing Bletchley – The Codebreaking Outstations from Eastcote to GCHQ.*
6. *Ultra*, Bletchley Park Magazine, Issue No. 18 Autumn 2022.

Glossary: People

1. Outstation Eastcote.
2. Source WRNS Officers 1939–45 online listings.
3. N/Archives HO391/12 1966 Escape of George Blake from HM Prison Wormwood Scrubs
4. The rear bumper of the van was not in place, only the supporting brackets. The brackets were then severely distorted due to the impact of the getaway car with the van.
5. Newmanry was the machine section using advanced codebreaking machines.
6. Do not confuse with Highgrove, which was used by the Prince of Wales.
7. i.e. autumn 1943.
8. Now referred to as the Churchill Rooms, open to the public as a museum.
9. PORES.
10. Initially three country houses were selected: Adstock, Gayhurst and Wavendon.
11. A film of this event, which is a remake of the original, was released in 2022.
12. The first three letters of the SIGSALY acronym indicating SIGNAL.
13. Vocoder is a general term for voice-encryption system, and versions have been used in the pop audio industry, with Cher being famous for one of her songs being heavily synthesised in part.
14. Churchill would write 'Action This Day' agreeing to almost unlimited resources for Bletchley Park when four codebreakers there signed a letter requesting urgent action.
15. The author recalls when at grammar school being challenged by a friend as to why my mother and I were not going to visit the coffin of Churchill at

Westminster Abbey to pay our respects, as he had planned to do with his parents. I didn't really have an answer, but as my parents and brother were from the Baltic States, and had only just obtained British citizenship, the role of Churchill to our family was perhaps not as pertinent or clear as it would be to a family whose parents fought under Churchill.

16. Reverend William Montgomery and Dilwyn Knox were the other codebreakers who worked alongside De Grey on the Zimmerman telegram in GC&CS. De Grey had been nicknamed 'the Dormouse' by a colleague.
17. There would be numerous models of Enigma and variations of those models. Some would have complex attachments to further improve security.
18. VE day was formally 8 May 1945.
19. Source: www.Firstworldwar.com
20. The use of the British 'Ruperts' around Caen was shown in the film *The Longest Day*.
21. Camouflage techniques were also taught in several American art colleges to students who went on to apply it on vehicles and equipment. This was all part of the deception techniques used.
22. Hollerith machines were effectively tabulating sorters or processors of punched cards that had data on them.
23. Staff at Bletchley Park and associated secret bases were formally written to after the war to remind them of the need for secrecy to be maintained continuously.
24. National Archives HW 14/9 Freeborn's requirements for equipment for Hut 7. See also HW 50/72 Dossier on Hollerith Machinery. Historical notes on use of Hollerith equipment under Mr Freeborn in Hut 7 at GC&CS.
25. N/A HW 25/22 Use of Hollerith punched card equipment in Bletchley Park.
26. The article 'Knockout Punch' in the Bletchley Park Magazine indicates there were differences of opinion and conflict between Freeborn and Bletchley Park management in prioritisation of processing data. Other sources confirm this further.
27. N/A HW 25/22 ditto.
28. Spelling of Elizebeth is correct, and not a misprint.
29. National Archives KV2/65, KV2/66, KV2/69, KV2/71 KV2 268, KV2/4213, KV2/4207, KV2/4193 communications by letter and W/T.
30. Pujol travelled to Venezuela.
31. The cracking of the four-wheel Enigma rotor coded messages using captured enemy code books from U-boat *U-559* after many months of stalemate by the codebreakers, resulted in identifying positions of enemy U-boats in 'wolfpacks'. The Admiralty made good use of this intelligence but the Allies had to be careful not to give too much away. The Germans would get suspicious if convoy courses were changed too frequently away from the gathering wolfpacks.
32. Post-war, during the Cold War period, the speaking clock would play a role in providing accurate time communication for British Strategic Command via its control base in High Wycombe in a possible nuclear attack situation, and also to communicate to police stations for the instruction to provide warning sirens for the general public.

ENDNOTES

33. Source: University Thesis on All The King's Men, British Codebreaking Operations 1938–43, author Andrew J. Avery, East Tennessee University.
34. Mavis Lever and Keith Batey, codebreakers at Bletchley Park, did the decrypts of the decoded Italian message that indicated an attack was imminent against the British.
35. Source: www.islandecho.co.uk
36. Thesis by PhD student Rachel Boon in 2020. University of Manchester, The Post Office Engineering Research Station, Dollis Hill 1933–1958.
37. Thesis by PhD student Rachel Boon in 2020. University of Manchester, The Post Office Engineering Research Station, Dollis Hill 1933–1958.
38. When Arthur Scherbius tragically died prematurely in an accident others took over the running of the company, and developed other versions of the Enigma machine, more sophisticated versions in some cases.
39. J. Agar, *Turing and the Universal Machine*.
40. With considerable input from Harold 'Doc' Keen on the engineering side at BTM.
41. Gordon Welchman, *The Hut Six Story*, Addendum II.
42. AMT/C/31 Report of AMT's visit to The National Computing Machine Laboratory at Dayton, Ohio, Dec 1942.
43. National Archives/King's College Archive Centre, Cambridge. AMT/B/9.
44. Publisher M&M Baldwin clarified this in some detail in October 2020 via letter for the author of this glossary. For further detail see the appendix Points of Interest on Intelligence and Codebreaking.
45. See the appendices for a simple summary of events relevant to *The Hut Six Story* provided via publishers M&M Baldwin.
46. Eileen Lawrence, another codebreaking veteran and a Wren, met Kay at the Bletchley Park veterans day in September 2022 and they exchanged experiences. Eileen commented to the author that she learned more at that veterans' lunch about wartime listening stations than she had been allowed to during the war.
47. Bombe registers are on loan to the National Archives in two volumes.
48. Some reports say 'Bomba' was from the name of a popular Polish ice cream!

Commentary on People

1. A radio presenter and interviewer told the author that until he had read the book *Backing Bletchley* he was convinced there was only one codebreaking Bombe machine based on what he saw in the film *The Imitation Game*.
2. HMS *Anderson* near Colombo, Ceylon.
3. Some staff used a wooden stick to help turn the wheels and make it easier to operate.
4. Gordon Welchman, *The Hut Six Story*, Chapter The First Year.
5. The Bletchley Park Roll of Honour can be accessed and searched online.
6. Some may have argued that the machine shown in the film *The Imitation Game* was a mere prototype Bombe, but nevertheless the absence of a scene showing

numerous machines being operated would give a misleading impression to the viewing public.
7. Checking machines were manual machines of three to four wheels that could be turned in both directions by the operator.
8. Three Americans working at Bell Laboratories in the US were John Bardeen, Walter Brattain and William Shockley and they jointly developed the modern transistor.
9. Stefan Krah was a professional violinist and amateur cryptographer.
10. Arguably, the Americans had the benefit of learning about the British Bombe, and experimenting with improved circuits and similar. They also probably had access to more materials and resources.

Glossary: Places

1. Sri Lanka is the modern name for Ceylon.
2. The author's parents and brother came from Estonia, one of the three Baltic States, and they had first-hand experience of the Russians during wartime. They left Estonia to start a new life in Britain in the mid-1940s, and were advised by the Home Office not to return as their children would be conscripted into the Russian Army if they did so.
3. National Archives CAB 114/34 1941-45 Establishment of Voluntary Interceptors in the Royal Observer Corps.
4. Source: Bentley Priory Museum.
5. Also, Italian, and some smaller sections were accommodated here for translation and for codebreaking.
6. N/A. HW 14/57 Redesignation of name from 15 November 1942 to HMS *Pembroke V*.
7. N/A. HW 14/43 Use of Ultra code word in lieu of 'Special' for all SIGINT material.
8. Robinson was used as a name from Heath Robinson, as the machine looked as though it was thrown together from different parts.
9. Drayton Parslow was the data processing Hollerith section that started at Bletchley Park but grew to unmanageable proportions as regards the need to store millions of punched cards. Drayton Parslow was managed by a BTM manager and the staff were mainly women.
10. National Archives HW14/3. Official designation of GC&CS in future to be Government Code and Cipher School. (1/1/1940-28/2/1940)
11. The American 6813th Technical History 1945 reformatted by Tony Sale © 2003.
12. Hut 18 (formerly Hut 8) was used for these temporary radio receivers.
13. N/A. HW 14/57 Hut 6 planning of resourcing H/speed Bombes.
14. Gordon Welchman, *The Hut Six Story*, Addendum III.
15. The 'Super-Bombe' was known as Giant. It was later dismantled into its four component Bombes. See *Backing Bletchley*, Chapter 8: Wrens and Bombes, by the author for details.
16. Source: *ICL: A Business and Technical History*.

ENDNOTES

17. BTM relied upon its contracts for calculation of the census of certain foreign countries, but wartime activities with building and modifying codebreaking machines would take up a proportion of the factory, and the resources. Computer development post-war is mentioned in *Grace's Guide to British Industrial History* and also in *ICL: A Business and Technical History*.
18. Source GCHQ website, Bletchley Park Page.
19. Around 10,000 acres for the military base with around 7,000 personnel.
20. The Channel Islands military museum on Jersey is full of examples of equipment, papers, maps and items from the war. It is situated at the end of a long beach, St Ouen, not far from the Jersey Pearl site.
21. The National Archives has documents that indicated GCHQ was proposed as the new title for Bletchley Park as far back as 1940. HW14/3.
22. A test carried out at the Pentagon, Washington, and Chopmist Hill listening station identified a spy transmission test within seven minutes of it being transmitted, the fastest of all Y-stations.
23. N/A 64/28 Admin of GC&CS outstation Drayton Parslow 30/4/1944–16/4/1946.
24. Source: Ruislip Online, information from a civil servant typist who worked at Eastcote post-war.
25. The author cannot recollect which of the sites this 'lashing' of printer to stabilise it occurred at, but could have been GCHQ Eastcote or even Bletchley Park.
26. Source: Ruislip Online from DTI staff personnel magazine articles.
27. This was confirmed to the author by the museum archivist at GCHQ in September 2019 via email.
28. Some of the envelopes marked 'GCHQ Bletchley Park' were exhibited at an exhibition at the London Science Museum, in 2019 or early 2020.
29. Source: Ruislip Online, entry of edited report from a DTI official writing in a DTI staff magazine, and who had detailed knowledge of the Eastcote base post-war.
30. The final plan agreed for D-Day was communicated to General Eisenhower, Churchill and HM King George VI shortly before D-Day on 15 May 1944 at St Paul's Boys' school in Hammersmith, London. A plaque exists to commemorate the meeting at the site on the boundary wall on the main road.
31. See 'Garbo'.
32. At time of writing British and other NATO troops are in Estonia, and help to protect it and the other Baltic States from a potential Russian threat.
33. Rejewski, Zygalski and Rozycki, cryptographers.
34. Russia invaded Poland two weeks after the Germans, yet Britain did not declare war on Russia.
35. We know that Outstation Eastcote in Middlesex had Siemens relays in some of the codebreaking Bombes.
36. VIs would be recruited largely from ham amateur radio enthusiasts; mostly men but some women too.
37. Harrow School is a fee-paying public school in Harrow on the Hill.
38. The exact address of the safe house at Crespigny Road, Hendon, is open to debate, as some books show No. 15 while other reports indicate 35.

39. General Slim in India made certain complaints about lack of intelligence at the time of the conflict with the Japanese, but other reports indicated he had sufficient intelligence to support the British and Indian armies, and use this to his advantage against the Japanese. See Captain F.W. Winterbotham's account in his book *The Ultra Secret*.
40. N/A HW 55/1.
41. N/A 192/420.
42. N/A HW 55/1.
43. A photograph of the assembly of Bombe machine components by women in the BTM factory and possibly also the Letchworth Spirella factory is available at the Garden City Collection Museum at Letchworth captioned 'Wizards with Wires'.
44. The Spirella company had reserved a bed at the local hospital in case a member of staff fell ill, and it paid for this facility.
45. Lime Grove would be the main entrance/exit and the route to and from Eastcote, where cafes and shops could be accessed by personnel on their breaks. Locals in the houses along Lime Grove would frequently see Wrens and military personnel walk up and down the road, but not be aware of their activities on the base.
46. American 6813th Technical History 1945, reformatted by Tony Sale, 2003.
47. i.e. the House of Commons.
48. Military History Matters online map of 'Sinking the Bismarck – The last voyage of the Bismarck' identifying interception of various British Naval forces and coastguard aircraft gathering intelligence in May 1941.
49. The author visited the site to inspect some flooring in a gymnasium a few weeks prior to the IRA attack. A colleague had commented that the incoming visitors' security had seemed somewhat casual at the time.
50. Twelve SIGSALY units total is the correct number of SIGSALY units made but some reports indicate only ten machines. The cryptomuseum website indicates twelve.
51. Shipping crossings for convoys across the Atlantic amounted to 85,775, whereas the losses principally due to German U-boats and similar enemy action amounted to 654 ships, around 0.75 per cent of the total. Merchant ship losses, not all in convoys, amounted to some 2,200 ships and 14 million tons. Source: World War II Infographics.
52. The total U-boats produced between 1939 and 1945 amounted to 1,170.
53. World War II Infographics.
54. Information verified by email from Museum of GCHQ to author dated 10 September 2019.
55. A film, *The Heroes of Telemark*, would be made in the 1960s with Kirk Douglas leading the raid in Norway.
56. Wrens arriving at Outstation Eastcote from Mill Hill training facility were often shocked at the drab surroundings encountered at the base.
57. The public footpath at Eastcote dividing the site into two created security problems for the base managers and armed Royal Marines would be needed at strategic points.

ENDNOTES

58. Local public houses near the outstation were off limits for most due to a local rule to avoid loose tongues by codebreaking support personnel within a certain radius of the outstation. This would have been lifted post-war, when Eastcote became GCHQ.
59. Bletchley Park was also sometime referred to as GCHQ before it closed down and Eastcote took over the reins after the war, prior to GCHQ relocating to Cheltenham in the early to mid-1950s.
60. One publication indicated there were three Colossi sent to Eastcote after the war, but this is not confirmed and it is much more likely just two were transferred.
61. This fact was also confirmed to the author in an email from Bletchley Park some years ago.
62. It is not known if Churchill did look over the substantial, wide, open fields at Eastcote on his honeymoon, the site of the eventual largest codebreaking outstation, but it is probably the case that he did so, as it was directly opposite Highgrove House, where Churchill stayed with his new wife.
63. N/A HW 14/43.
64. Although GCHQ had been used on occasions at Bletchley Park previously, it was probably an unofficial name, Bletchley being known as GC&CS, and only became official when GCHQ was established at Eastcote in April 1946. A bank account was established in the name of GCHQ for the site.
65. i.e. Adstock, Gayhurst and Wavendon outstations, which preceded Outstations Stanmore and Eastcote.
66. Bletchley Park was identified as *Pembroke V* in 1941–45 for the purposes of WRNS codebreaking activities, along with codebreaking outstations.
67. N/A HW 14/57 November 1942.
68. N/A HW 8/96.
69. Sourced from the biography *Alastair Deniston*, Chapter 'Berkeley Street', by Joel Greenberg.
70. The author recollects that a podcast on Scarborough listening station was broadcast by Bletchley Park some time ago.
71. Jennings, Christian, *The Third Reich is Listening*.
72. SIGSALY was protected within communication cable ducts in London to prevent enemy interference and there would be sensors to detect any interference along the cable route.
73. One of the SIGSALY machines was positioned on an American ship used at the Battle of Midway. Britain was allocated only one machine out of the ten built by the Americans.
74. Parachutes were also made by Irvin's down the road at Letchworth, an American-owned company. Irvin's subcontracted some of their work to Spirella, before BTM used the workers for Bombe component production.
75. Source: *ICL: A Business and Technical History*.
76. The local Territorial Army Reserve sometimes holds events and demonstrations on the land of the St Paul's boys' school site, showing their operation of weaponry and communications equipment.

77. Thesis by PhD student Rachel Boon in 2020, University of Manchester, The Post Office Engineering Research Station, Dollis Hill 1933–1958.
78. The Molotov–Ribbentrop non-aggression pact of August 1939 signed in Moscow.
79. At time of writing the situation in Ukraine is dominating the news. The entry in this glossary is intended to be a very brief summary of the wartime situation in and around Ukraine, and many historians will have specific views as to how things evolved and when and how specific European territory was claimed. The author does not claim to be an expert on the subject but does have in-depth knowledge and some family history of the Baltics during the Second World War and the period leading up to it, which was not far from the area of Ukraine.
80. Lend-Lease, the basis of the Act agreed by Congress in the USA in 1941, amounted to $49 billion dollars of aid to its allies, being almost a fifth of its total wartime expenditure. The British Empire received some $30.7 billion, the largest share of the pot.
81. Morris Moses & John Wade, *Spycamera – The Minox Story*.
82. The author lectured at the museum on the seventy-fifth anniversary of the D-Day assault, on D-Day and codebreaking in 2019.
83. See listings of British Y-stations in the appendices to this glossary.
84. N/A HW41/401 Lists and locations of Y-stations. This information is provided year by year, and at the end of the war the listings of those either shut down or planned to be shut down and demolished after 1945.
85. *Enigma* was released in Britain in 2001 and adapted from a novel.
86. HMS *Anderson* in Ceylon near Colombo. GC&CS. N/A HW4. Also relevant is FRUEF.
87. Many used American-made military radios lent to the British were dumped down wells after the war as the US did not want them sent back.
88. One assumes that the EU may possibly be an additional member as time passed.
89. Sweden and Finland applied to join NATO in 2022 following Russia attacking Ukraine.

Commentary on Places

1. The super-bomb was named Giant and built at BTM.
2. Author Jennings, Christian.
3. Fortitude South was part of Operation Bodyguard.
4. The first SIGSALY machine would be installed at the Pentagon.
5. Spirella was originally a corset and foundation wear company and had a factory in Letchworth, Hertfordshire.
6. See listings of British Y-stations within the appendices to this book.
7. N/A. HW41/401 Lists and Locations of Y-Stations – N/A HW 50/15/3 Relations with Y-Stations and GC&CS.

Index

A

Abbots Cliff House 80
Adstock 60, 137, 140, 142, 187, 197, 213, 219
Africa 21, 40, 43, 48, 53, 70, 79, 80, 97, 98, 99, 111, 112, 119, 129, 131, 152, 153, 156, 167, 168, 178, 192
Alexander 2, 3, 8, 70, 88, 117, 119
Arlington Hall 82, 163, 164, 165
Arizona 80, 143
Army 8-11, 14, 20, 22, 25, 26, 37, 39, 40-43, 49, 50, 51, 53-55, 60, 62, 75, 78, 80-83, 86, 88, 89, 93, 98, 99, 103, 109-111, 114, 115, 119-122, 127, 133, 143, 148, 150, 152, 156, 158, 163-168, 176, 179, 181, 186, 187, 189, 192, 193, 197, 216, 219
Atlantic 13, 57, 99, 135, 136, 187, 223
Australia 24, 77, 82, 83, 89, 95, 106, 163, 168, 169, 180, 183, 195

B

Baker Street 83, 128, 129
Baltic Sea 53, 83, 84
Baltic States 84, 109, 127, 148, 159, 160, 206
Barbarossa 6, 53, 84, 98, 147, 148, 183
Barnet 42, 85, 128, 179
Batey 2, 33, 34, 35, 67, 215
Battle of Britain Bunker 145, 163, 212
Battle of Britain House 84, 85
Baudot 2, 3, 27, 112, 124, 191, 193, 213
Beaumanor 85, 86, 98, 167
Bentley Priory 86, 140, 156, 204, 212, 216
Berkeley Street 86, 128, 219

Berlin 3, 22, 30, 33, 43, 49, 57, 60, 75, 86, 87, 102, 103, 109, 113, 125, 142, 149, 152, 153, 155, 163, 167, 181, 192, 193
Blagrove 3, 77
Bletchley / Bletchley Park 2-13, 15-20, 23, 25, 28, 29-73, 75-77, 79, 82, 84, 86, 87-94, 97, 98, 100-114, 116-119, 121-131, 135-144, 147-149, 153-156, 159-162, 165-168, 170, 171, 173-180, 182, 186, 187, 189, 191-195, 198, 204
Blake 3, 4, 5, 213
Block C Bletchley 19, 91, 118
Block D Bletchley 91
Blunt 4
Bodyguard 22, 143, 158, 165, 191, 193, 220
Bombe 4, 10, 11, 12, 13, 16, 29, 30, 31, 32, 36, 39, 40, 42, 43, 44, 45, 47, 50, 52, 53, 54, 56, 57, 58, 60, 61, 62, 63, 65, 66, 68, 69, 70, 71, 72, 74, 75, 76, 77, 78, 79, 88, 89, 90, 91, 92, 93, 95, 99, 100, 105, 106, 107, 113, 115, 117, 118, 119, 123, 125, 126, 128, 137, 138, 139, 140, 141, 143, 147, 149, 155, 156, 157, 159, 161, 162, 164, 165, 166, 171, 173, 174, 178, 179, 180, 191, 193, 195, 197, 198, 201, 210, 215, 216, 217, 218, 219
Bourne 4
Broadway Bldgs. 91
BTM 19, 20, 28, 29, 30, 31, 32, 44, 52, 53, 56, 57, 63, 76, 78, 79, 90, 91, 92, 100, 104, 105, 118, 126, 138, 155, 174, 186, 191, 193, 197, 207, 208, 211, 215, 216, 217, 218, 219, 220
Bundy 127
Burgess 4, 5

C

Cairncross 4, 5, 149
Cabinet war rooms 7, 92, 93, 99, 101, 128, 129, 133, 134, 179, 194
Cadix 97, 191
Cambridge 3-5, 8, 10, 15, 23, 24, 33, 37, 38, 41, 56, 57, 63, 88, 93, 191, 203, 215
Canada 12, 77, 93, 94, 113, 168, 169, 183
Canaris 5
Caughey 5
Ceylon 43, 60, 66, 77, 80, 89, 94, 116, 122, 123, 161, 167, 180, 190, 215, 216, 220
Channel Islands 95, 96, 204, 209, 217
Chateau des Fouzès 97
Cheltenham 2, 8, 29, 48, 90, 97, 106-108, 112, 136, 139, 145, 146, 164, 172, 198, 219
Chesterfield Street 97
Chicksands 97, 98, 167, 188
China 3, 98, 148, 159, 183, 186
Chopmist Hill 98, 99, 217
Churchill 4-8, 10, 13, 28, 29, 31, 37, 38, 47, 54, 56, 58, 67, 68, 71, 72, 90-93, 99, 101, 115, 122, 125, 128-130, 132-134, 139, 140, 145, 146, 151, 156, 158-161, 173, 175, 176, 179, 194, 204, 213, 214, 217, 219
Churchill Rooms See Cabinet War rooms
Colossus 5, 7, 12, 13, 15, 16, 17, 18, 23, 27, 29, 37, 39, 40-44, 46, 48, 51, 54, 55, 61, 63, 64, 68, 72, 73, 77, 88, 90, 101, 102, 106, 113, 124, 129, 139, 149, 159, 162, 171, 178, 183, 192, 197, 198
Cooper 8, 107
Cumming 8

D

Dayton, Ohio 10, 11, 12, 58, 99, 100, 163, 215
D-Day 6, 13, 15, 17, 22, 23, 25, 28, 37, 43, 74, 75, 89, 93, 96, 105, 108, 112, 113, 120, 123, 125, 127, 128, 134, 135, 137, 138, 142, 146, 150, 153, 155, 156, 158, 159, 163, 165, 171, 176, 178, 179, 189, 192, 193, 194, 197, 206, 210, 217, 220
De Grey 9, 214
Denmark Hill 80, 100, 124, 128, 167, 188
Derby House 101
Desch 10, 11, 12, 62, 63, 75, 100
Denniston 9, 10, 33, 48, 56, 61, 88, 94, 110, 206
Dönitz 12, 13, 142
Dollis Hill 6, 7, 15, 18, 25, 27, 39, 40, 41, 44, 45, 51, 52, 54, 61, 69, 72, 90, 93, 99, 101-103, 128, 131, 142, 145, 159, 160, 163, 179, 194, 215, 220
Donibristle 29, 201
Dorset 98, 103, 108, 115, 129, 212
Douglas Fairbanks Jnr. See Fairbanks Jnr.
Drayton Parslow 16, 19, 20, 28, 89, 91, 104, 105, 118, 208, 216, 217
Du Boisson 13

E

Eastcote x, 2, 4, 5, 8, 18, 24, 29, 32, 35, 48, 52, 54, 58, 60, 63, 67, 68, 90, 97, 102, 105, 106, 107, 108, 112, 115, 123, 126, 127, 128, 136, 137, 138, 139, 140, 141, 142, 143, 145, 157, 162, 163, 164, 166, 172, 173, 175, 177, 179, 187, 197, 198, 200, 201, 204, 205, 206, 207, 208, 209, 210, 213, 217, 218, 219
Eisenhower 13, 25, 128, 129, 134, 150, 156, 217
Ellis 13, 14
English Channel 13, 93, 95, 108
Enigma 2, 4, 6, 8, 9-13, 16, 18, 20, 22, 23, 25-28, 30, 32-34, 36, 37, 39, 40, 42-51, 57, 59, 60, 61, 63-65, 66, 67-75, 78-83, 88, 91, 95, 97, 100, 101, 108, 110-113, 115, 117, 118, 119, 121, 122, 125, 129, 135, 136, 138, 142, 144, 148, 153, 154, 156-158, 161, 162, 164, 165, 167, 170, 171, 174, 175, 191-194, 200, 202, 203, 214, 215, 220

INDEX

Estonia 84, 109, 127, 160, 204, 216, 217
ETOUSA 54, 89, 123, 127, 138, 147, 162, 186
Etrétat 109, 115
Ewing 9, 14, 146, 147

F

Fairbanks Jnr. 14, 15, 133, 150
Fenson 15
Finland 84, 109, 110, 127, 157, 169, 220
FISH 23, 27, 55, 60, 88, 112, 124, 125, 135, 182, 192, 193, 195, 197, 210
Fletcher 15
Flicke 15, 16, 126
Flowerdown 110, 167
Flowers 12, 13, 15, 16, 17, 18, 39, 40, 41, 43, 44, 45, 51, 61, 64, 71, 72, 73, 76, 77, 90, 101, 102, 103, 171, 198
Fort Mead, Maryland 110, 163
Fortitude 22, 74, 112, 135, 137, 150, 153, 165, 176, 178, 191, 193, 220
Fortitude North 112, 137, 150, 191, 193
Fortitude South 22, 74, 112, 135, 153, 165, 176, 178, 191, 193, 220
Foss 18, 19, 33, 107
France 4, 6, 9, 12, 13, 15, 22, 26, 30, 43, 48, 57, 60, 72, 73, 75, 78, 80, 84, 87, 95, 96, 97, 103, 108, 109, 110, 111, 112, 113, 115, 127, 129, 135, 137, 142, 143, 144, 150, 158, 176, 183, 191, 193
Frankfurt Am Main 112
Freeborn 19, 20, 28, 29, 76, 91, 104, 105, 118, 182, 193, 214
Freebornery 20, 193
Fricke 20, 114
Friedman 20, 21, 122
FUSAG 43, 75, 123, 127, 143, 165, 186

G

Gano 21, 156
Garbo 13, 22, 23, 44, 74, 113, 115, 127, 143, 145, 151, 153, 155, 179, 217
Garcia-See Garbo
Gayhurst 90, 140, 141, 142, 187.
   See OSG

GCHQ 2, 8, 14, 18, 19, 23, 24, 25, 29, 35, 48, 52, 55, 56, 58, 62, 63, 67, 89, 90, 94, 97, 105, 106, 107, 108, 110, 112, 116, 126, 127, 128, 129, 136, 137, 139, 140, 142, 145, 146, 154, 162, 164, 166, 169, 170, 172, 179, 183, 186, 197, 198, 202, 204, 205, 206, 209, 211, 213, 217, 218, 219
Geheimschreiber 157, 193
Germany 3, 5, 7, 9, 12, 13, 22, 25, 26, 27, 29, 32, 34, 37, 40, 42, 43, 47, 49, 54, 61, 70, 84, 86, 87, 93, 98, 103, 109, 111-113, 121, 125-127, 135, 144, 147-150, 154, 157, 158, 160, 162, 164, 181, 183, 210
Gibraltar 113, 127, 131, 152, 190
Golombeck 23
Good 8, 23, 24, 38, 56
Grabeel 24
Grazier 25
Greece 35, 40, 114, 121, 129, 131, 152, 155, 183
Green Hornet 93, 151, 193
Greenock 151, 152, 153, 178
Greenwich 3, 114

H

Hall 25
Hammersmith 13, 22, 128, 255, 217
Hanslope Park 85, 102, 114
Hardelot 115
Harpenden 115, 188
Harris 25
Harrow 104, 115, 130, 147, 156, 204, 217
   Harrow School 104, 115, 130, 217
Hayes 26, 120
Hayward 26, 27, 102, 103, 171
Heath Robinson see also Robinson 13, 15, 193, 194, 216
Hebern 27
Hendon 17, 115, 179, 217
Highgrove House 5, 115, 116, 140, 214
Hitler 5, 6, 7, 8, 12, 13, 16, 22, 27, 28, 40, 46, 51, 52, 61, 64, 68, 70,

223

71, 75, 86, 96, 101, 108, 112, 113, 121, 139, 143, 146, 148, 153, 171, 172, 173, 175, 178, 181, 192
HMS Anderson 43, 80, 89, 95, 116, 123, 190, 215, 220
HMS Pembroke 3, 4, 29, 88, 115, 116, 143, 193, 194, 195, 216
HMS Tullichewan 117
Hollerith 16, 19, 20, 28, 29, 76, 79, 89, 91, 104, 105, 116, 118, 126, 182, 193, 197, 214, 216
Hollingberry 29, 209
Hooper 29
Hughes 29, 200, 209, 211
Hut Six 2, 15, 30, 39, 56, 91, 117, 118, 216
Hut Seven 19, 63, 89, 91, 105, 116, 118, 214
Hut Eight 2, 23, 34, 39, 58, 91, 118, 119, 216

I

India 55, 60, 77, 82, 119, 120, 122, 180, 218
Ireland 26, 29, 97, 120
Irvin 30, 219
Isle of Wight 42, 120
Italy 40, 47, 70, 79, 87, 113, 121, 122, 149, 152, 183
Ivy Farm 80, 100, 101, 122, 123, 128, 159, 167, 170, 173, 194

J

Japan 2, 6, 10, 19, 21, 38, 43, 45, 46, 47, 57, 60, 63, 66, 77, 78, 81, 82, 83, 86, 87, 89, 94, 95, 98, 99, 110, 116, 118, 119, 120, 122, 128, 131, 132, 133, 134, 143, 148, 159, 160, 161, 162, 163, 165, 167, 172, 180, 183, 186, 199, 218
Jeffreys 30
Jeffrey's sheets 30
Jenkins 30, 38, 46
Jones E 30, 31, 106
Jones RV 31, 108

K

Keen 7, 10, 27, 31, 32, 44, 48, 56, 67, 77, 92, 114, 121, 174, 215
Kensington 122, 166
Kent 5, 60, 75, 78, 80, 88, 96, 100, 108, 116, 122, 123, 128, 141, 142, 143, 147, 150, 159, 162, 167, 179, 182, 194
Kenya 80, 95, 123, 180, 190
Kesselring 32
Kew 123, 204, 210, 221
Knockholt 5, 43, 52, 60, 78, 80, 88, 97, 100, 101, 109, 122, 123-125, 128, 142, 150, 159, 167, 168, 170, 173, 179, 182, 188, 194, 222
Knox 9, 10, 33, 34, 35, 47, 60, 67, 154, 186, 214
Koch 34, 49, 50
Konigsberg 125, 160, 182
Krah 74, 216
Kriegsmarine 12, 52, 58, 89, 101, 118, 193
Kroger 34
Kursk 5, 54, 125, 147, 148

L

Lauf 15, 16, 114, 126
Laughton-Matthews 34
Lawrence, Eileen 200, 209, 211, 215
Letchworth 19, 20, 28, 30, 31, 32, 44, 52, 53, 56, 57, 63, 69, 72, 78, 79, 88, 90, 91, 92, 100, 104, 105, 118, 126, 138, 140, 155, 156, 174, 175, 179, 191, 204, 207, 210, 218, 219, 220
Lever 2, 33, 34, 35, 40, 67, 121, 215
Lime Grove 126, 127, 145, 218
Lisbon 113, 127, 145
Listening Stations-14, 20, 26, 39, 52, 60, 61, 67, 70, 77, 79, 80, 82, 85, 86, 90, 93, 97, 98, 99, 108, 109, 114, 115, 117, 118, 125, 134, 135, 142, 143, 153, 154, 155, 167, 168, 170, 176, 179, 180, 189, 190, 215
Lithuania 84, 109, 127, 160
Little Brickhill 127

INDEX

London vi, 3, 6, 7, 8, 10, 13, 15, 16, 17, 21, 22, 25, 29, 32, 34, 35, 37, 39, 40, 42, 44, 44, 52, 53, 61, 80, 82, 83, 85, 86, 87, 91, 92, 97, 99, 100, 101, 105, 107, 114, 115, 116, 120, 122, 128, 129, 130, 131, 133, 134, 136, 137, 139, 142, 144, 145, 151, 152, 155, 156, 157, 158, 159, 160, 161, 163, 166, 167, 172, 175, 177, 178, 179, 186, 187, 194, 201, 204, 212, 217, 219
Lorenz 13, 16, 27, 41, 43, 44, 45, 46, 52, 54, 55, 56, 59, 60, 61, 69, 72, 88, 100, 149, 192, 193, 194, 195, 197
Loutsa 129
Lovell 35, 36, 103, 129
Lywood 36

M

Maclean 5, 37
Malta 129, 131, 152, 190
Malvern 36, 39, 63, 72, 90, 103, 104, 115, 129, 130, 136, 172
Marston Montgomery 130
Masterman 37
Mediterranean 7, 12, 16, 35, 40, 42, 43, 67, 70, 79, 113, 121, 129, 130, 136, 152, 154, 193
Menzies 37-150
Michie 23, 30, 37, 38, 46, 56, 58, 59, 64, 70, 71
Midway Island 122, 131, 132
MI5 4, 22, 29, 37, 42, 74, 75, 85, 102, 115, 127, 145, 159, 179, 183, 191, 201
Mill Hill 68, 128, 131, 144, 166, 177, 179, 200, 218
Milner-Barry 2, 38, 39, 70, 117
Molotov 84, 109, 147, 220
Morell 39
Morgan 39
Morse 2, 5, 23, 39, 40, 41, 42, 43, 52, 59, 60, 71, 78, 80, 82, 86, 88, 100, 101, 109, 110, 112, 114, 119, 123, 124, 128, 131, 134, 135, 136, 150, 153, 160, 163, 167, 168, 170, 171, 182, 189, 192, 193, 194, 213

Murray Hill 132
Mussolini 40, 121
Myers 40

N

National Archives 32, 123, 124, 140, 189, 190, 202, 204, 208, 210, 211, 214, 215, 216, 217
National Physical Laboratory 58, 134, 158, 202
Nazi 2, 5, 6, 7, 9, 10, 12, 13, 15-17, 20, 22, 23, 25-29, 31, 32, 34, 36, 37, 38, 40, 42, 43, 45, 46-48, 50, 53, 54, 56-59, 63, 64, 68, 70, 71, 73, 74, 75, 77, 78, 79, 80, 83, 84, 86-88, 91, 93, 94-97, 99, 100, 106, 109-113, 115, 117, 120-123, 125-128, 131, 133-137, 139, 142-145, 147-155, 157-161, 164, 167, 168, 171, 174, 176, 181, 183, 192, 193, 194, 195, 210
Neumann 41, 42
Newman 17, 18, 23, 38, 39, 40, 41, 44, 56, 58, 61, 62, 72, 77
New York 134, 138, 151
New Zealand 2, 36, 77, 134, 168, 180
Non-Morse 2, 5, 23, 41, 43, 52, 59, 60, 80, 86, 88, 100, 101, 109, 112, 123, 124, 128, 150, 160, 167, 168, 170, 171, 182, 192, 193, 213
Noordwijk 134
Normandy 13, 15, 27, 61, 93, 108, 109, 112, 120, 134, 135, 137, 143, 153, 155
North Africa 21, 43, 48, 53, 80, 97, 99, 111, 112, 129, 131, 152, 156, 168, 178, 192
North Atlantic 13, 57, 99, 135, 136, 187, 223
North Sea 79, 136, 137, 178
Northwood Hills 97, 106, 107, 136, 209
Norway 48, 83, 87, 137, 150, 157, 162, 167, 171, 178, 193, 218

O

Official Secrets Act 4, 7, 17, 18, 29, 32, 37, 53, 59, 62, 63, 68, 73, 76, 138, 140, 145, 162, 174, 200
Operation Sealion 108, 121, 151

225

OSA Adstock 137, 187
OSE Eastcote 52, 54, 60, 105, 106, 137, 140, 145, 157, 172, 187, 198
OSG Gayhurst 140, 187
OSS Stanmore 86, 120, 140, 156, 157, 187, 198
OSW Wavendon 141, 187
Outstations 3, 6, 7, 10, 29, 30, 32, 36, 50, 60, 68, 69, 71, 72, 75, 79, 88, 91, 92, 105, 116, 117, 118, 119, 120, 122, 128, 131, 135, 137, 138, 140, 141, 142, 143, 155, 156, 157, 161, 170, 173, 174, 176, 179, 180, 194, 195, 197, 198, 200, 201, 204, 210, 213, 219

P

Pacific 43, 47, 70, 77, 80, 81, 94, 95, 98, 120, 122, 131, 143, 161, 162, 165, 179, 180
Paddock 6, 93, 101, 128, 142, 194
Page 42, 43, 206
Palmer Street 142
Paris 9, 43, 48, 60, 110, 111, 142, 154, 192, 193
Pas de Calais 13, 22, 23, 43, 75, 96, 109, 112, 135, 142, 176
Patton 43, 127
Payne 43, 44
Pearl Harbor 6, 21, 45, 46, 95, 98, 110, 122, 131, 132, 143, 160, 161, 165
Pembroke 3, 4, 29, 68, 88, 105, 115, 116, 117, 122, 127, 131, 137, 140, 141-144, 177, 189, 193-195, 204, 207, 208, 216, 219, 222, 223
Pembroke V 3, 4, 29, 68, 88, 105, 115, 116, 122, 127, 131, 137, 140, 141, 142, 143, 144, 177, 194, 195, 216, 219
Philpott 32, 44, 174
Poland 5, 7, 47, 48, 51, 53, 54, 60, 65, 70, 73, 80, 84, 97, 111, 112, 113, 144, 148, 160, 164, 183, 217
Polish 22, 23, 30, 45, 47, 48, 51, 53, 58, 64, 65, 66, 73, 80, 97, 111, 127, 131, 144, 156, 159, 164, 190, 210, 215

Portugal 22, 127, 145
Pound The 123, 159, 194
Pujol 22, 23, 44, 74, 75, 115, 127, 145, 153, 214
PORES 17, 18, 25, 44, 45, 54, 101, 102, 168, 171, 179, 187, 213
Post Office Research Station 41, 45, 88, 101

R

Radley 17, 25, 26, 44, 45
RAF 26, 30, 31, 35, 36, 37, 40, 42, 63, 64, 68, 72, 78, 83, 85, 86, 88, 91, 93, 96, 98, 99, 103, 106, 107, 108, 110, 111, 116, 119, 120, 122, 124, 129, 130, 134, 135, 136, 138, 139, 140, 141, 143, 145, 146, 150, 151, 156, 157, 158, 163, 167, 168, 176, 178, 179, 180, 181, 187, 188, 189, 192, 195, 201, 218
RAF Eastcote 106, 145
RAF Uxbridge 145, 146, 163
Roberts 45, 46, 88
Robinson 7, 13, 15, 17, 39, 41, 44, 46, 54, 55, 61, 63, 68, 88, 102, 104, 129, 192, 193, 194, 216
Rochefort 45, 132
Roll of Honour 4, 20, 29, 35, 69, 90, 215
Rommel 99
Roosevelt 7, 8, 46, 47, 54, 56, 57, 93, 98, 128, 134, 151, 158, 160, 161, 164, 175, 179
Room 40 9, 14, 25, 33, 87, 146, 147, 149, 166, 194
Rotor 10, 11, 12, 25, 30, 31, 34, 40, 41, 44, 49, 50, 51, 58, 59, 65, 70, 91, 100, 101, 117, 119, 135, 136, 138, 141, 142, 144, 154, 155, 158, 161, 162, 164, 165, 166, 194, 214
Rozycki 47, 48, 64, 97, 217
Ruislip 84, 85, 105, 106, 139, 147, 187, 204, 209, 217
Ruislip Woods 138, 147, 173
Russia 3, 4, 5, 6, 7, 8, 9, 13, 15, 24, 28, 36, 37, 47, 53, 54, 56, 57, 62, 64, 66, 70, 77, 82, 84, 86, 87, 95, 98, 102,

INDEX

103, 106, 109, 110, 111, 112, 113, 125, 126, 127, 144, 147, 148, 149, 150, 154, 155, 156, 157, 159, 160, 161, 162, 163, 169, 183, 195, 208, 216, 217, 218, 220

S

Sale 27, 48, 90, 159, 178, 216, 218
Sandridge 80, 88, 149, 150, 167, 189
Sandy Hook 14, 150, 178
Scarborough 89, 150, 188, 189, 219
Scherbius 9, 34, 48, 49, 50, 112, 192, 215
Schmidt 50, 51, 111, 144
Schreyer 51, 64, 71
Scotland 3, 8, 14, 22, 29, 38, 53, 60, 68, 105, 117, 131, 136, 150, 151, 152, 153, 160, 167, 177, 188, 193, 201
Secret Writer 54, 55, 56, 157, 193, 194, 195
Selfridges 99, 133, 134, 151, 159, 161, 163, 175, 179, 198
Sicily 15, 37, 43, 131, 150, 152, 155
Signal City 151, 152, 178, 208
SIGABA 194
SIGSALY 7, 13, 47, 56, 58, 93, 114, 132, 133, 134, 151, 152, 159, 161, 178, 179, 187, 193, 194, 198, 213, 218, 219, 220
Sinclair 52, 87, 94, 110
Slowikowski 53, 80
South Africa 153
Spain 22, 113, 131, 145, 152-155
Spaso House 154
Spirella 30, 53, 78, 92, 126, 155, 174, 175, 179, 218, 219, 220
SS 21, 84, 114, 120, 142
St Malo-Paramé 115, 155
Stalin 6, 7, 47, 53, 54, 98, 113, 147, 148, 158, 159
Stanmore 29, 31, 32, 44, 54, 63, 68, 86, 90, 102, 116, 128, 137, 138, 140, 141, 142, 143, 156, 157, 163, 173, 175, 177, 179, 187, 197, 201, 204, 210, 212, 219
Stewart 54

St James' Street 37, 128, 155
Stowe 140, 156, 173
St Paul's school 22
Swaffield 54
Swakeleys House 157
Sweden 50, 84, 110, 157, 168, 169, 220
Switzerland 21, 49, 79, 87, 158

T

Teddington 134, 158
Tehran 7, 54, 15
Teleprinter 2, 5, 12, 13, 16, 25, 27, 32, 38, 39, 41, 46, 55, 59, 60, 63, 69, 71, 88, 100, 106, 112, 117, 123, 124, 125, 128, 149, 152, 153, 157, 159, 160, 167, 168, 170, 172, 173, 191, 192, 193, 195, 197, 213
Telemark 83, 128, 137, 178, 218
Tester 41, 54, 56
Testery 38, 41, 45, 46, 54, 55, 56, 88, 100, 125
Tiltman 19, 20, 55, 88, 156
Timms 56
TNMOC 48, 90, 159, 177, 178, 187, 212, 213
Toms 105, 139
Tower of London 159
Travis 10, 56, 88, 106, 107, 141
TRE 36, 39, 63, 72, 90, 103, 104, 115, 129, 130, 136, 172, 187
Triton 89, 119, 136, 194, 195
Truman 7, 8, 11, 47, 56, 57, 100, 128, 134, 151, 161, 164, 179
Turing 2, 5, 8, 10, 11, 16, 17, 18, 19, 23, 25, 31, 32, 37, 38, 39, 41, 42, 45, 46, 50, 51, 55, 56, 57, 58, 59, 60, 61, 62, 64, 65, 66, 70, 71, 75, 76, 77, 88, 90, 92, 93, 100, 102, 114, 115, 117, 119, 126, 133, 144, 152, 158, 159, 161, 165, 166, 171, 174, 179, 191, 202, 203, 205, 206, 207, 215
Tutte 41, 46, 59, 60, 67, 88, 100
Tunny 5, 26, 27, 30, 32, 55, 56, 59, 80, 88, 102, 112, 125, 135, 195
Twenty Committee 37, 128, 155, 179
Twinn 60

WW2 CODEBREAKING PEOPLE AND PLACES

U

U-Boats 12, 28, 36, 67, 91, 99, 101, 108, 113, 135, 136, 142, 150, 172, 175, 176, 193, 195, 214, 218

Ukraine 53, 109, 125, 148, 160, 182, 197, 220

United States of America 45, 80, 132, 160

USA 6, 10-13, 15, 16, 19, 21, 24, 33, 34, 36, 37, 47, 53, 54, 56, 57, 58, 63, 80, 81, 82, 92, 97, 98, 99, 100, 103, 110, 113, 122, 123, 126, 127, 133, 134, 136, 138, 147, 149, 157, 160, 161, 162, 163, 164, 165, 166, 167, 168, 169, 172, 176, 178, 183, 220

Uxbridge 145, 146, 163, 204, 209, 212

Uzès 97, 111, 191

V

Valentine 60

Vint Hill Farms 163

Virginia 15, 24, 82, 163, 164, 178

Von Rundstedt 22, 23, 60, 61, 109, 142

W

Warsaw 10, 48, 111, 144, 164

Washington 11, 20, 37, 47, 58, 62, 75, 82, 94, 95, 100, 119, 151, 161, 164, 165, 217

Watergate House 166

WATU 101, 187, 208

Wavendon 43, 44, 90, 140-142, 187, 197, 213, 219

Welchman 2, 5, 8, 10, 17, 30, 31, 32, 38, 39, 45, 56-59, 61, 62, 63, 65, 69, 88, 91, 92, 115, 117, 118, 126, 159, 162, 171, 173, 174, 198, 206, 215, 216

Wenger 62, 100

Whaddon Hall 89, 166

Whitehall 6, 7, 9, 166, 187

Wimbledon 128, 131, 166

Wingate 62

Woburn Abbey 166, 177, 195

World Powers of cooperation (UK/USA Agreement) 97, 168

Wormwood Scrubs 3, 4, 85, 209, 213

Wrens 3, 4, 20, 29, 30, 35, 43, 44, 54, 55, 63, 66, 67, 68, 69, 71, 72, 77, 80, 88, 89, 90, 94, 95, 101, 104, 105, 106, 113, 114, 116, 117, 118, 119, 122, 123, 128, 131, 134, 137, 138, 139, 140, 141, 142, 143, 144, 147, 150, 151, 152, 153, 161, 162, 165, 166, 167, 173, 177, 180, 195, 197, 198, 200, 204, 209, 213, 216, 218

WRNS 3, 4, 5, 13, 29, 34, 35, 77, 88, 89, 105, 114, 116, 117, 122, 128, 143, 144, 167, 187, 192, 195, 200, 204, 209, 213, 219

Wynn-Williams 11, 12, 36, 39, 63, 75

Y

Yoxall 63

Y-Stations 8, 10, 14, 39, 63, 67, 69, 71, 79, 82, 84, 89, 94, 98, 117, 119, 123, 125, 136, 142, 153, 155, 161, 168, 176, 178, 180, 182, 189, 190, 209, 217, 220

Z

Zhukov 64, 148

Zuse 27, 51, 64, 71

Zygalski 30, 47, 64, 65, 73, 97, 144, 164, 217

Numbered

6812th US signals 54, 138, 147, 162, 208

6813th US signals 89, 127, 216, 218